Shugo Chara!

1

PEACH-PIT

Translated by
June Kato

Adapted by
David Walsh

Lettered by
North Market Street Graphics

DEL
REY

BALLANTINE BOOKS • NEW YORK

A Del Rey Trade Paperback Original

Shugo Chara! volume 1 copyright © 2006 by PEACH-PIT
English translation copyright © 2007 by PEACH-PIT
Original cover design by Akiko Omo

Published in the United States by Del Rey Books, an imprint of The Random House Publishing Group, a division of Random House, Inc., New York.

DEL REY is a registered trademark and the Del Rey colophon is a trademark of Random House, Inc.

Publication rights arranged through Kodansha Ltd.

First published in Japan in 2006 by Kodansha Ltd., Tokyo

ISBN 978-0-345-49745-1

Printed in the United States of America

www.delreymanga.com

9 8 7 6

Translator—June Kato
Adaptor—David Walsh
Lettering—North Market Street Graphics

Contents

Honorifics Explained

Throughout the Del Rey Manga books, you will find Japanese honorifics left intact in the translations. For those not familiar with how the Japanese use honorifics and, more important, how they differ from American honorifics, we present this brief overview.

Politeness has always been a critical facet of Japanese culture. Ever since the feudal era, when Japan was a highly stratified society, use of honorifics—which can be defined as polite speech that indicates relationship or status—has played an essential role in the Japanese language. When addressing someone in Japanese, an honorific usually takes the form of a suffix attached to one's name (example: "Asuna-san"), is used as a title at the end of one's name, or appears in place of the name itself (example: "Negi-sensei," or simply "Sensei!").

Honorifics can be expressions of respect or endearment. In the context of manga and anime, honorifics give insight into the nature of the relationship between characters. Many English translations leave out these important honorifics and therefore distort the feel of the original Japanese. Because Japanese honorifics contain nuances that English honorifics lack, it is our policy at Del Rey not to translate them. Here, instead, is a guide to some of the honorifics you may encounter in Del Rey Manga.

-san: This is the most common honorific and is equivalent to Mr., Miss, Ms., Mrs. It is the all-purpose honorific and can be used in any situation where politeness is required.

-sama: This is one level higher than "-san" and is used to confer great respect.

-dono: This comes from the word "tono," which means "lord." It is an even higher level than "-sama" and confers utmost respect.

-kun: This suffix is used at the end of boys' names to express familiarity or endearment. It is also sometimes used by men among friends, or when addressing someone younger or of a lower station.

-chan: This is used to express endearment, mostly toward girls. It is also used for little boys, pets, and even among lovers. It gives a sense of childish cuteness.

Bozu: This is an informal way to refer to a boy, similar to the English terms "kid" and "squirt."

Sempai/Senpai: This title suggests that the addressee is one's senior in a group or organization. It is most often used in a school setting, where underclassmen refer to their upperclassmen as "sempai." It can also be used in the workplace, such as when a newer employee addresses an employee who has seniority in the company.

Kohai: This is the opposite of "sempai" and is used toward underclassmen in school or newcomers in the workplace. It connotes that the addressee is of a lower station.

Sensei: Literally meaning "one who has come before," this title is used for teachers, doctors, or masters of any profession or art.

-[blank]: This is usually forgotten in these lists, but it is perhaps the most significant difference between Japanese and English. The lack of honorific means that the speaker has permission to address the person in a very intimate way. Usually, only family, spouses, or very close friends have this kind of permission. Known as *yobisute*, it can be gratifying when someone who has earned the intimacy starts to call one by one's name without an honorific. But when that intimacy hasn't been earned, it can be very insulting.

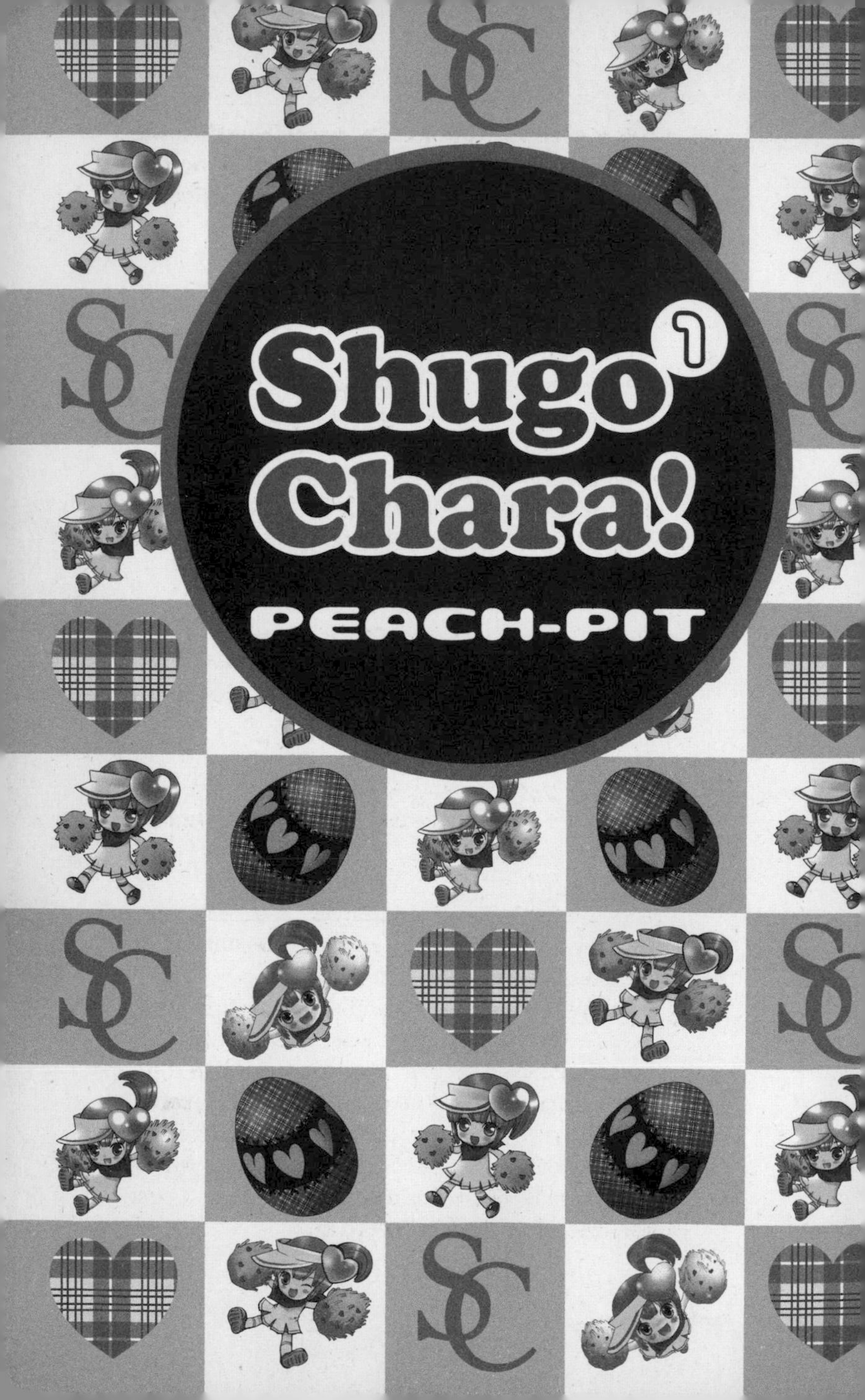
Shugo Chara! 1
PEACH-PIT

Shugo Chara!

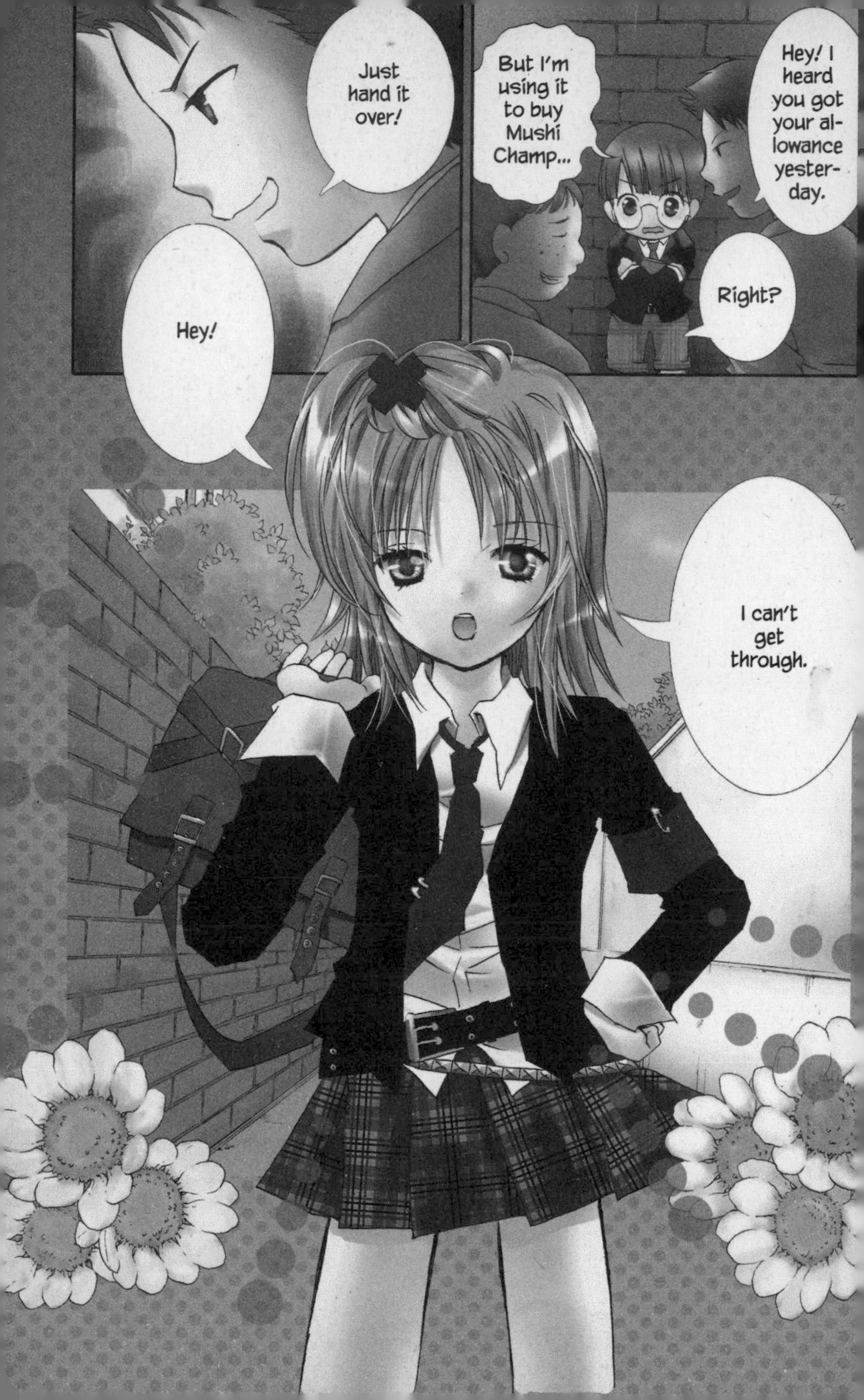
Hey! I heard you got your allowance yesterday.
Right?
But I'm using it to buy Mushi Champ...
Just hand it over!
Hey!
I can't get through.

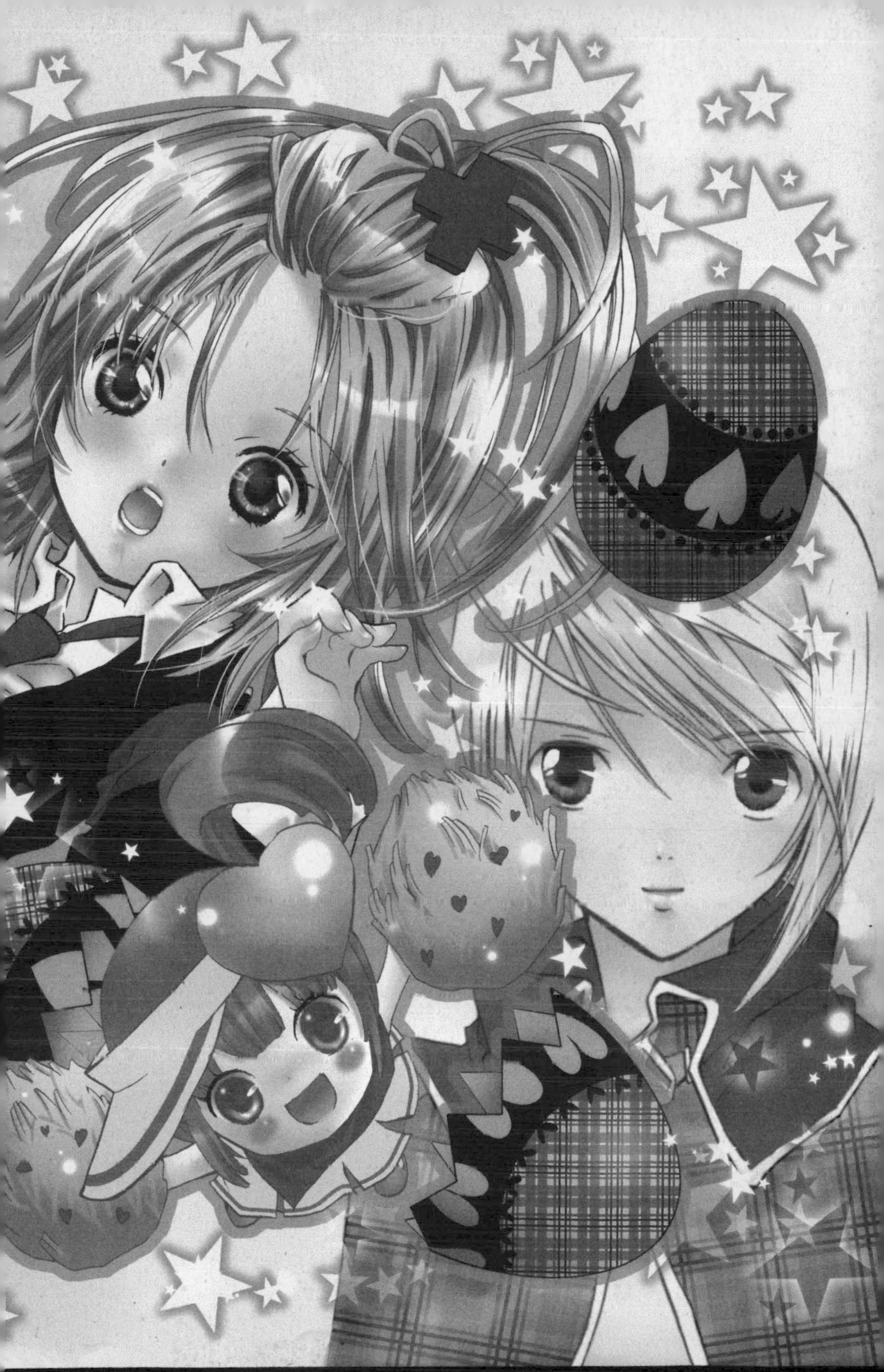

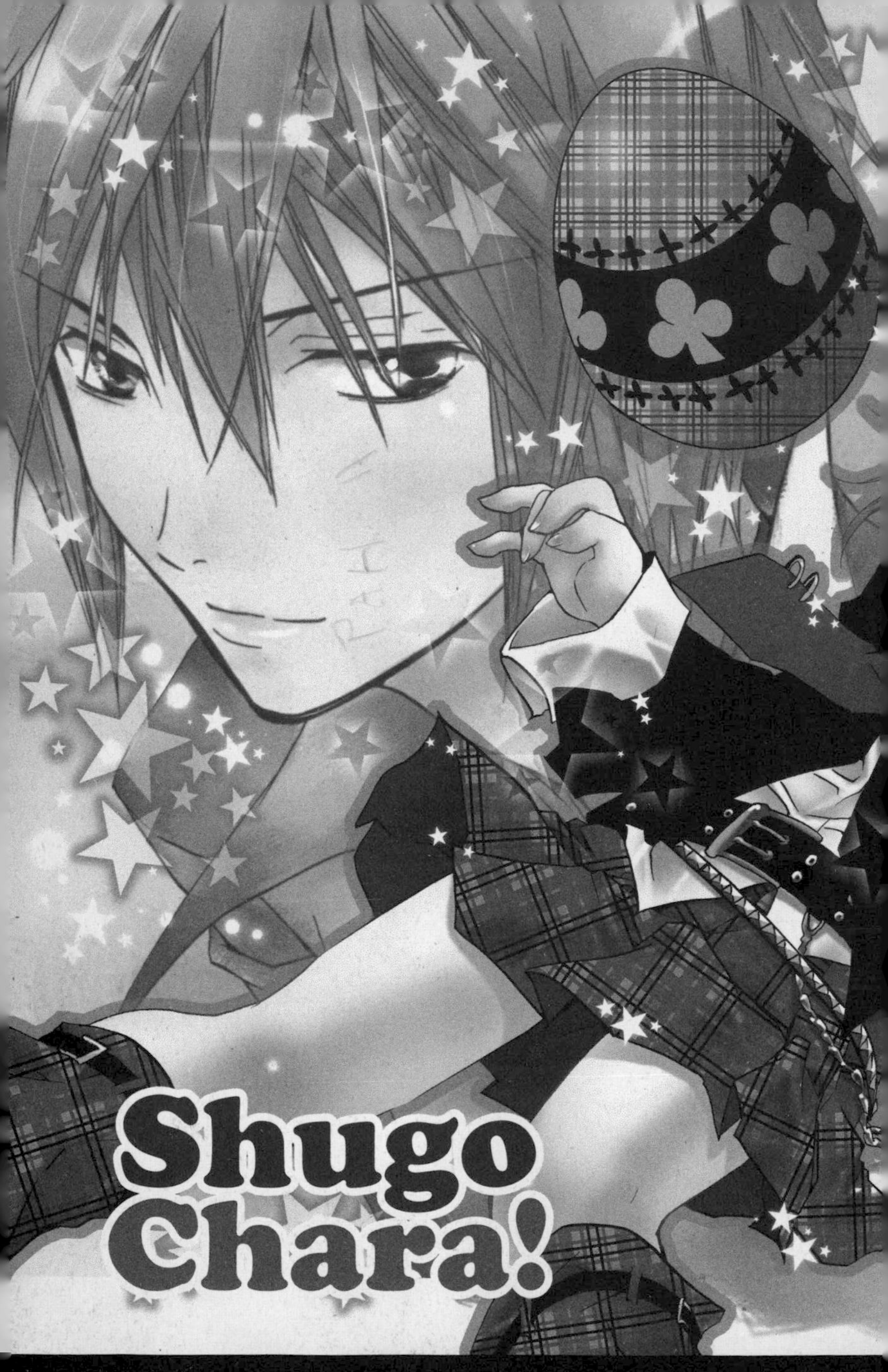
Shugo Chara!

Shugo Chara!

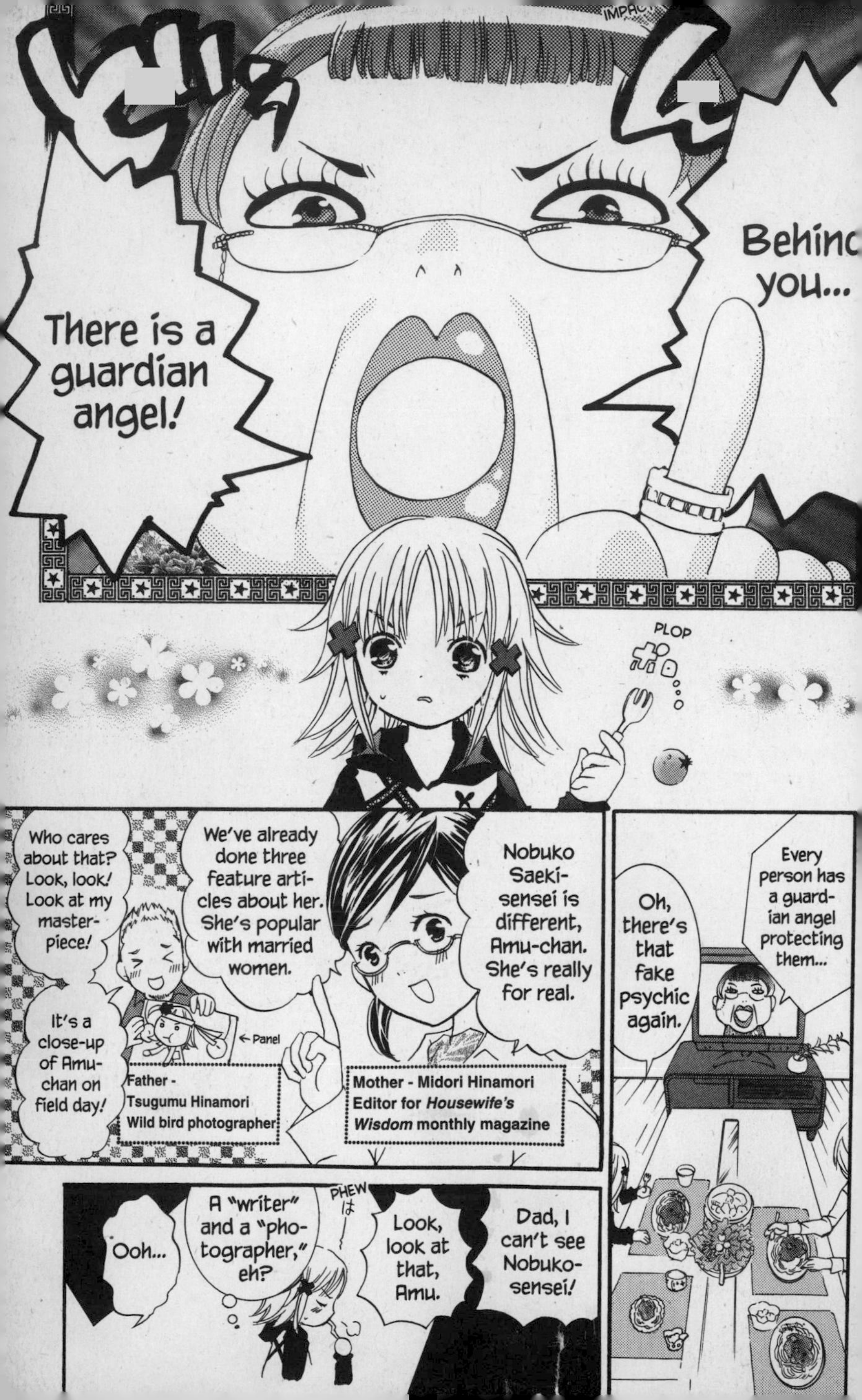
IMPAC
Behind you...
There is a guardian angel!
PLOP
Every person has a guardian angel protecting them...
Oh, there's that fake psychic again.
Nobuko Saeki-sensei is different, Amu-chan. She's really for real.
We've already done three feature articles about her. She's popular with married women.
Who cares about that? Look, look! Look at my masterpiece!
It's a close-up of Amu-chan on field day!
← Panel
Mother - Midori Hinamori Editor for *Housewife's Wisdom* monthly magazine
Father - Tsugumu Hinamori Wild bird photographer
Dad, I can't see Nobuko-sensei!
Look, look at that, Amu.
PHEW
A "writer" and a "photographer," eh?
Ooh...

SCREECH

She sounds like she's talking directly to me...

Amu-chan? You're done eating?

I am talking to you.

I'm not gonna depend on that.

A guardian angel is something that people rely on when they're struggling in life.

She is...

so cool.

Even though she's my own kid.

PATAN

Thank you for dinner.

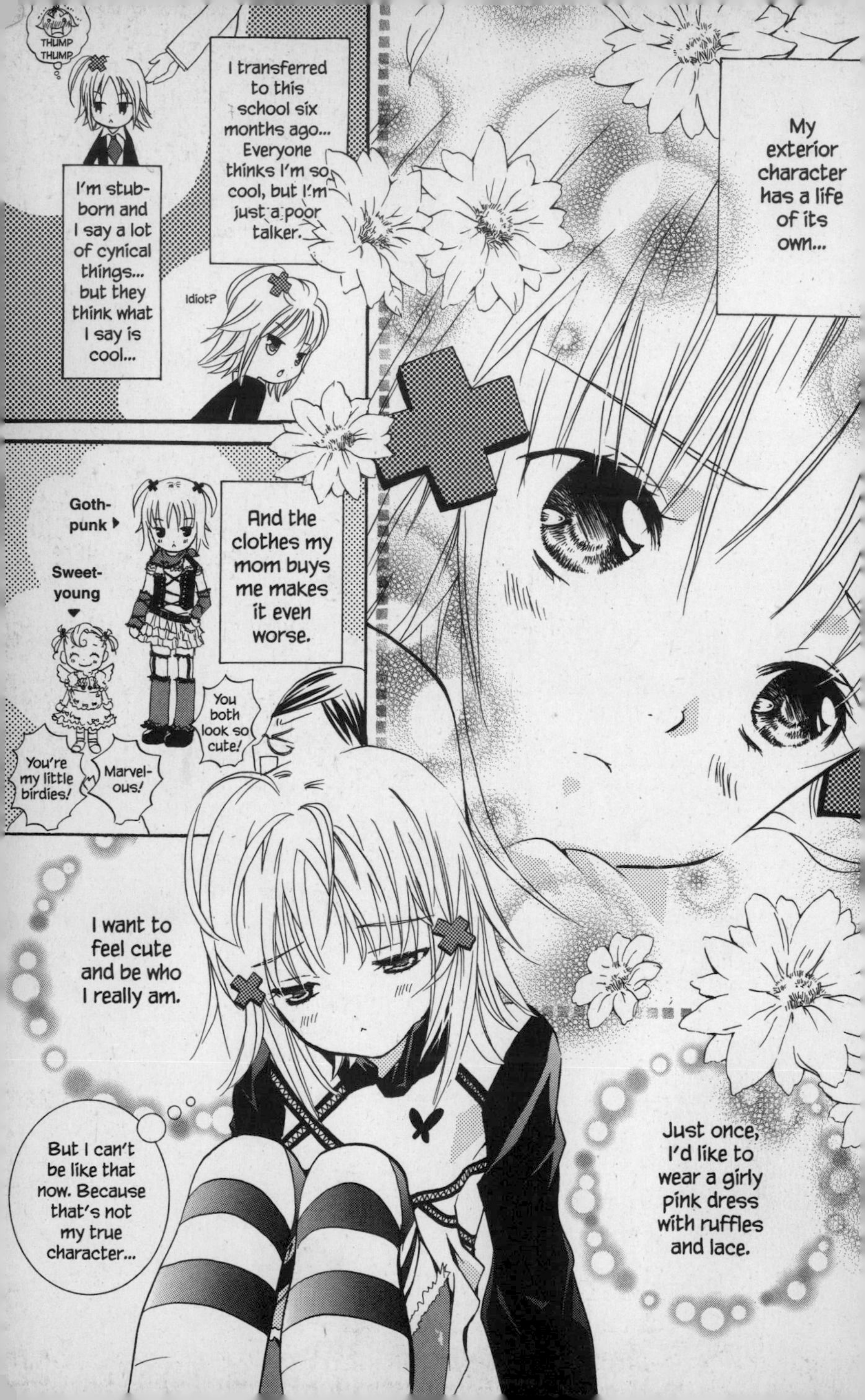
My exterior character has a life of its own...
I transferred to this school six months ago... Everyone thinks I'm so cool, but I'm just a poor talker.
THUMP THUMP
I'm stub-born and I say a lot of cynical things... but they think what I say is cool...
Idiot?
And the clothes my mom buys me makes it even worse.
You both look so cute!
Goth-punk
Sweet-young
Marvel-ous!
You're my little birdies!
Just once, I'd like to wear a girly pink dress with ruffles and lace.
I want to feel cute and be who I really am.
But I can't be like that now. Because that's not my true character...

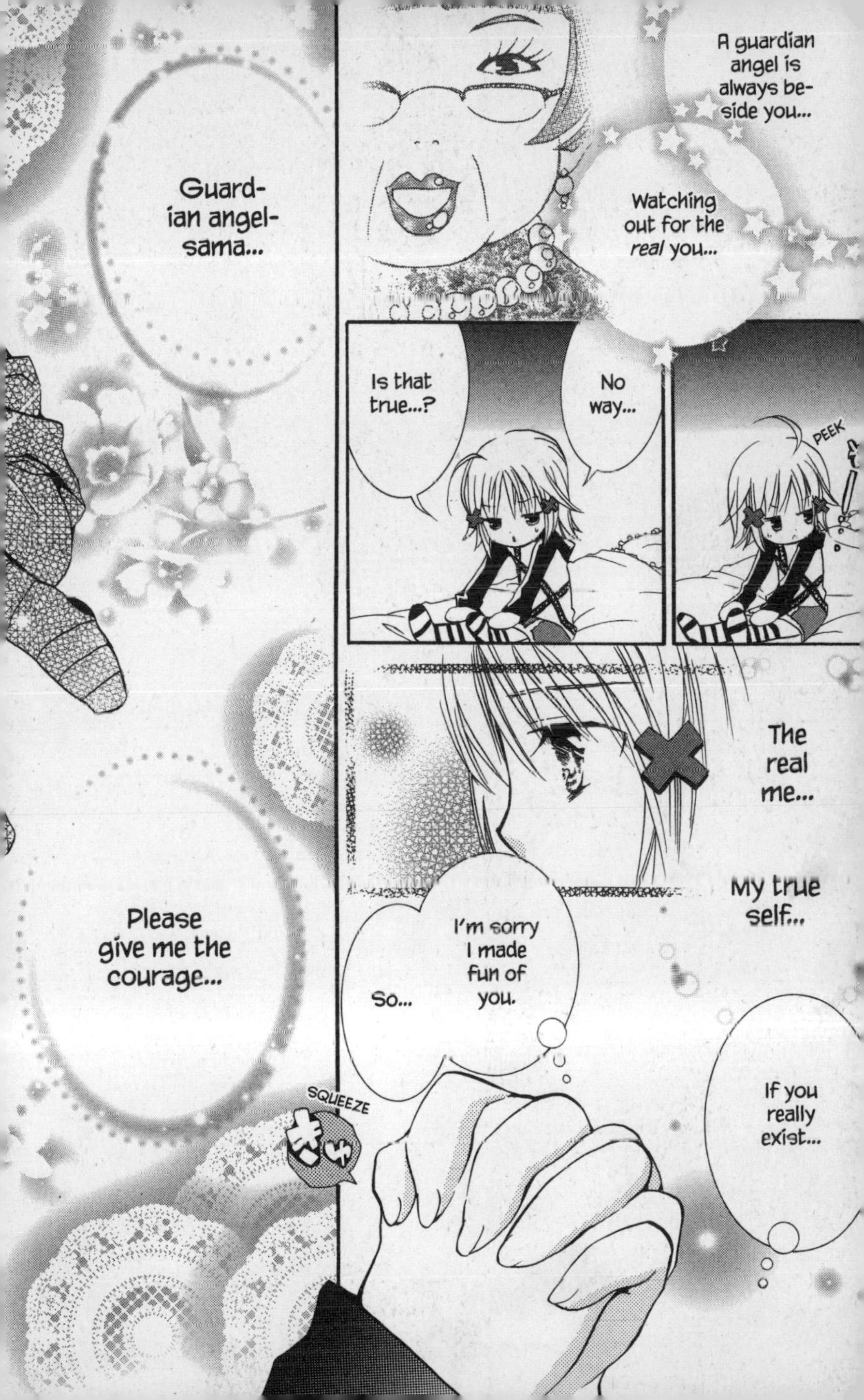

A guardian angel is always be-side you...
Watching out for the *real* you...
PEEK
No way...
Is that true...?
The real me...
My true self...
If you really exist...
I'm sorry I made fun of you.
So...
SQUEEZE
Guard-ian angel-sama...
Please give me the courage...

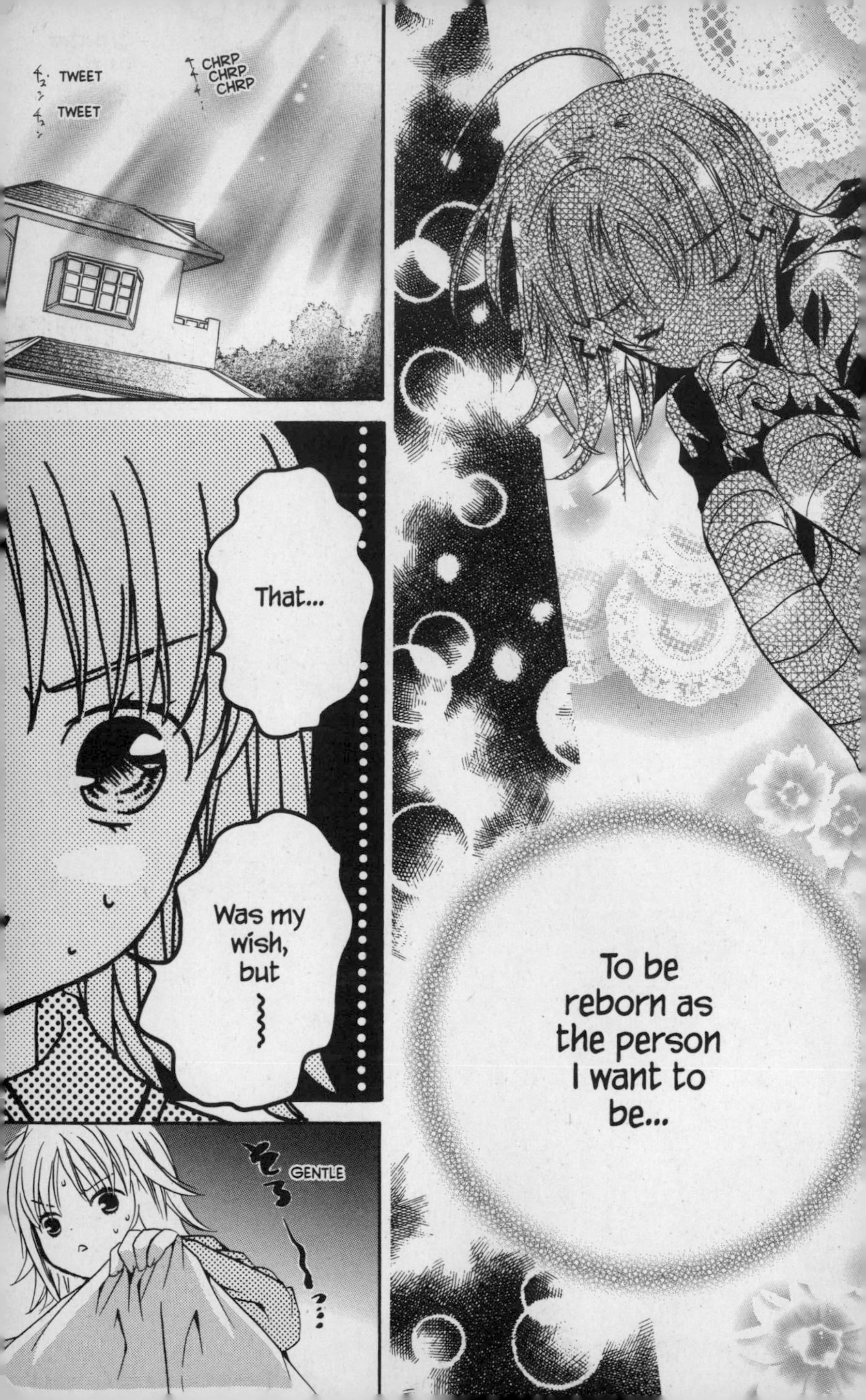
To be reborn as the person I want to be...
TWEET
TWEET
CHRP CHRP CHRP
That...
Was my wish, but ...
GENTLE

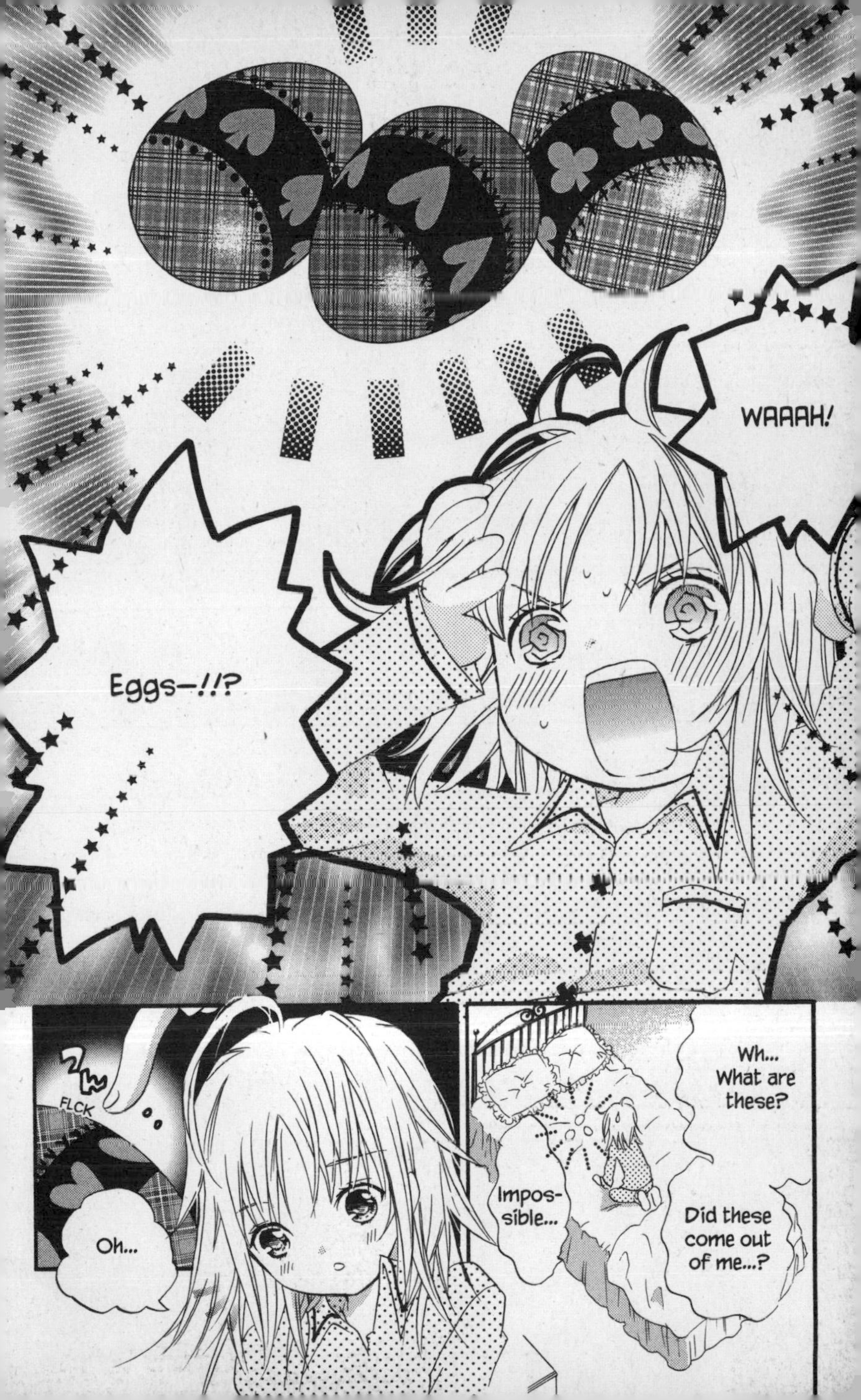
WAAAH!
Eggs-!!?
Wh... What are these?
Did these come out of me...?
Impos-sible...
FLCK
Oh...

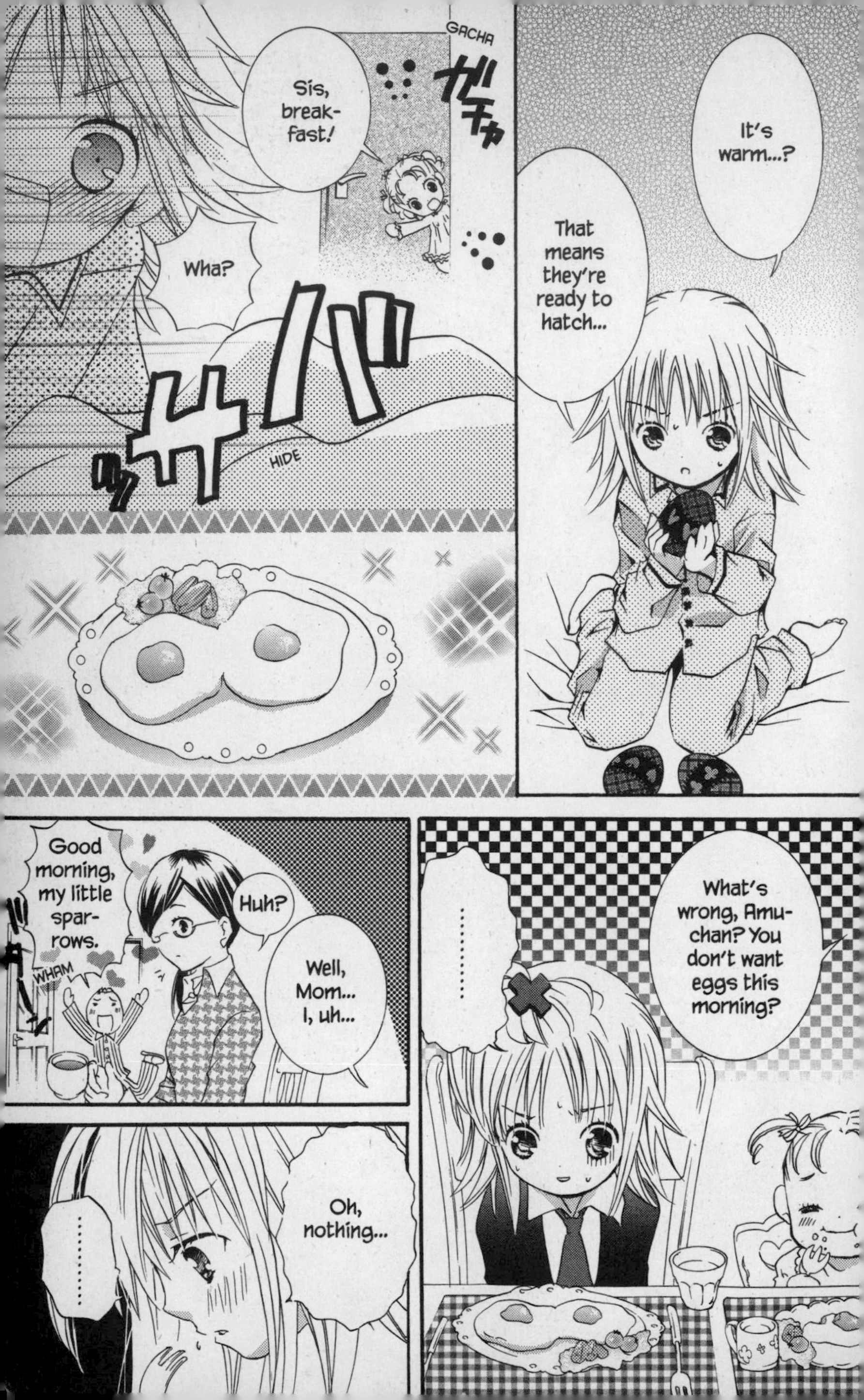
It's warm...?
That means they're ready to hatch...
GACHA
Sis, breakfast!
Wha?
HIDE
What's wrong, Amu-chan? You don't want eggs this morning?
......
Good morning, my little sparrows.
WHAM
Huh?
Well, Mom... I, uh...
......
Oh, nothing...

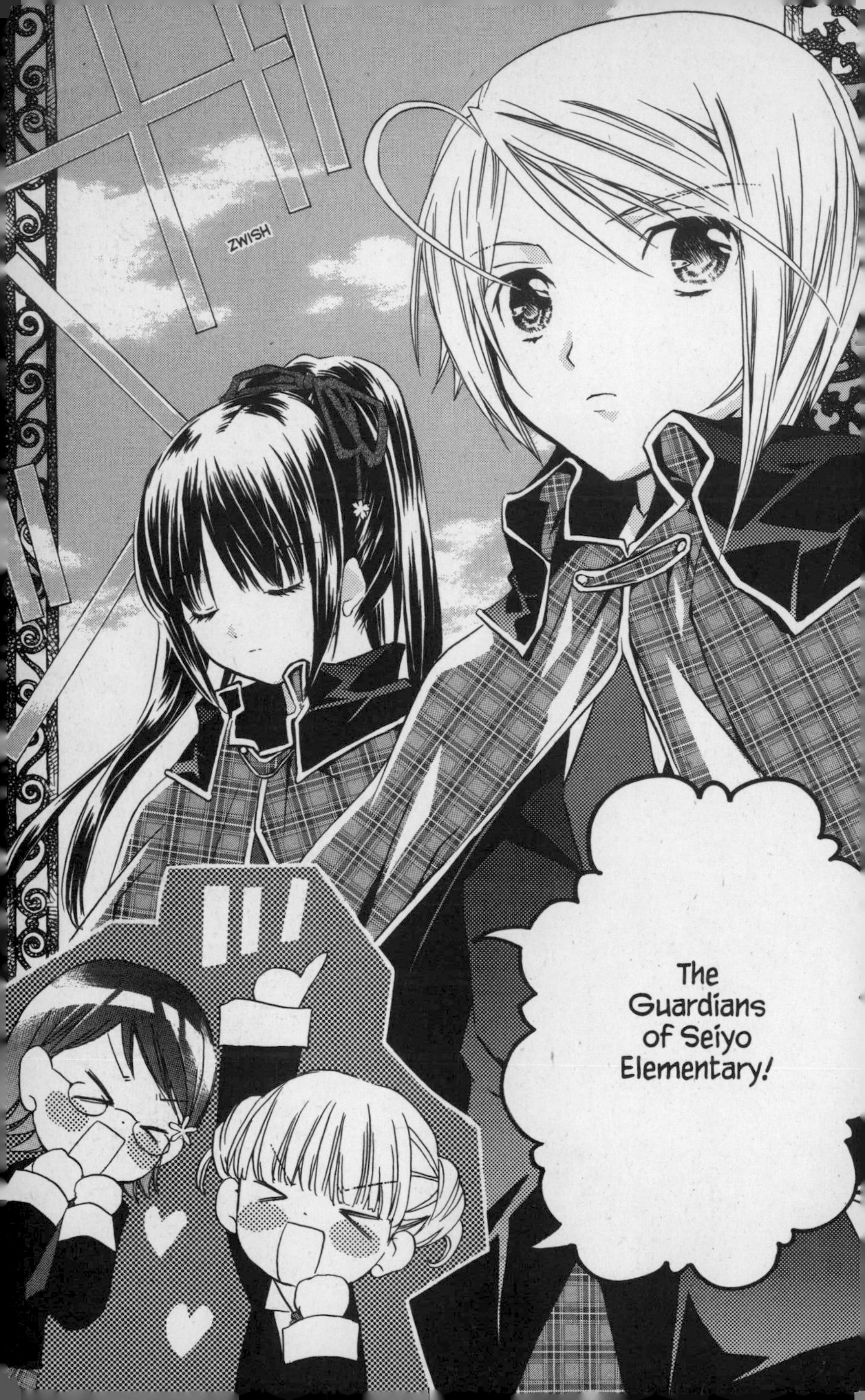
ZWISH
The Guardians of Seiyo Elementary!

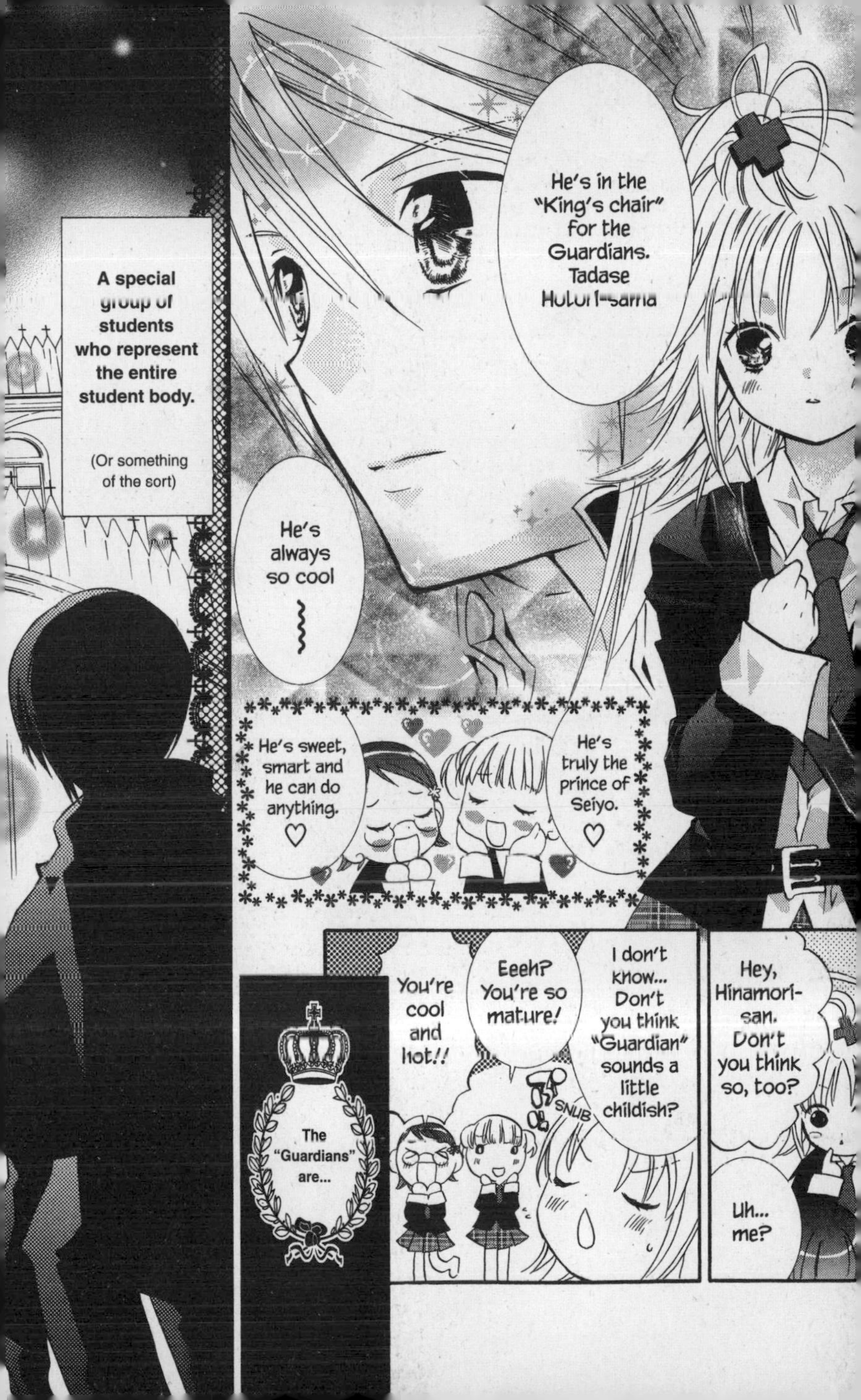
He's in the "King's chair" for the Guardians. Tadase Hotori-sama
He's always so cool ~
He's truly the prince of Seiyo. ♡
He's sweet, smart and he can do anything. ♡
Hey, Hinamori-san. Don't you think so, too?
Uh... me?
I don't know... Don't you think "Guardian" sounds a little childish?
SNUB
Eeeh? You're so mature!
You're cool and hot!!
The "Guardians" are...
A special group of students who represent the entire student body.
(Or something of the sort)

And after school there's a tea party in the Royal Garden that only the Guardians can attend...

The teachers listen and are more fair with them...

That's right! And it's also okay if the Guardians come to school late and leave early.

And especially...

That's too royal–!!

The Guardians have a royal cape that only they can wear!!

It's comprised of four posts: The K Chair, Q Chair, J Chair, and the A chair.

Once a year, only four out of all the students are chosen.

Everybody says Hinamori-san's gonna be the next Q chair.

Eh?

I bet it would look good on you!

Just once I wish I could wear that cape!

Guardians sound like they're really special.

I have no interest in wearing it.

CHATTER

Geez, not again.

They're all wrong.

I'm sorry. What everyone is saying...

They protect us from the harsh school rules and all kinds of trouble, and keep our personal information safe.

They are truly our Guardians!

What?

Huh? Do you think that matters?

Hinamori-san is a better choice.

Guardians treat all students as equals—

HO HO HO ホホホ...

I'm a superior student. I'm good looking and my family is in high standing...

And my father is the top benefactor to this school. Of course, I, Saaya Yamabuki, will be chosen.

Yeah.

Yeah.

CLAP CLAP CLAP

TUNED OUT

She irritates me... And she's only been at this school for six months...

Just wait and see.

Oh... Prince.

He's so cute...

Nice hair— He's so skinny he could snap in two...

But I don't like that cape....

I...

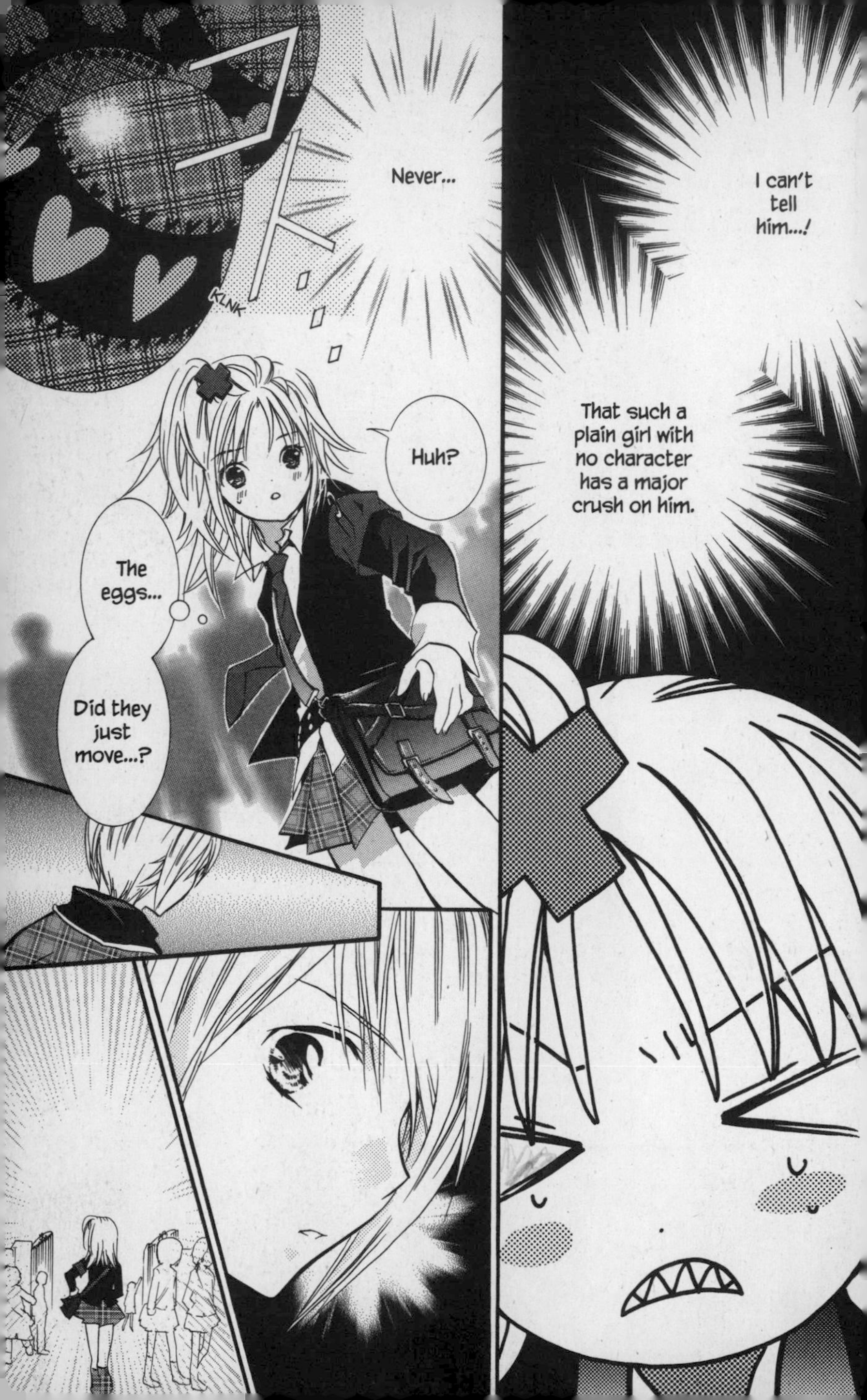
I can't tell him...!
That such a plain girl with no character has a major crush on him.
Never...
KLNK
Huh?
The eggs...
Did they just move...?

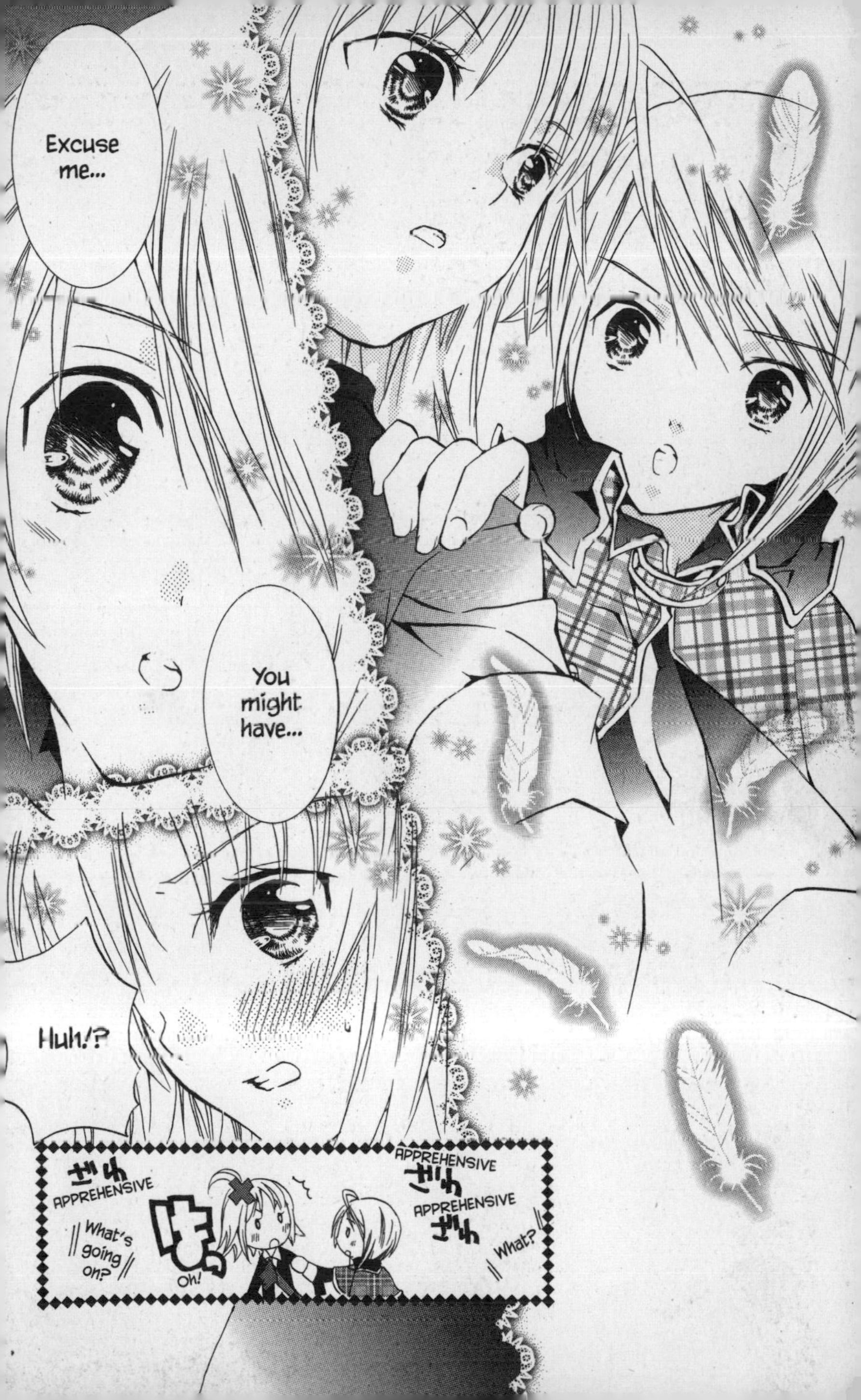

Excuse me...
You might have...
Huh!?
APPREHENSIVE
APPREHENSIVE
What?
APPREHENSIVE
Oh!
What's going on?

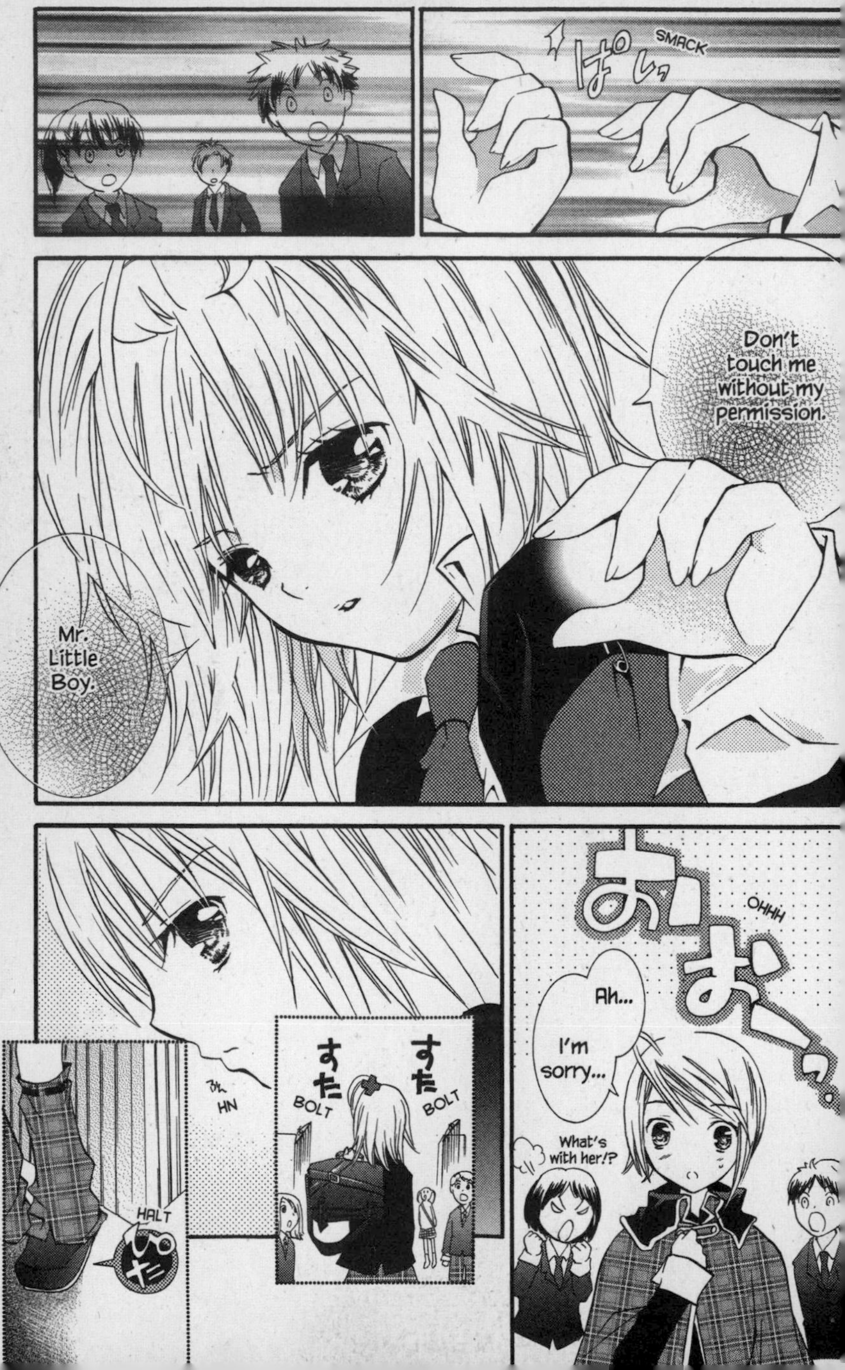
SMACK
Don't touch me without my permission.
Mr. Little Boy.
OHHH
Ah... I'm sorry...
What's with her!?
HN
すた すた
BOLT BOLT
HALT

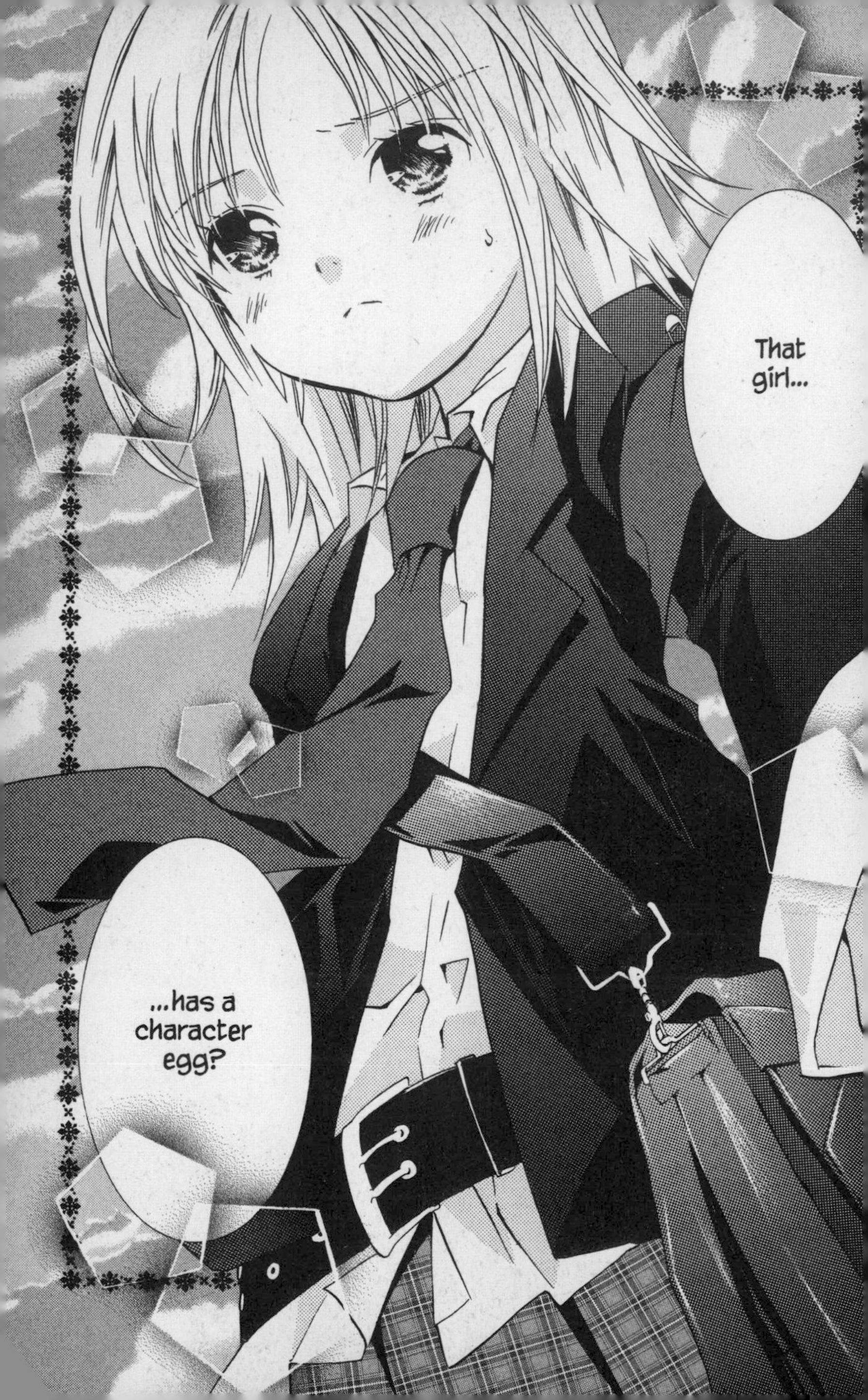
That girl...
...has a character egg?

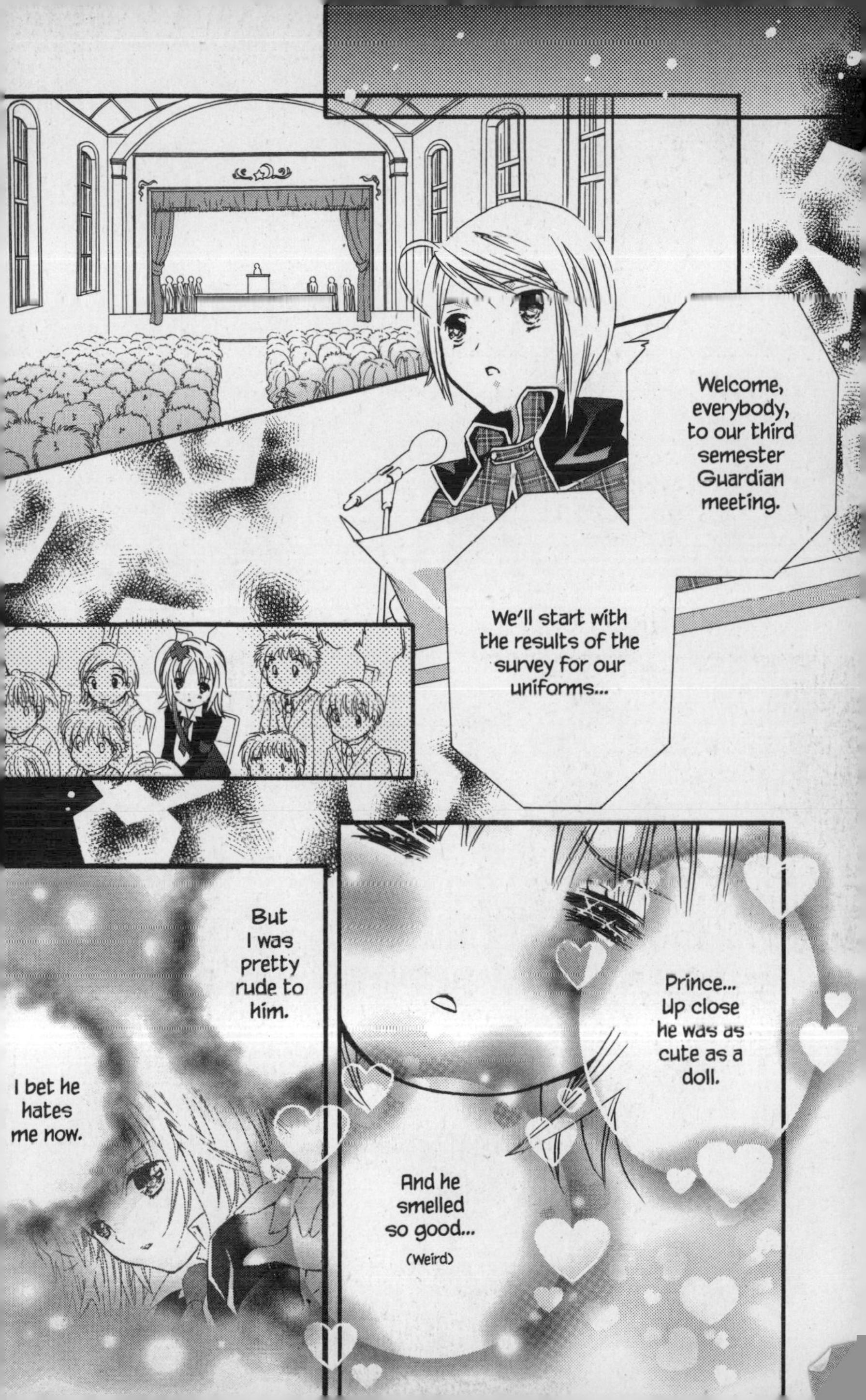
Welcome, everybody, to our third semester Guardian meeting.
We'll start with the results of the survey for our uniforms...
Prince... Up close he was as cute as a doll.
And he smelled so good...
(Weird)
But I was pretty rude to him.
I bet he hates me now.

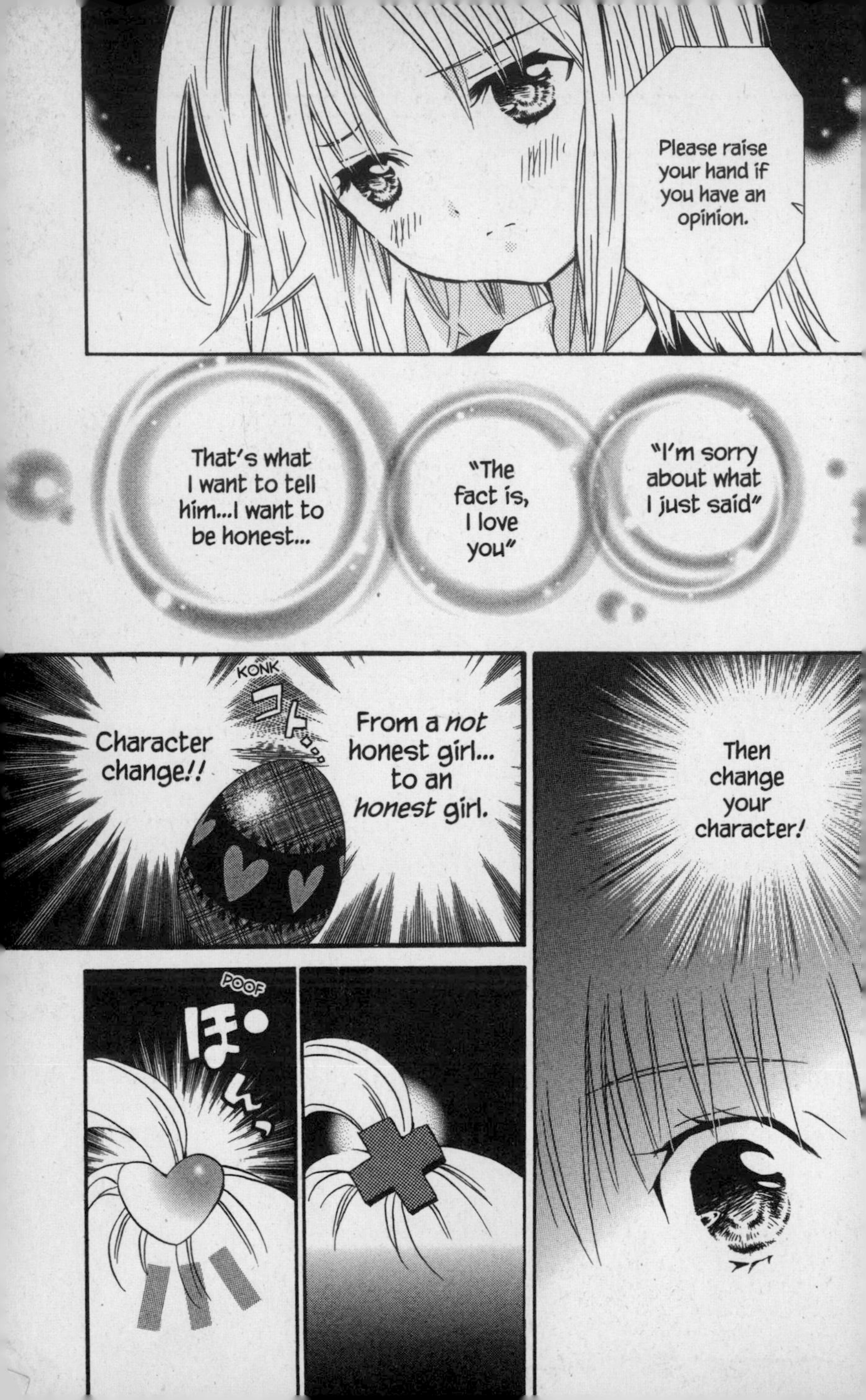
Please raise your hand if you have an opinion.
"I'm sorry about what I just said"
"The fact is, I love you"
That's what I want to tell him...I want to be honest...
Then change your character!
From a *not* honest girl... to an *honest* girl.
KONK
コト
Character change!!
POOF
ぽん

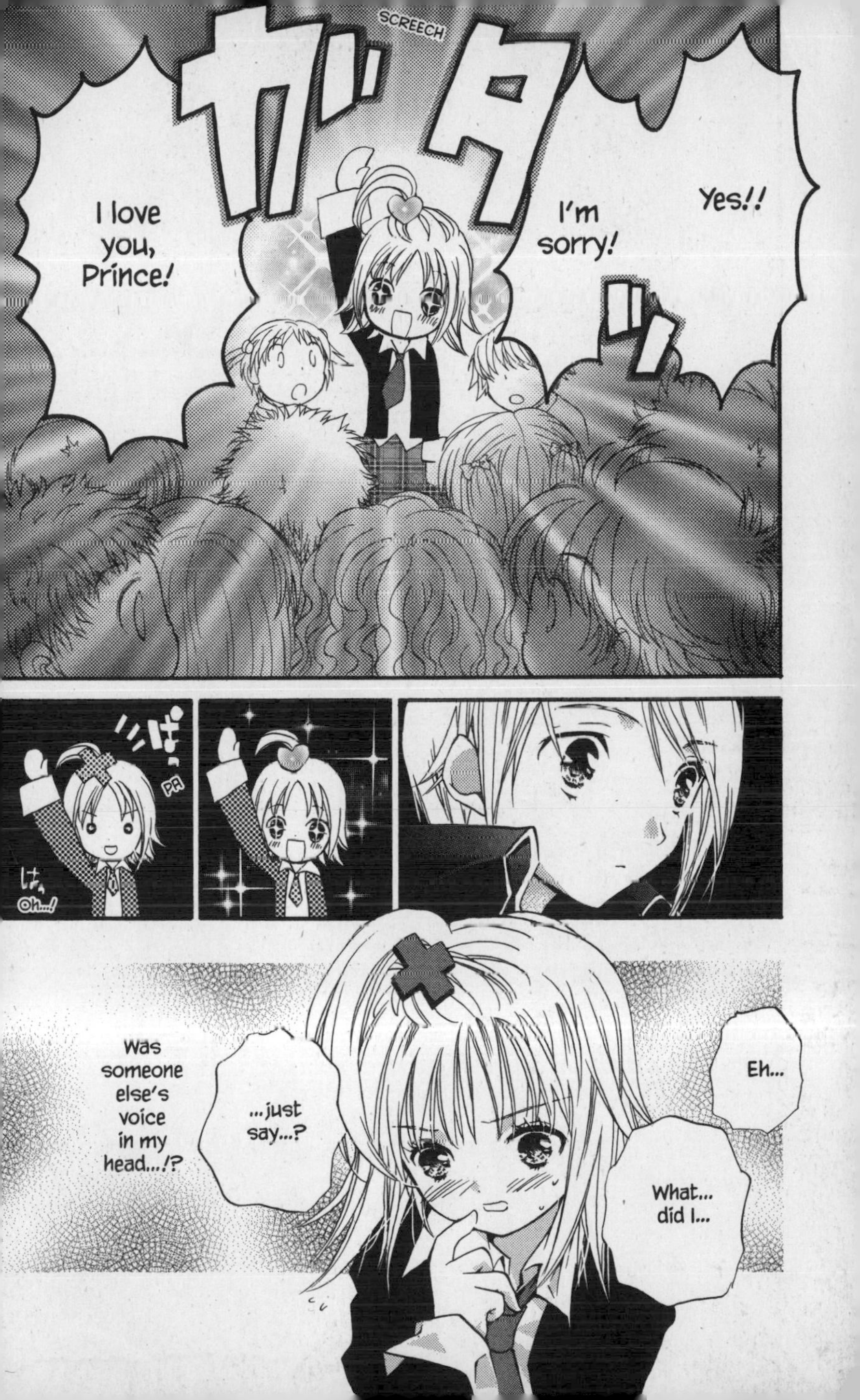
SCREECH
Yes!!
I'm sorry!
I love you, Prince!
PA
Oh...!
Eh...
What... did I...
...just say...?
Was someone else's voice in my head...!?

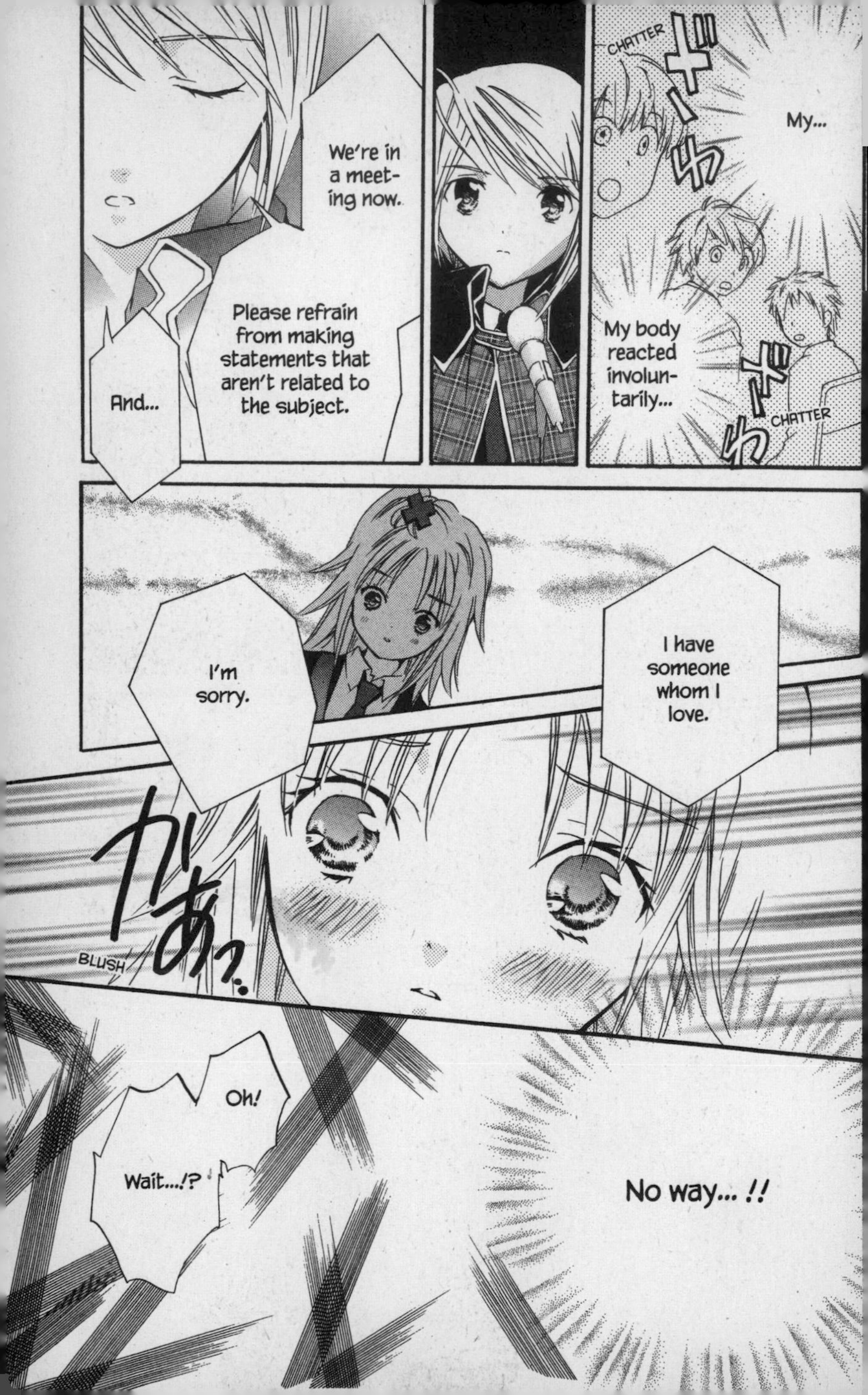
CHATTER
My...
My body reacted involuntarily...
CHATTER
We're in a meeting now.
Please refrain from making statements that aren't related to the subject.
And...
I have someone whom I love.
I'm sorry.
BLUSH
No way... !!
Oh!
Wait...!?

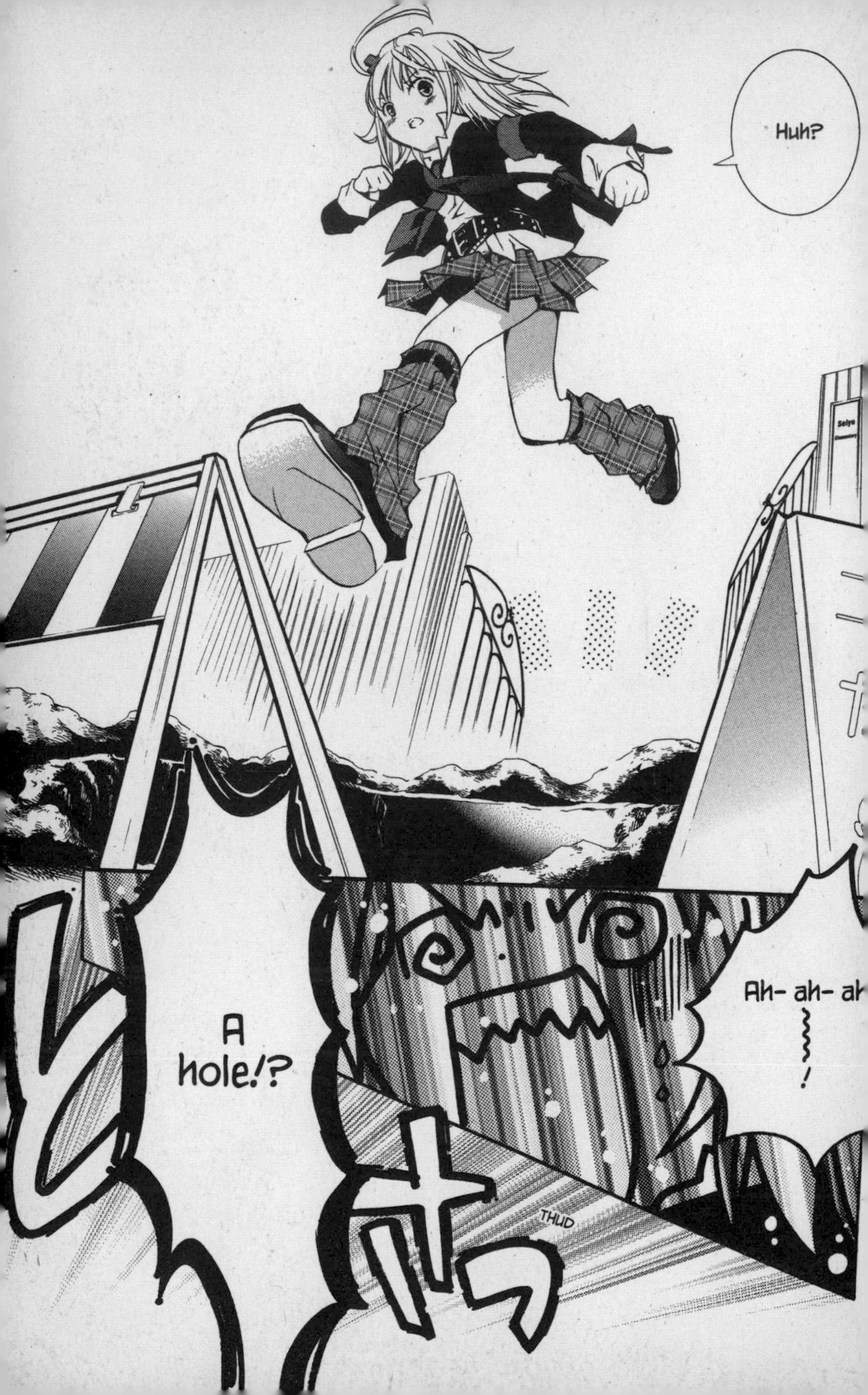
Huh?
Ah- ah- ah
!
A hole!?
THUD

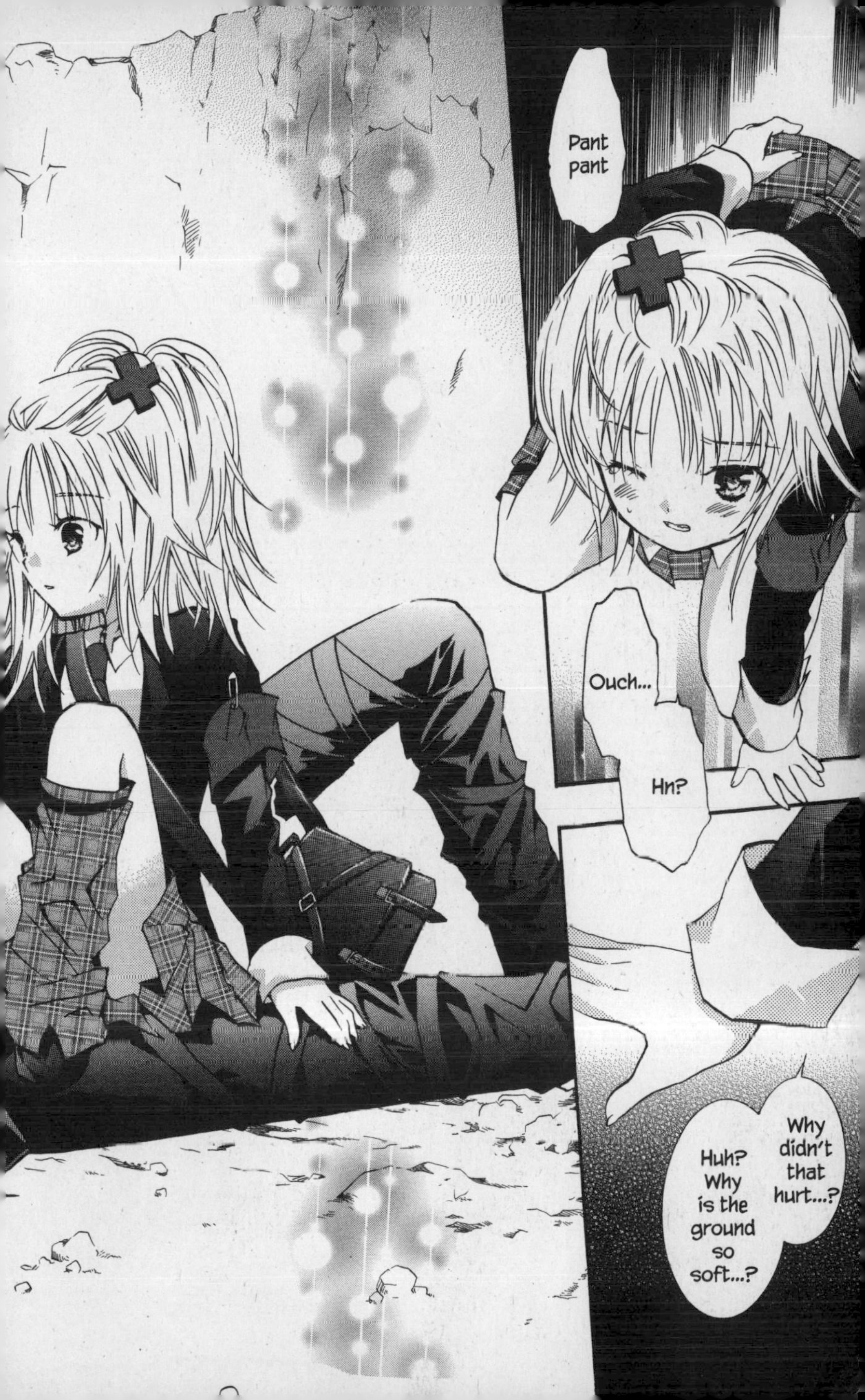
Pant pant
Ouch...
Hn?
Why didn't that hurt...?
Huh? Why is the ground so soft...?

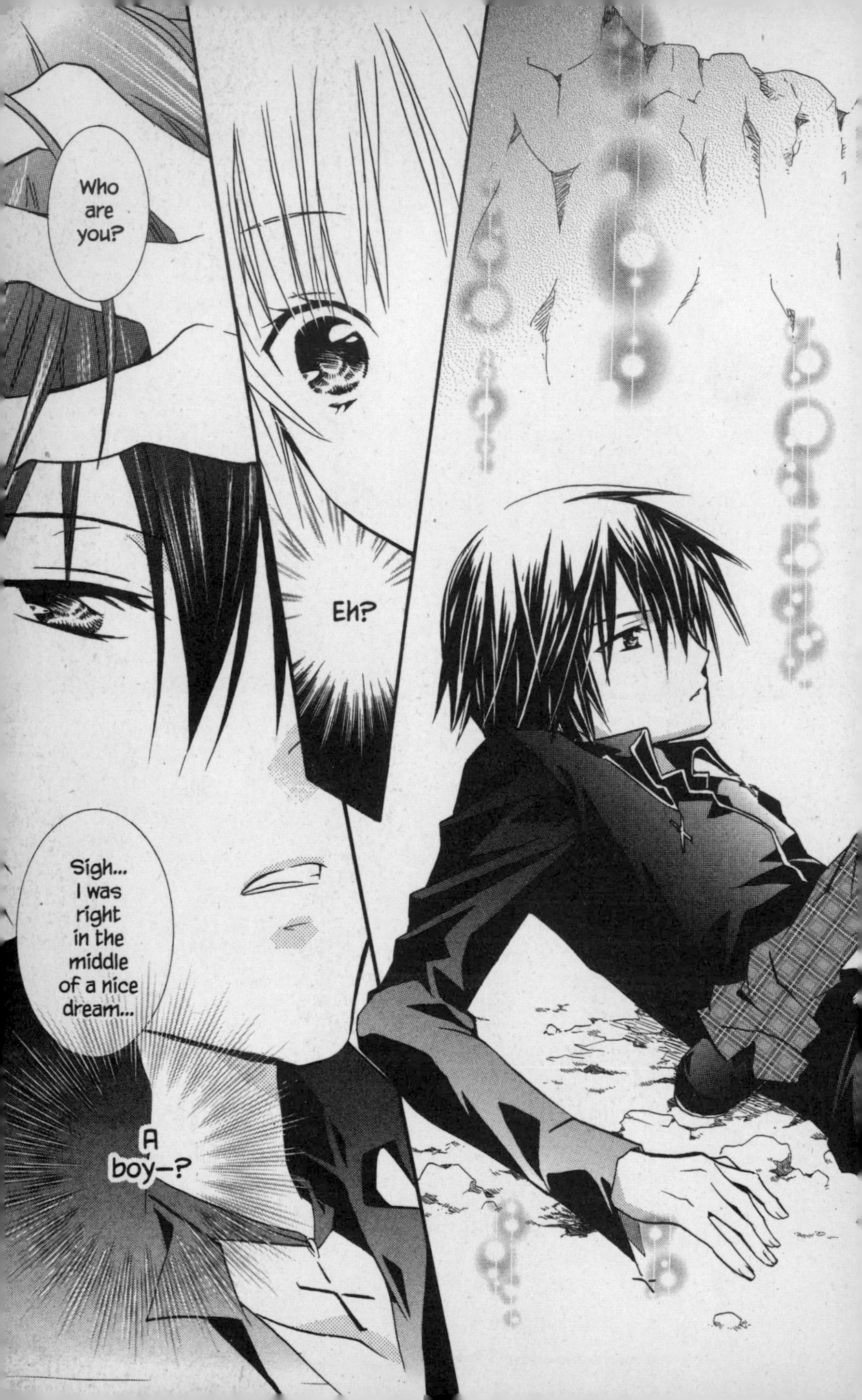
Eh?
Who are you?
Sigh... I was right in the middle of a nice dream...
A boy—?

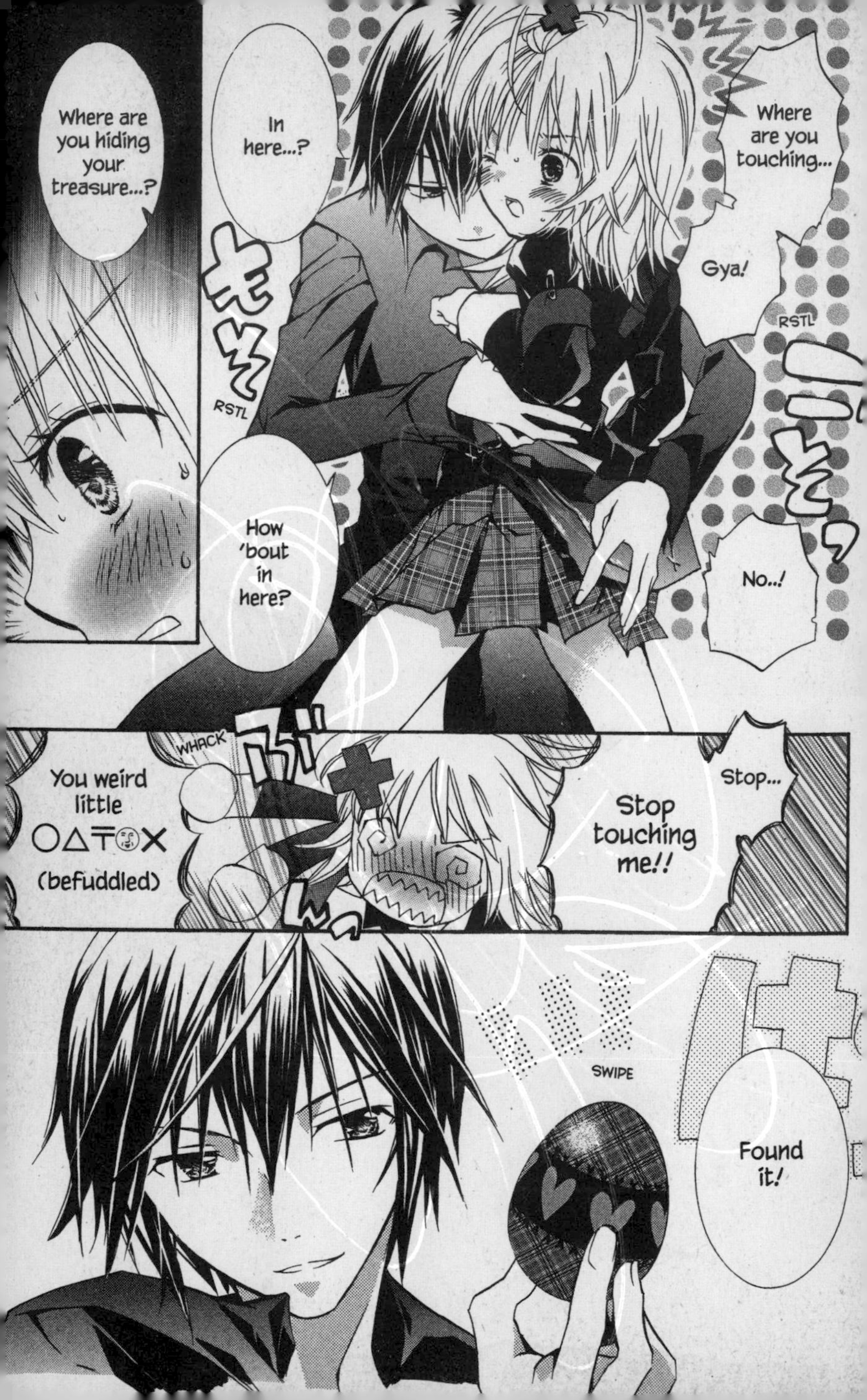

Where are you touching...
In here...?
Gya!
RSTL
No...!
RSTL
How 'bout in here?
Where are you hiding your treasure...?
Stop...
Stop touching me!!
WHACK
You weird little ○△T☺X (befuddled)
Found it!
SWIPE

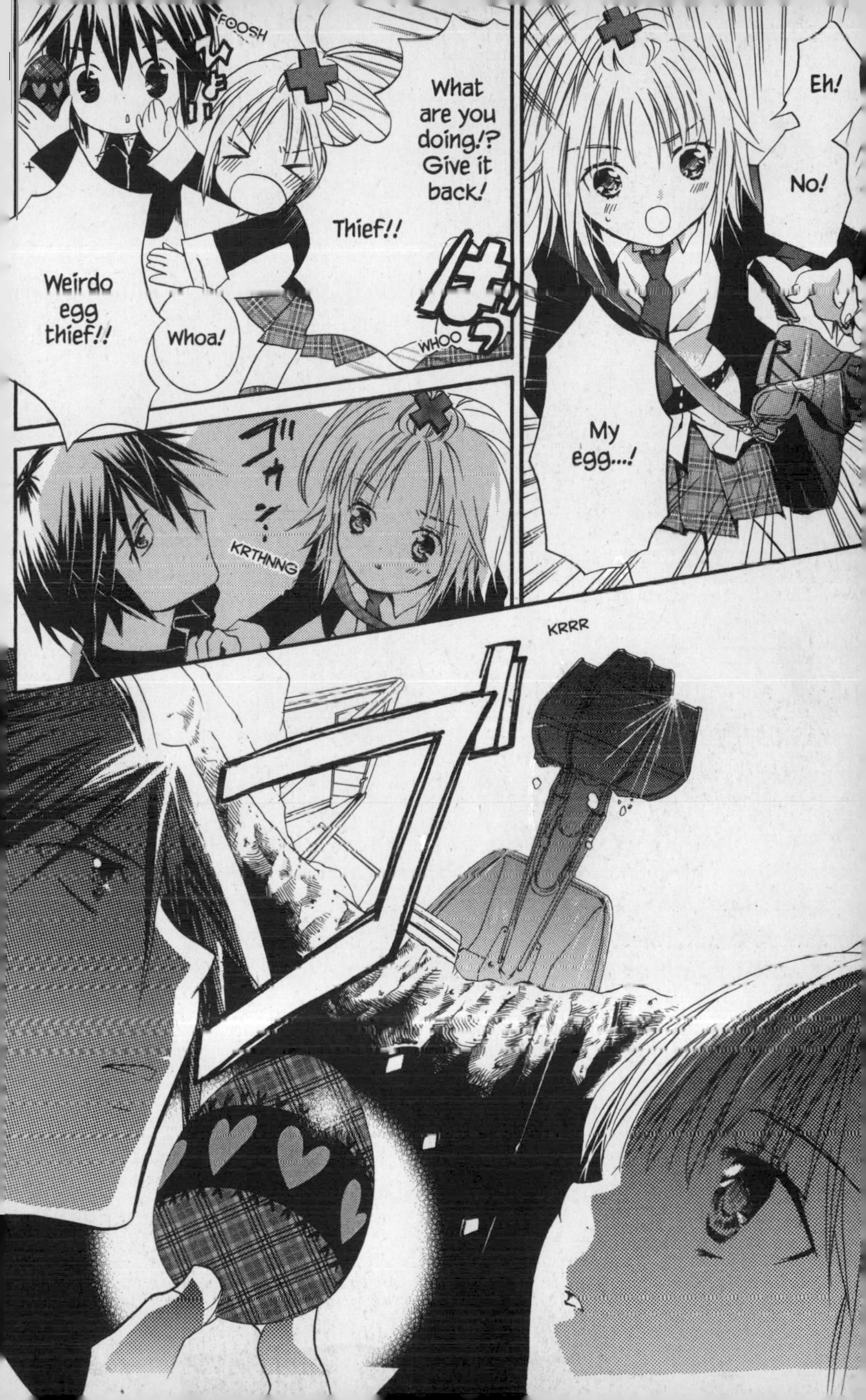
Eh!
No!
My egg...!
What are you doing!? Give it back!
FOOSH
Thief!!
WHOO
Whoa!
Weirdo egg thief!!
KRTHNNG
KRRR

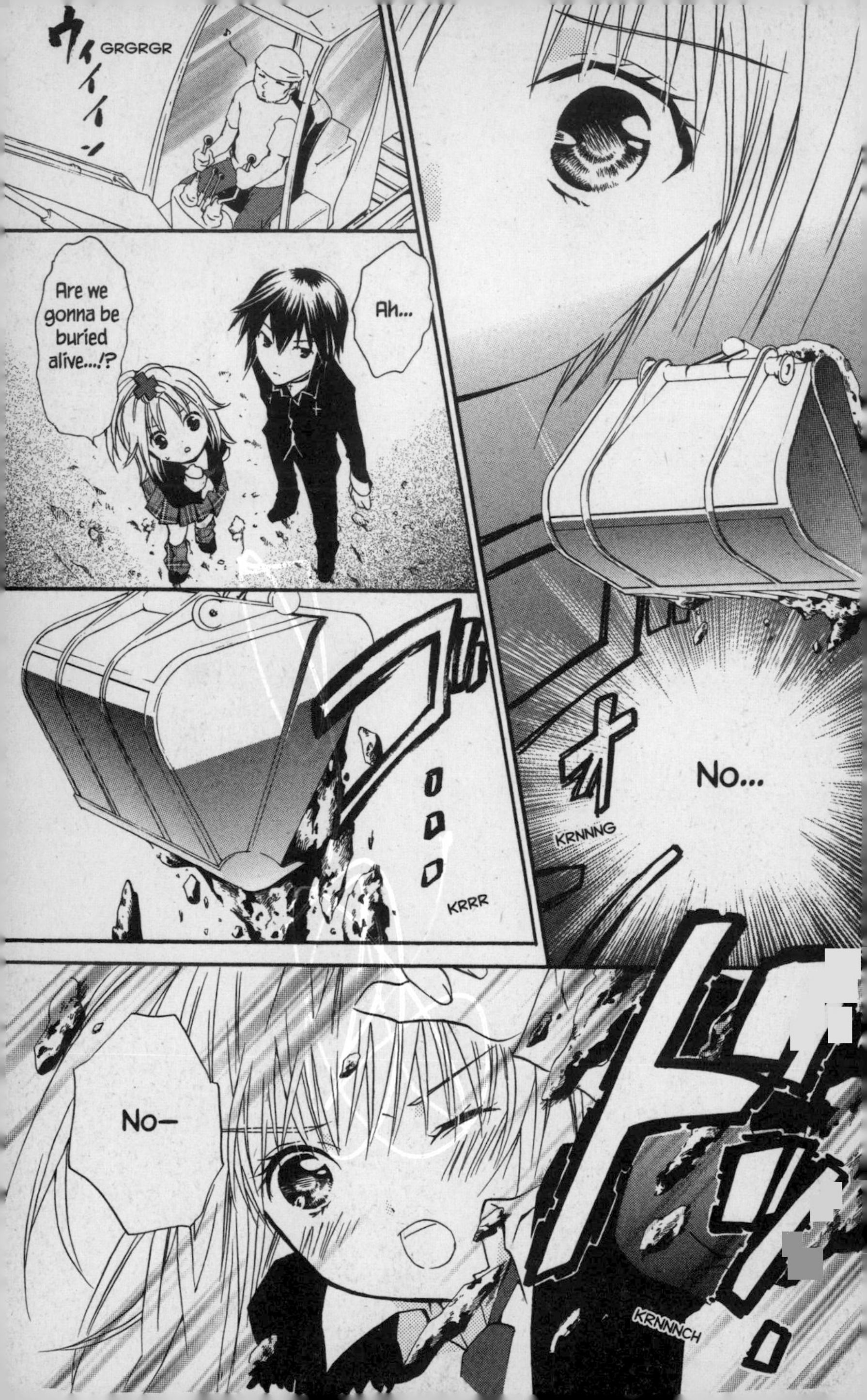
No...
KRNNNG
ウィイイーン
GRGRGR
Ah...
Are we gonna be buried alive...!?
KRRR
No–
KRNNNCH

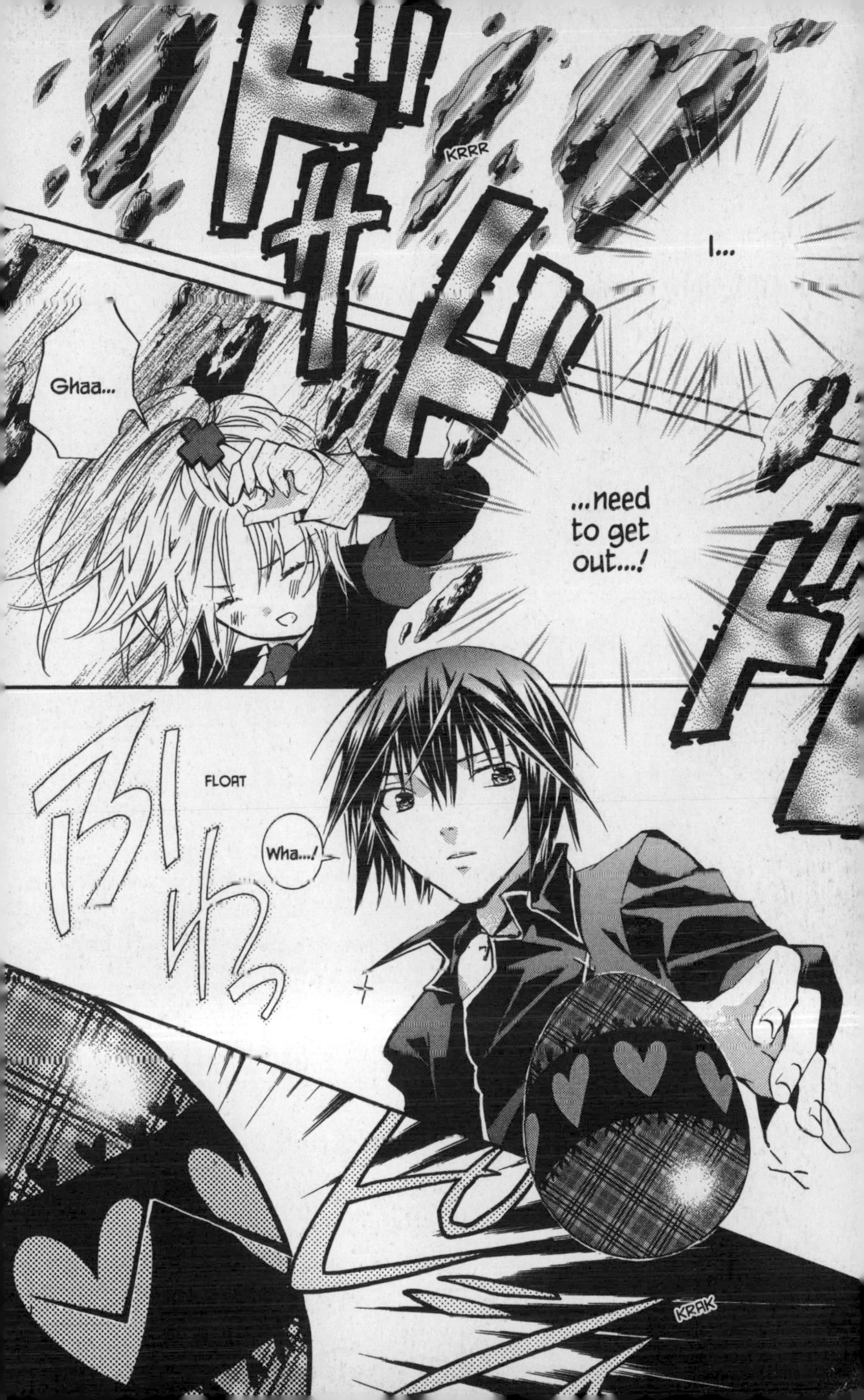
KRRR
I...
...need to get out...!
Ghaa...
FLOAT
Wha...!
KRAK

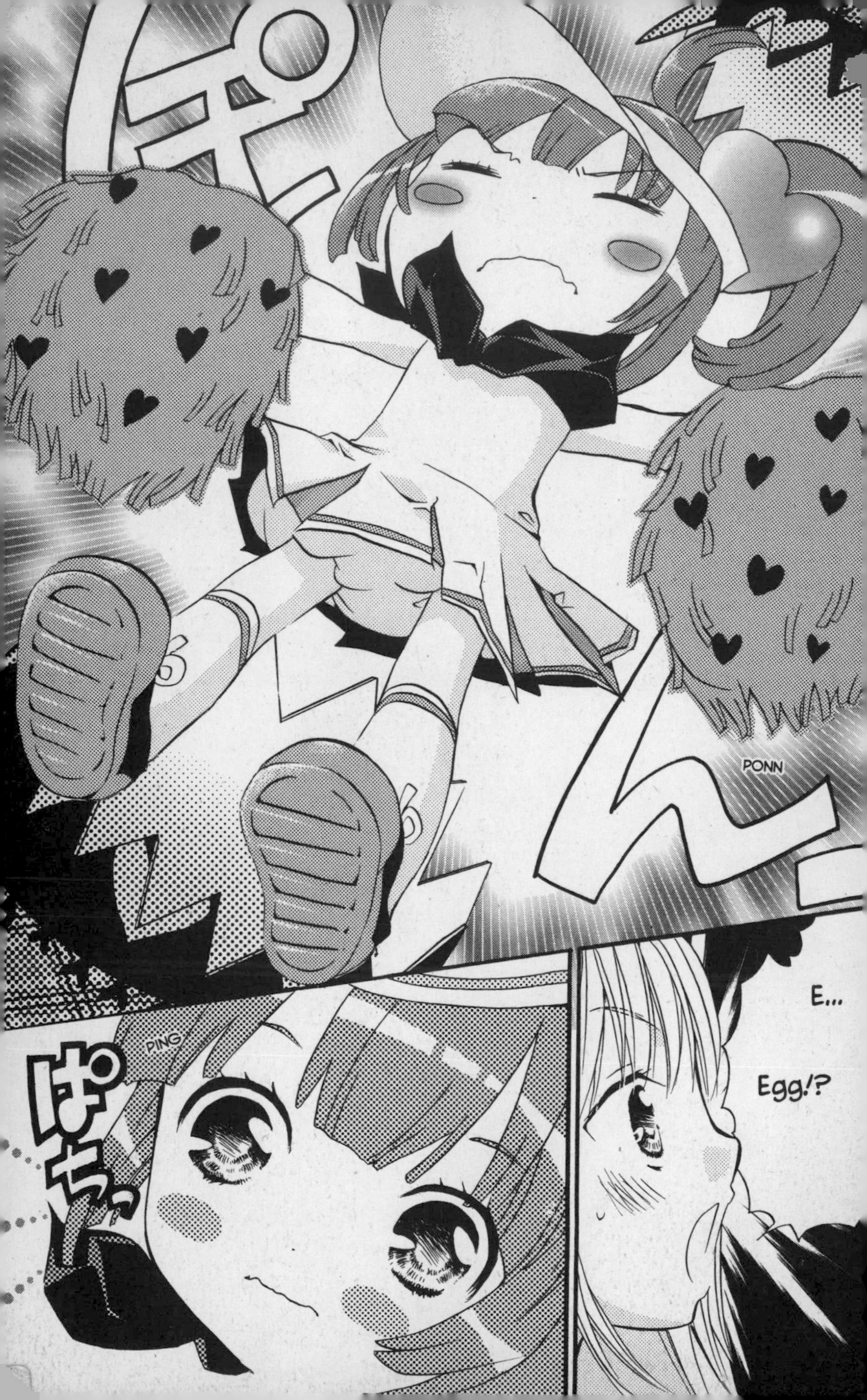
PONN
E...
Egg!?
PING
ぱちっ

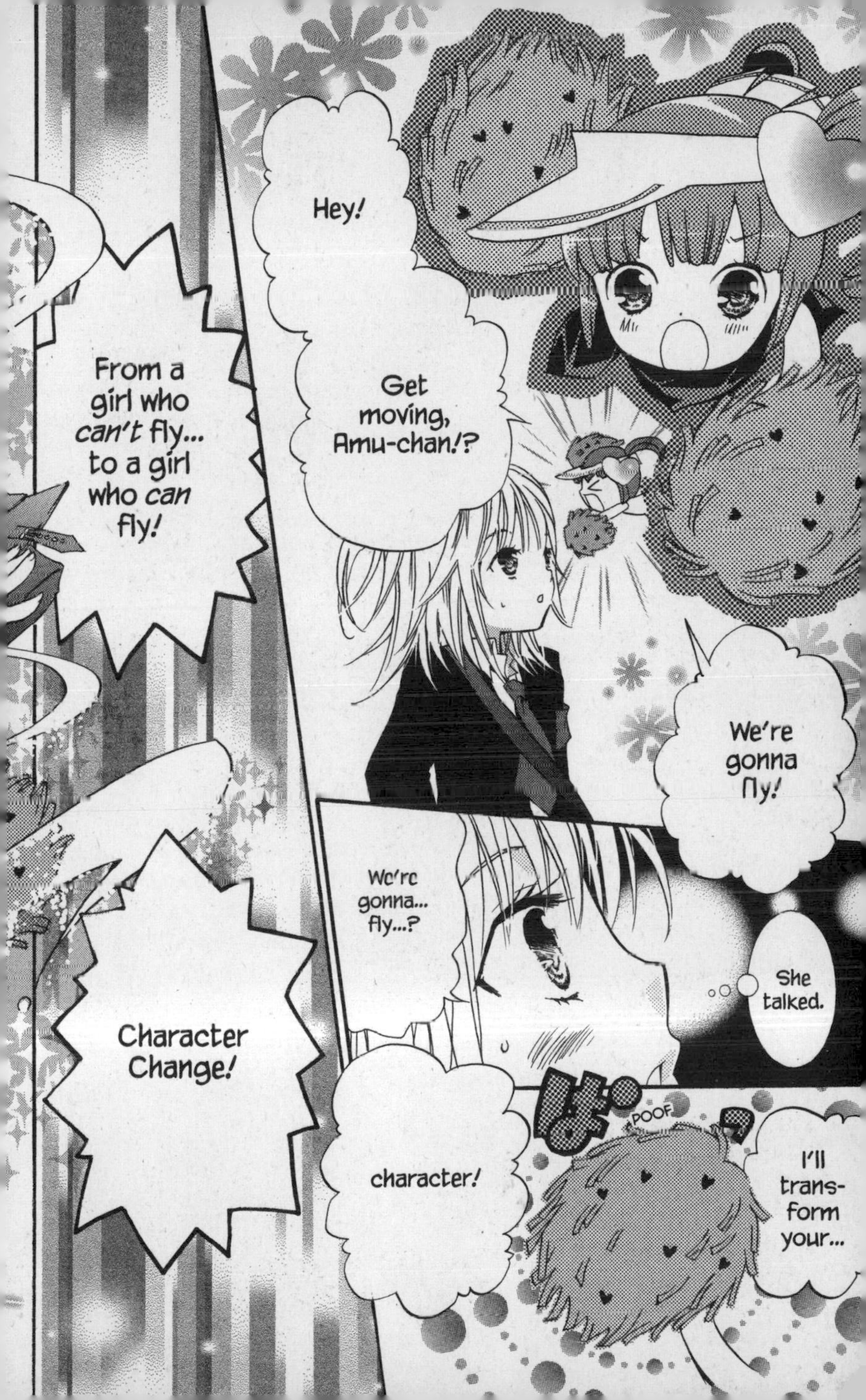
Hey!
Get moving, Amu-chan!?
We're gonna fly!
She talked.
We're gonna... fly...?
I'll trans-form your...
POOF
character!
From a girl who *can't* fly... to a girl who *can* fly!
Character Change!

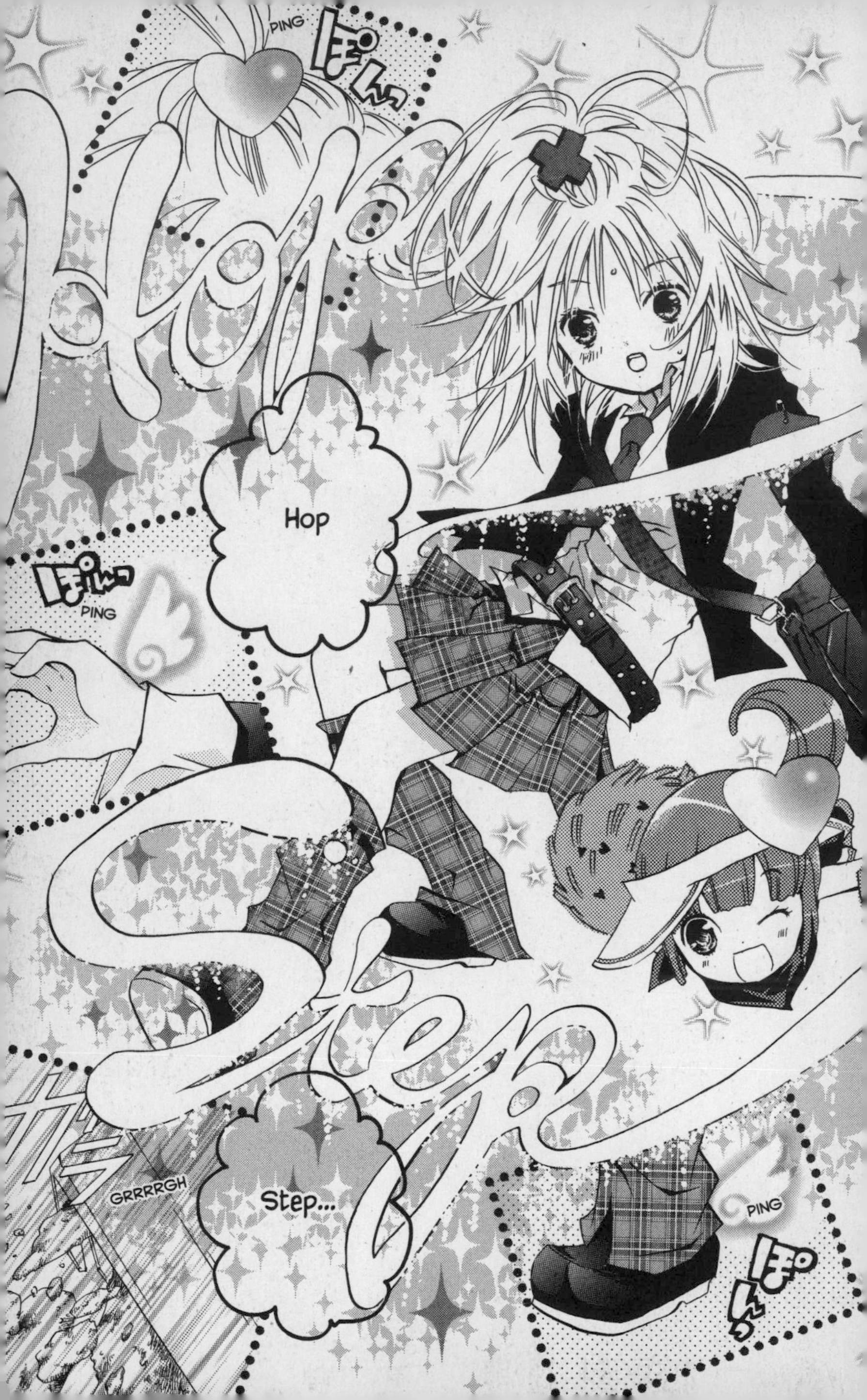
ぽんっ
PING
Hop
ぽんっ
PING
Step...
PING
ぽんっ
GRRRRGH

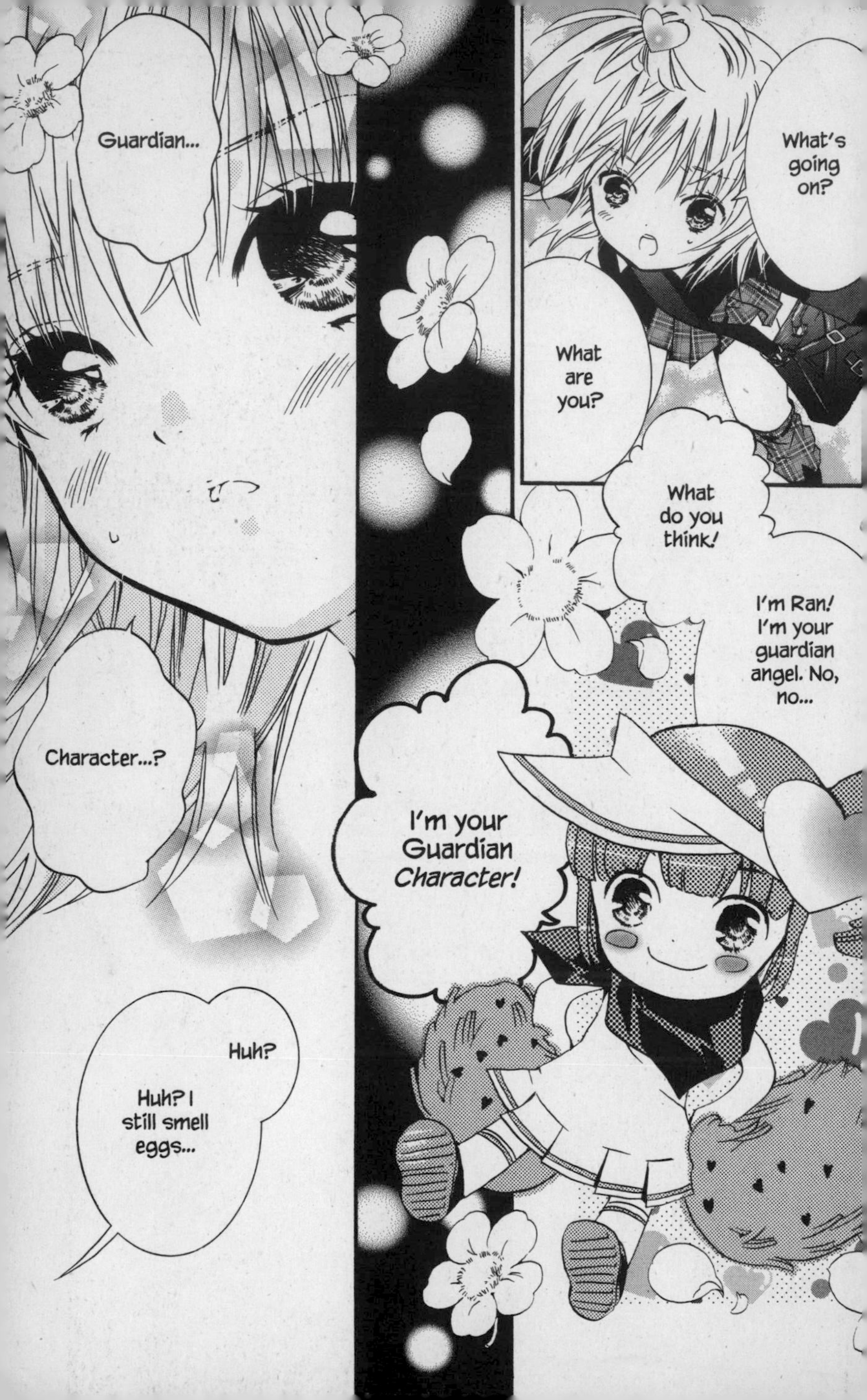
What's going on?
What are you?
What do you think!
I'm Ran! I'm your guardian angel. No, no...
I'm your Guardian *Character*!
Guardian...
Character...?
Huh?
Huh? I still smell eggs...

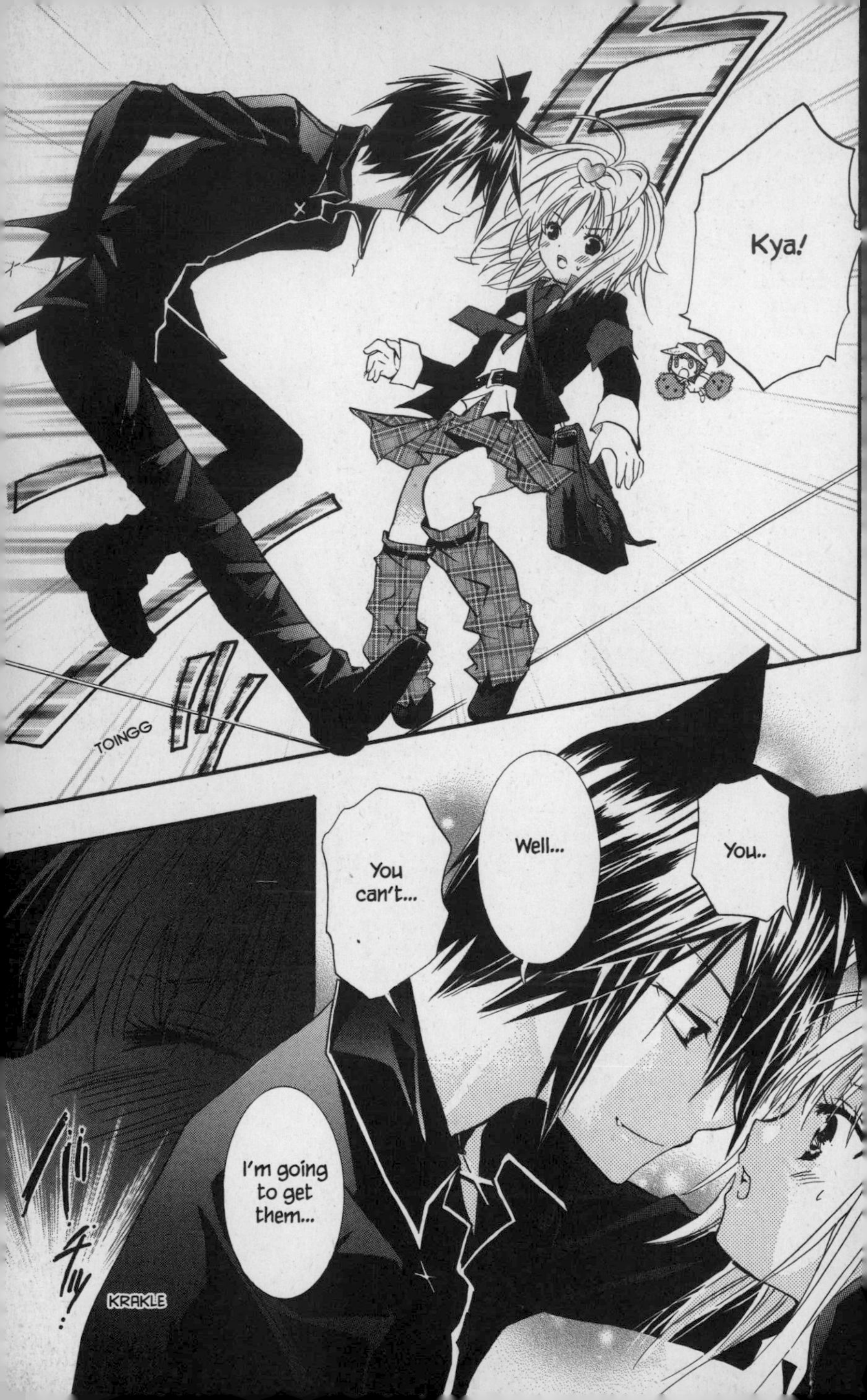
Kya!
TOINGG
You..
Well...
You can't...
I'm going to get them...
KRAKLE

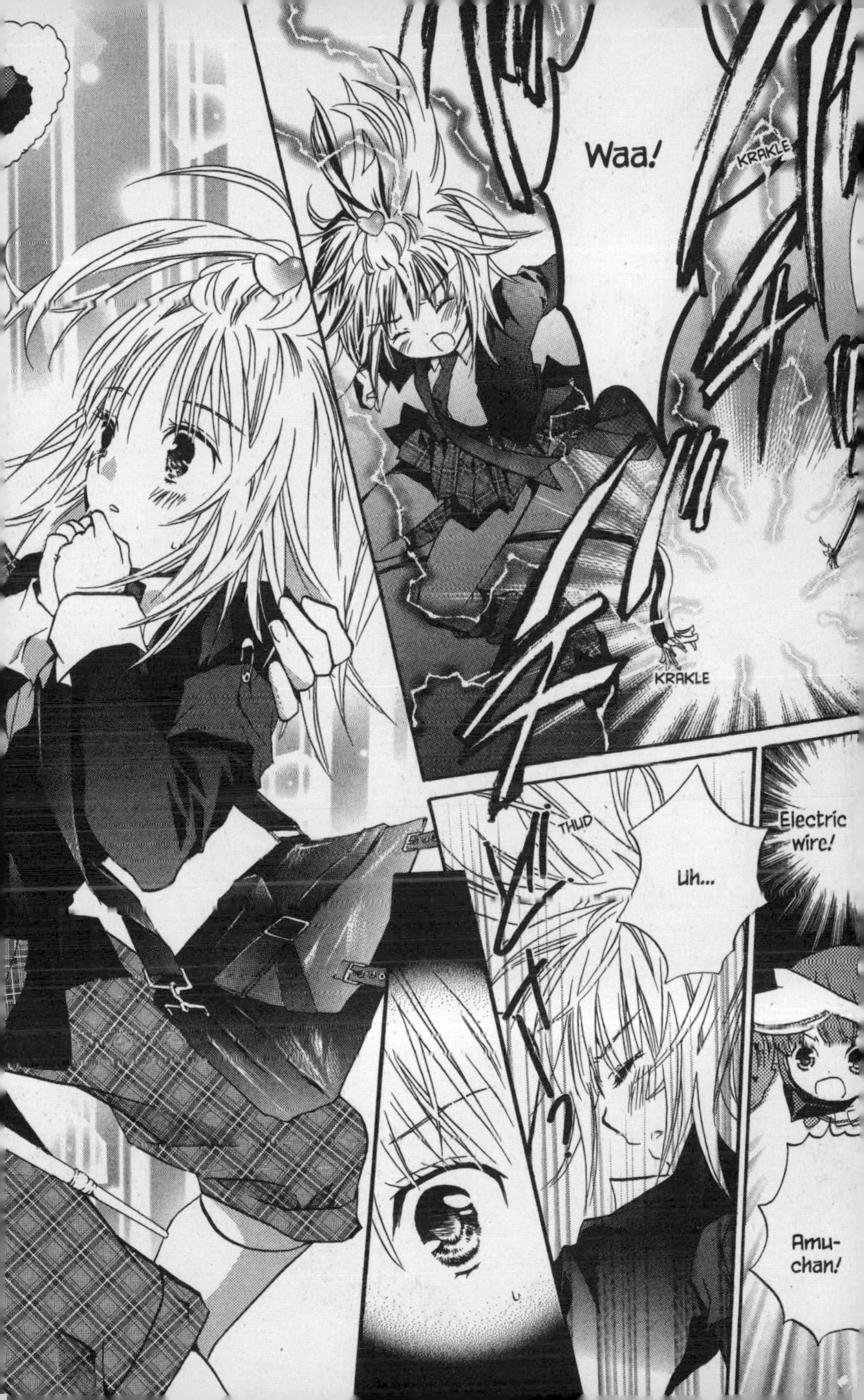
Waa!
KRAKLE
KRAKLE
Electric wire!
Uh...
THUD
Amu-chan!

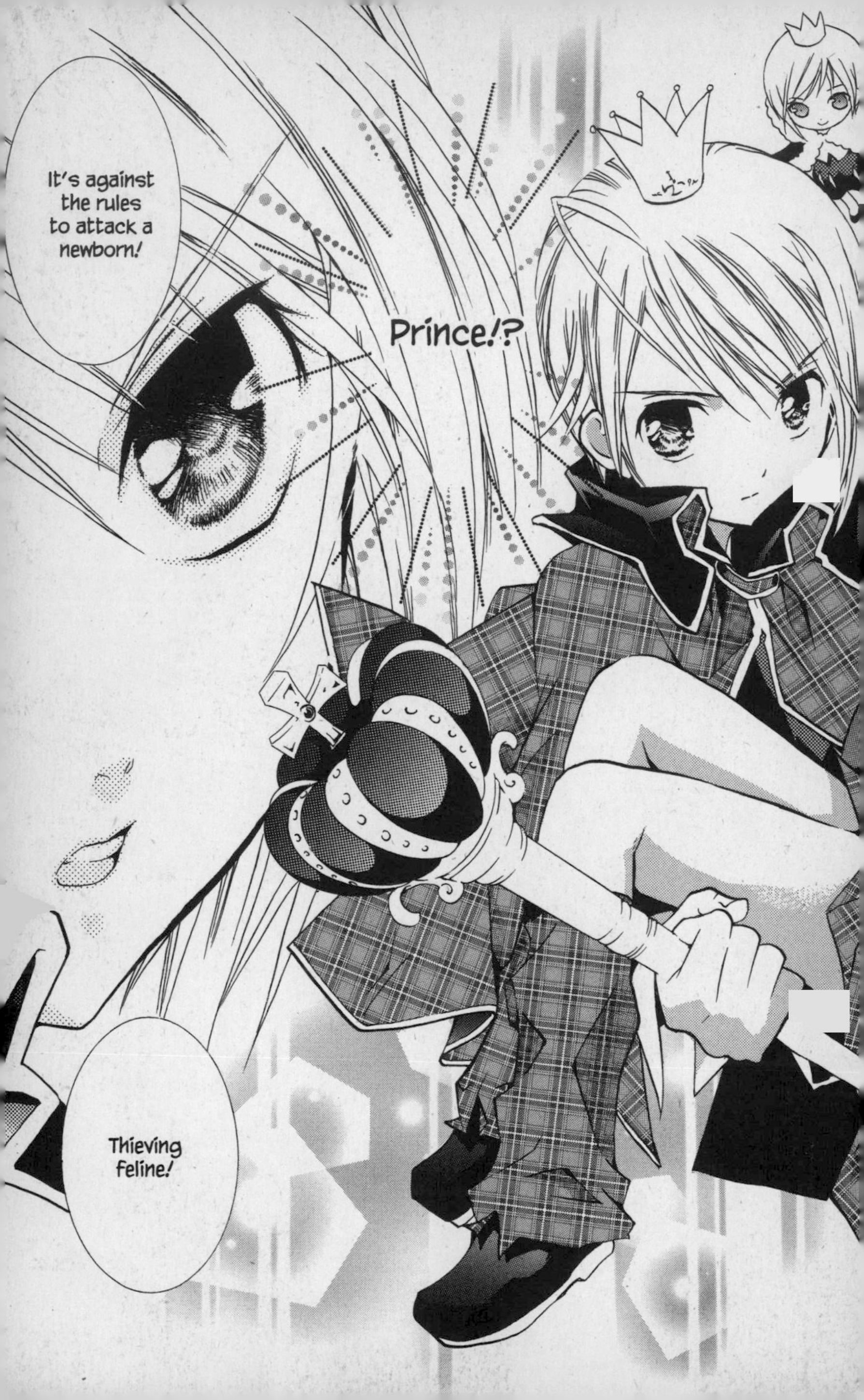
Prince!?
It's against the rules to attack a newborn!
Thieving feline!

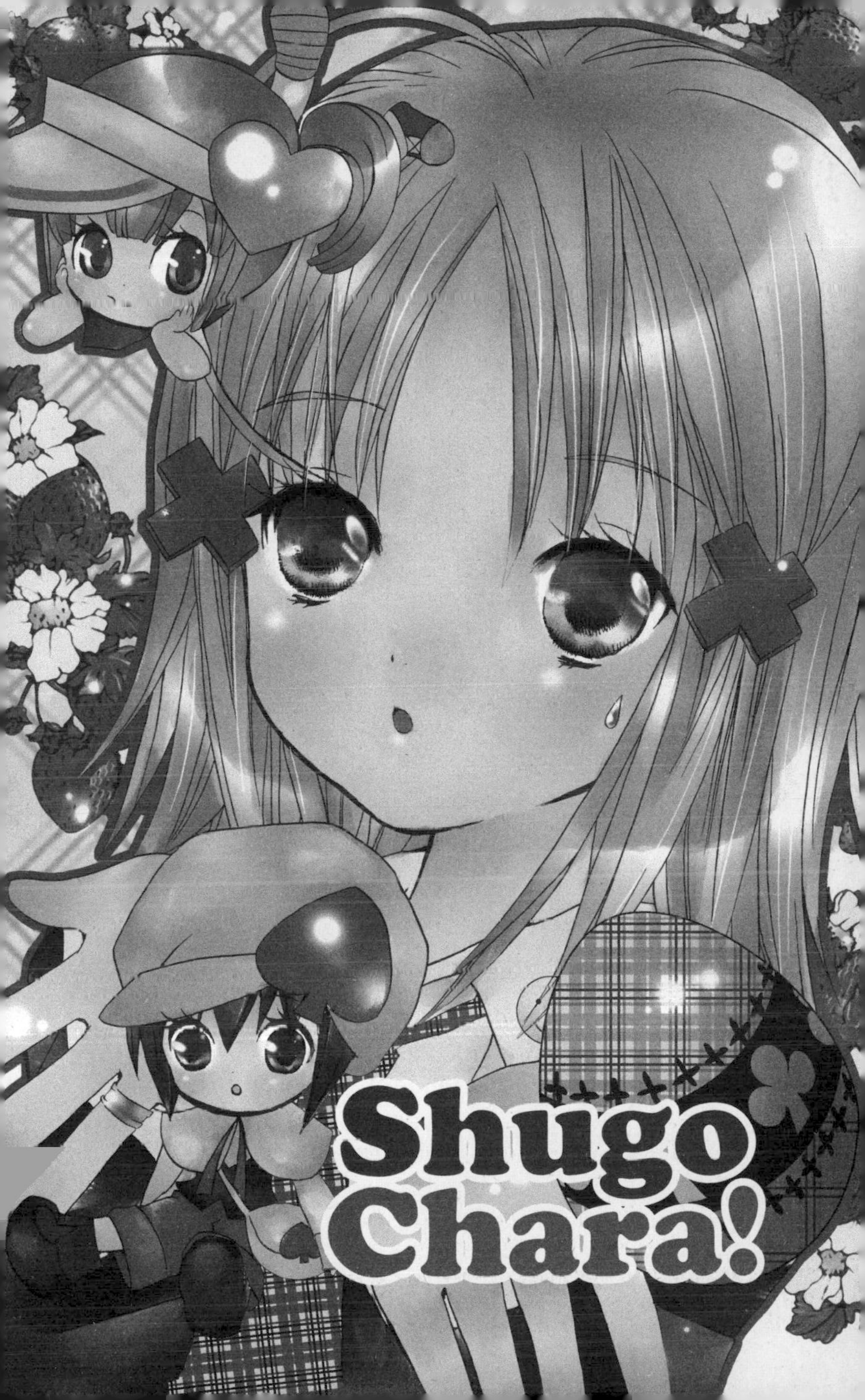
Shugo
Chara!

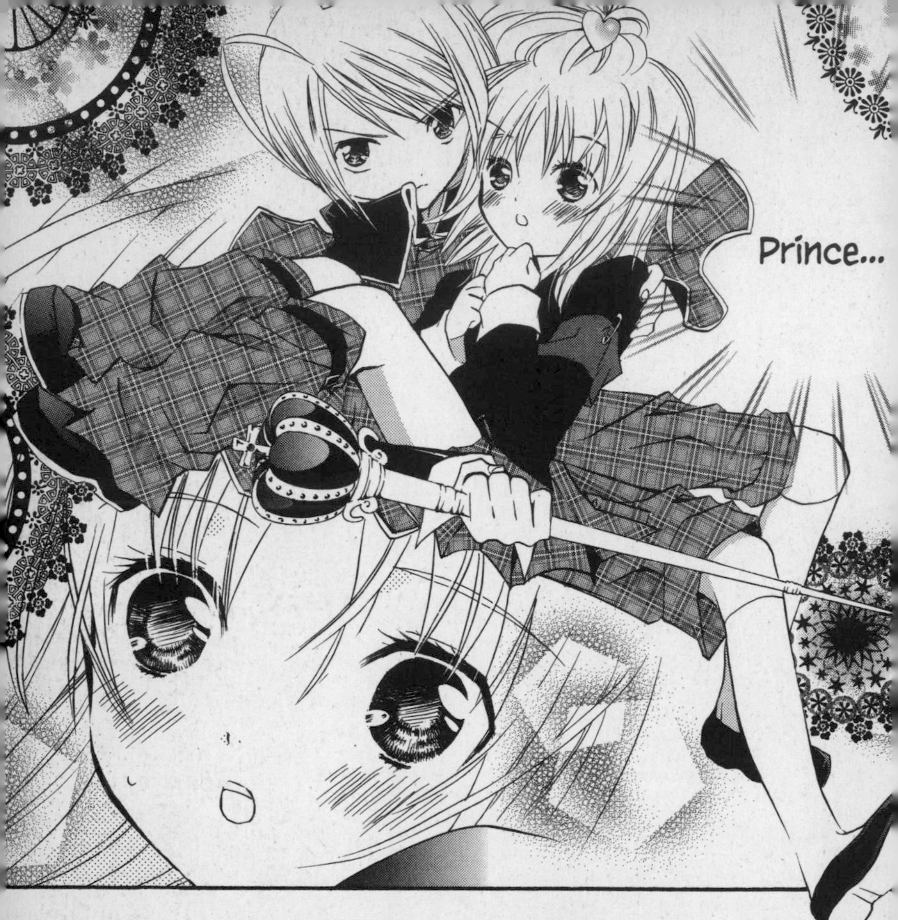
Prince...

Nice to meet you, everyone! We're PEACH-PIT.
We'd like to thank you for purchasing "Shugo Chara!" This is a free space we've been dreaming about having. We're very excited and hope you enjoy reading up to the end. ♡

We're thinking of using this free space to answer frequently asked questions from our fan mail (by the way...thank you for them!) or to just freely talk about whatever is on our mind.
Those of you who think, "the print's too small, I can't read it!" we apologize for that...please blow it up on a copy machine!

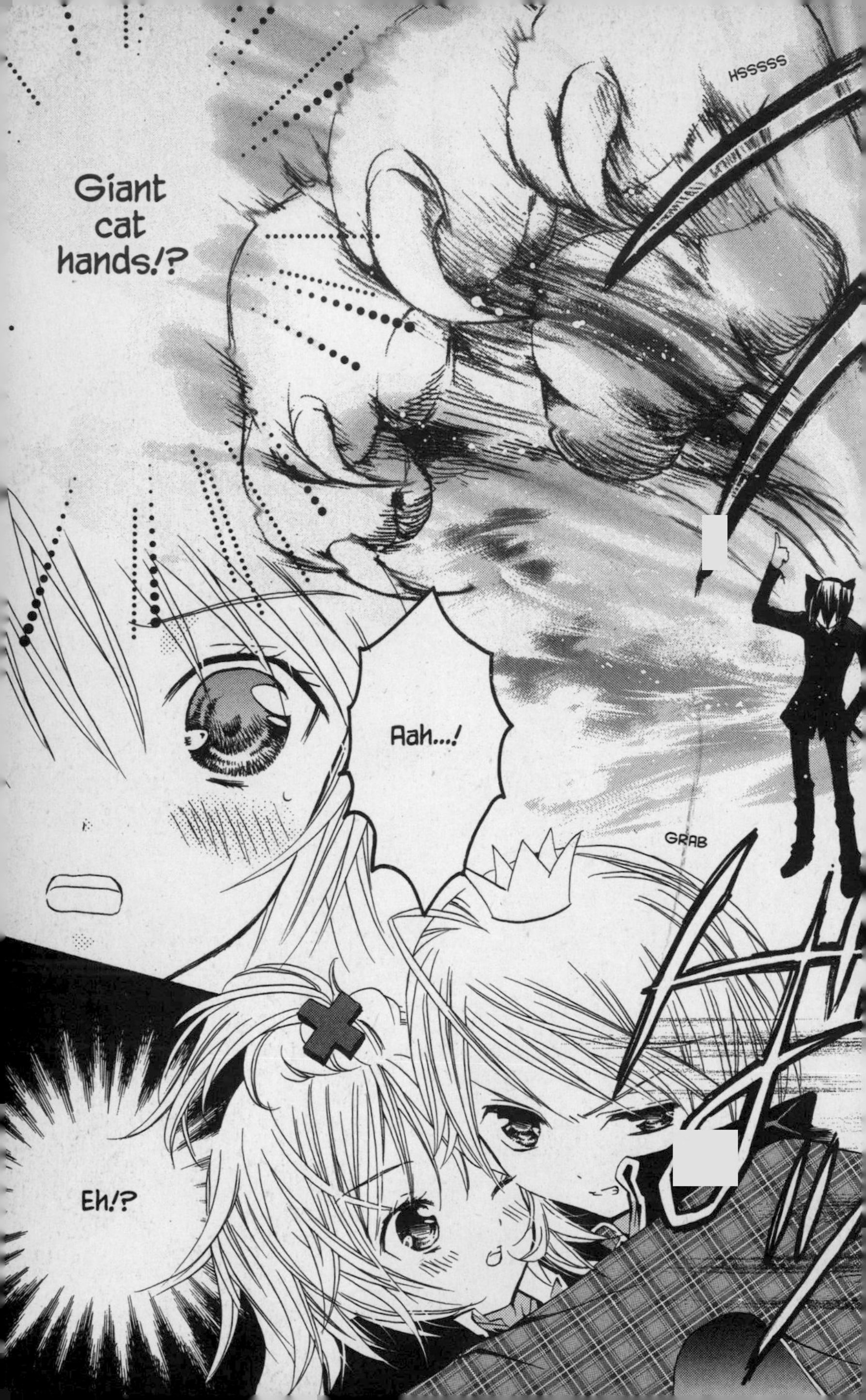
HSSSSS
Giant cat hands!?
Aah...!
GRAB
Eh!?

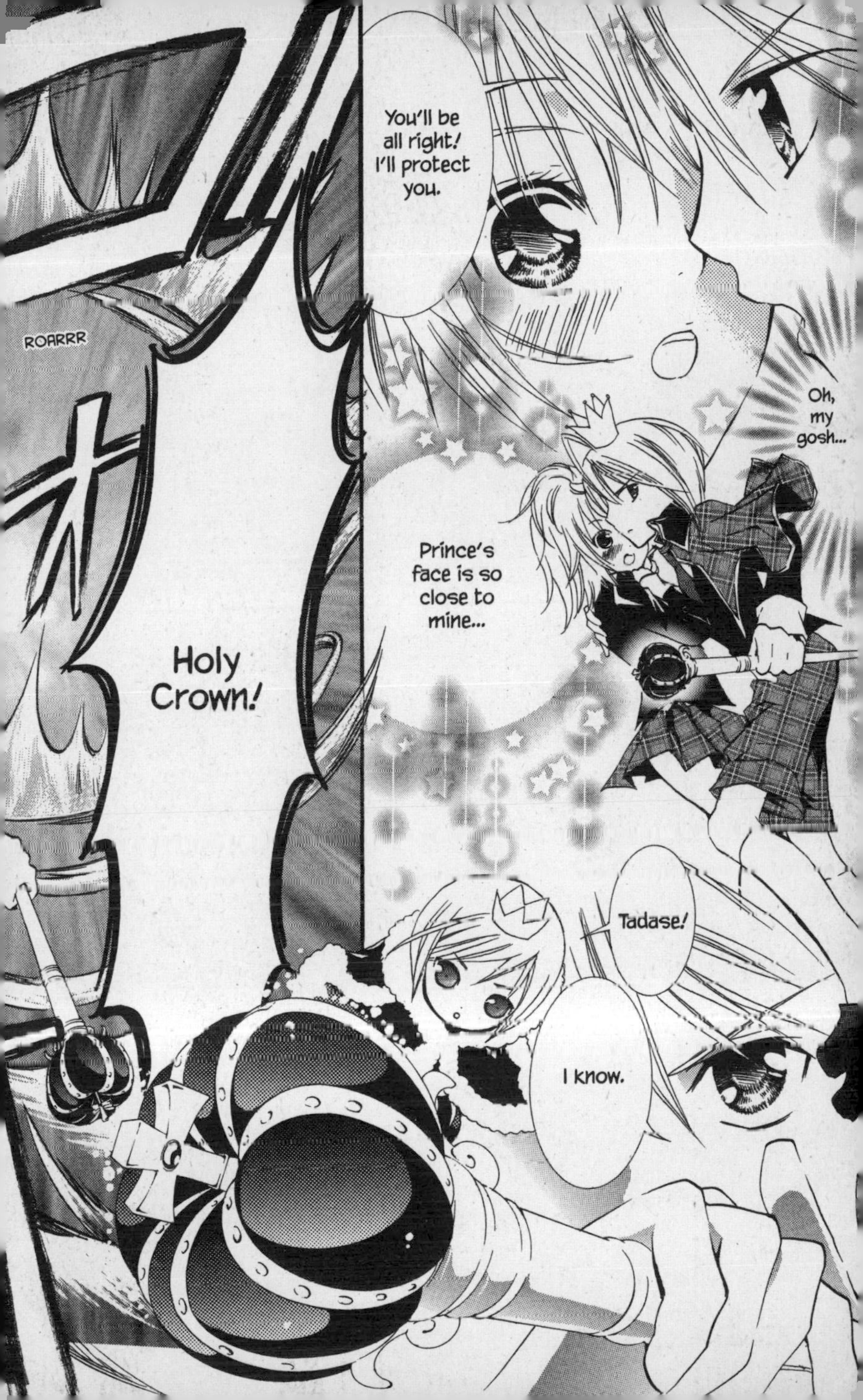
You'll be all right! I'll protect you.
Oh, my gosh...
Prince's face is so close to mine...
Tadase!
I know.
ROARRR
Holy Crown!

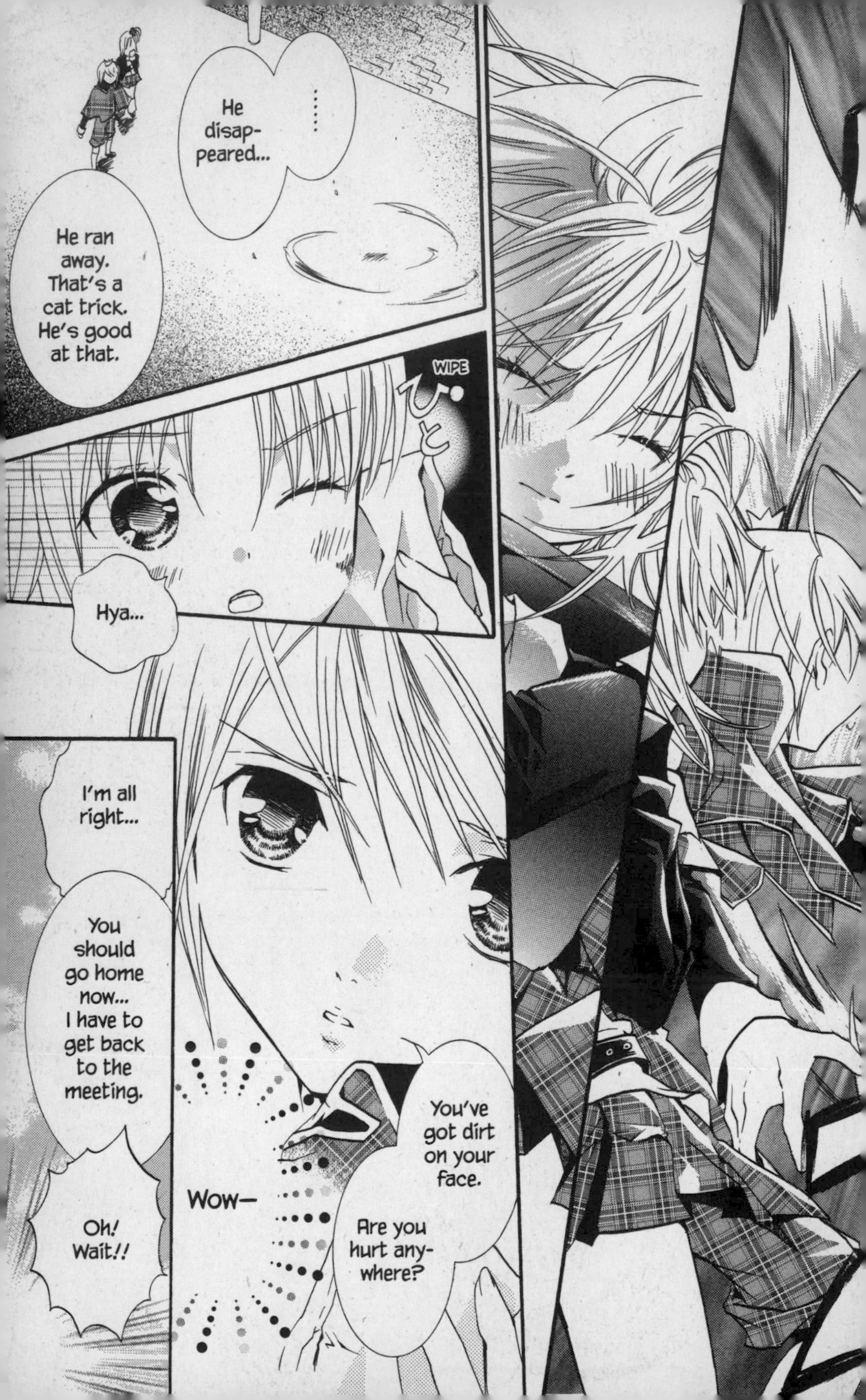
......
He disap-peared...
He ran away. That's a cat trick. He's good at that.
WIPE
ひと
Hya...
You've got dirt on your face.
Are you hurt any-where?
Wow—
I'm all right...
You should go home now... I have to get back to the meeting.
Oh! Wait!!

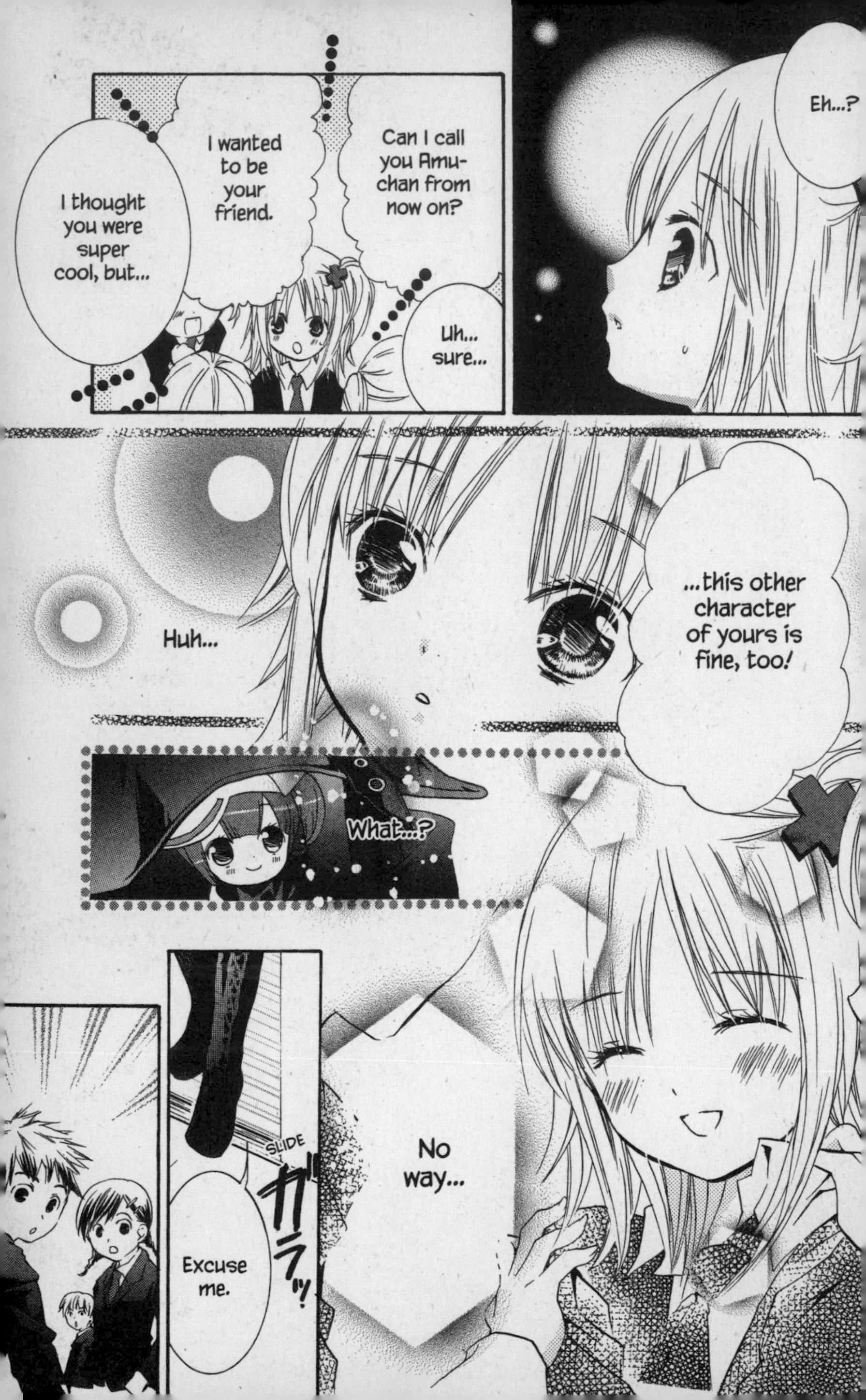
Eh...?
Can I call you Amu-chan from now on?
I wanted to be your friend.
I thought you were super cool, but...
Uh... sure...
...this other character of yours is fine, too!
Huh...
What...?
No way...
SLIDE
Excuse me.

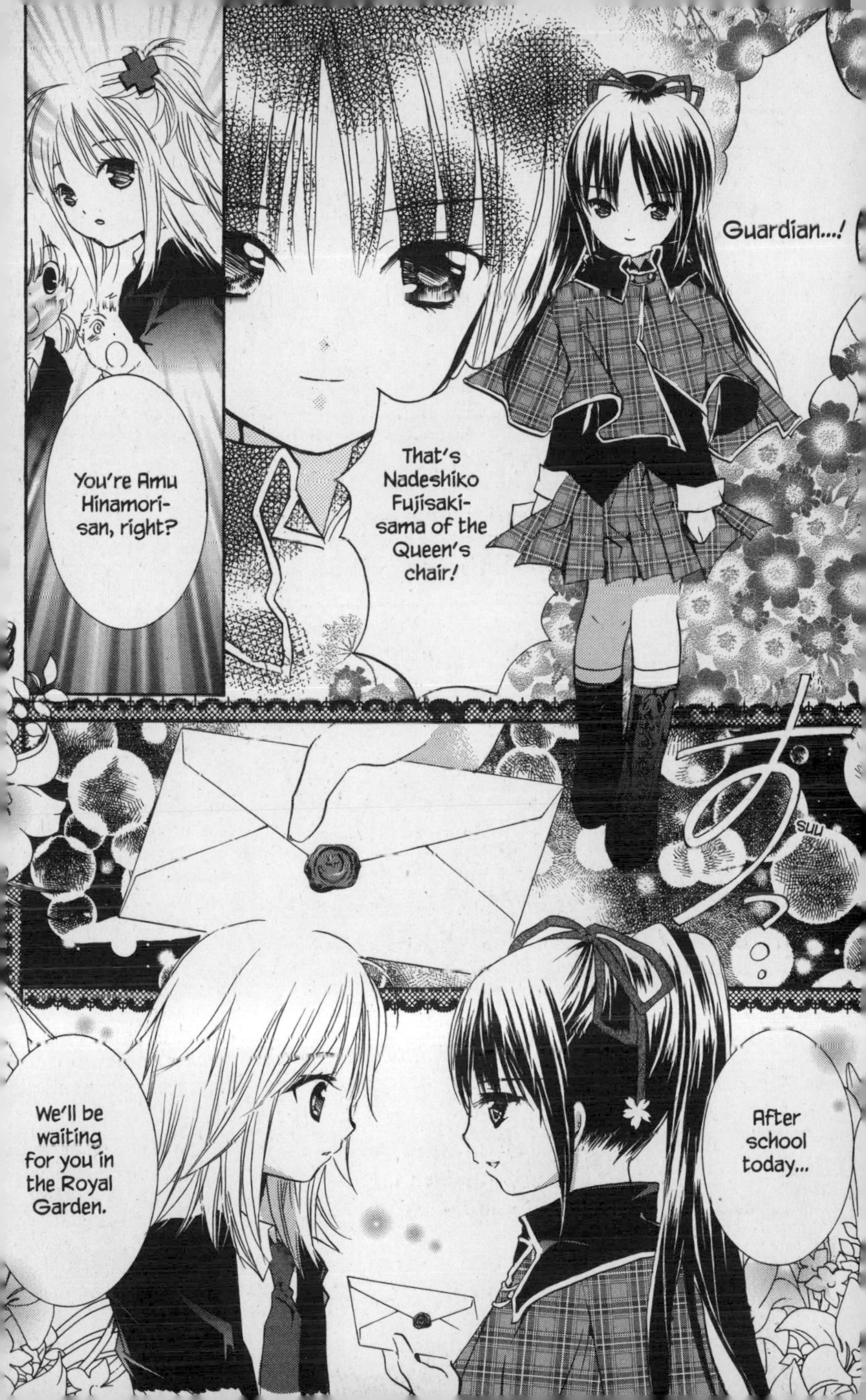
Guardian...!
That's Nadeshiko Fujisaki-sama of the Queen's chair!
You're Amu Hinamori-san, right?
suu
After school today...
We'll be waiting for you in the Royal Garden.

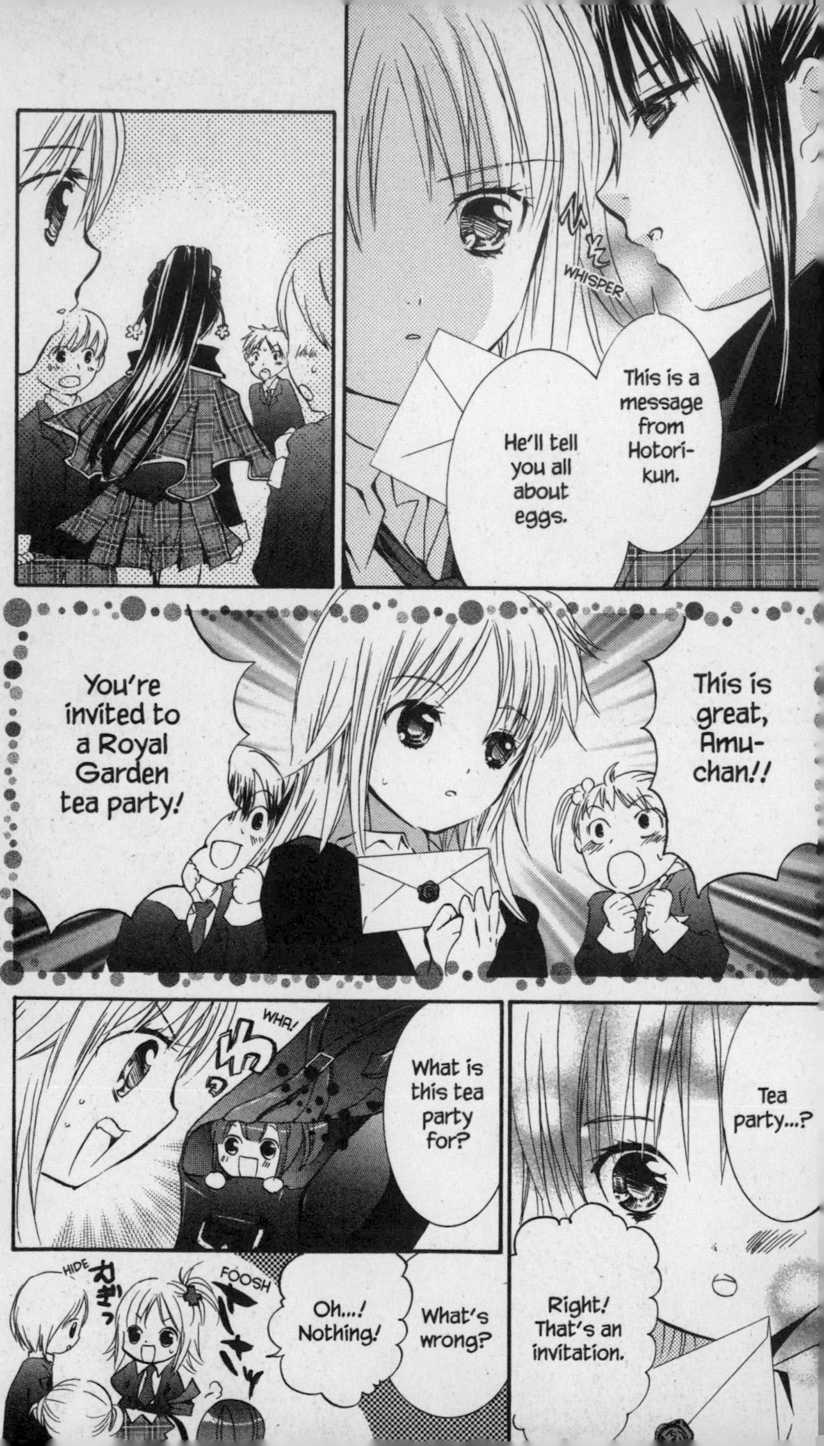
WHISPER
This is a message from Hotori-kun.
He'll tell you all about eggs.
This is great, Amu-chan!!
You're invited to a Royal Garden tea party!
Tea party...?
Right! That's an invitation.
WHA!
What is this tea party for?
What's wrong?
Oh...! Nothing!
FOOSH
HIDE

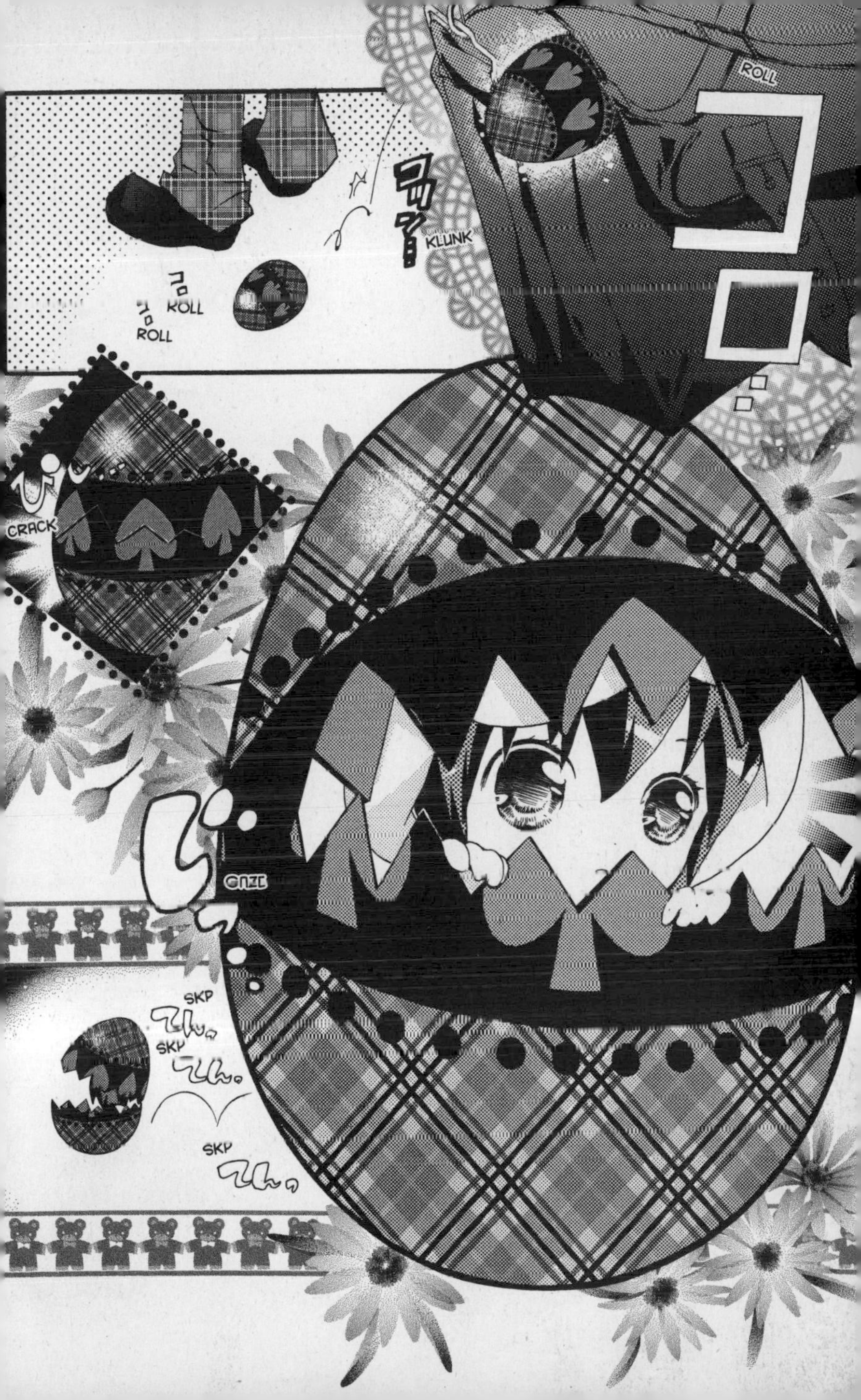

ROLL
KLUNK
ROLL
ROLL
CRACK
SKP
SKP
SKP

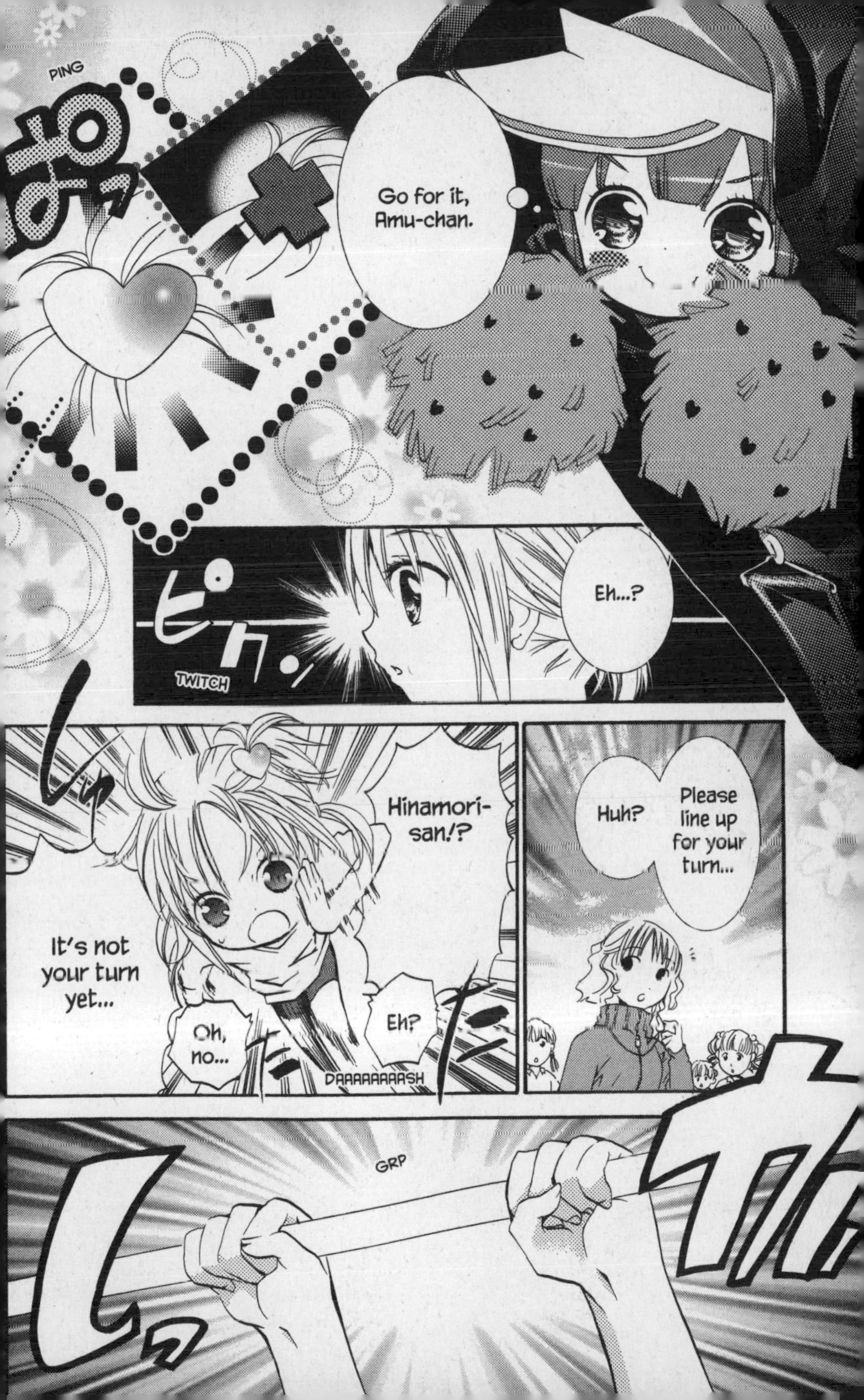
Go for it, Amu-chan.
PING
Eh...?
TWITCH
Please line up for your turn...
Huh?
Hinamori-san!?
It's not your turn yet...
Eh?
Oh, no...
DAAAAAAAAASH
GRP

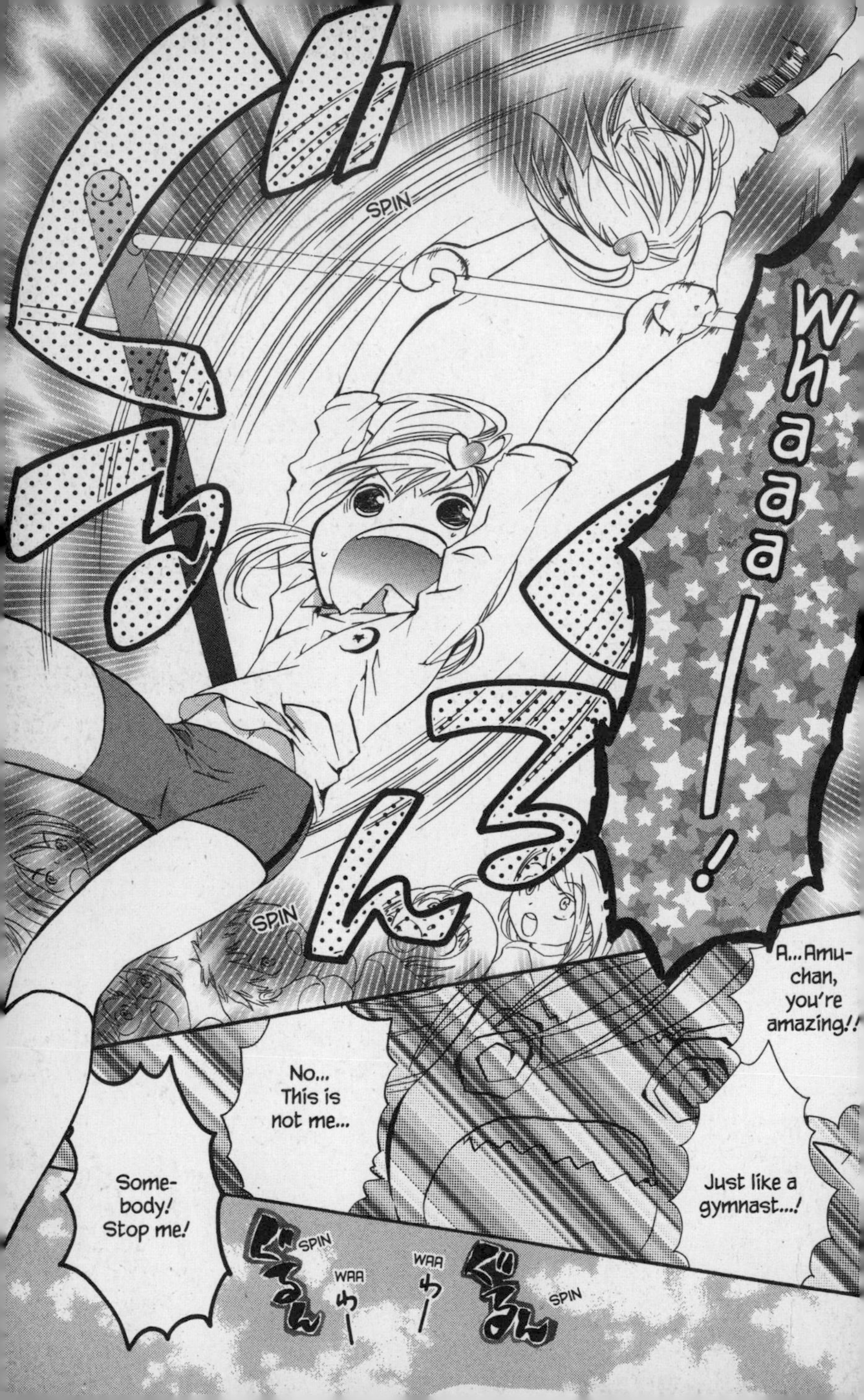
Whaaaa—!
SPIN
SPIN
A...Amu-chan, you're amazing!!
No... This is not me...
Just like a gymnast...!
Somebody! Stop me!
SPIN
WAA
WAA
SPIN

character profile

日奈森 あむ
Amu Hinamori

Birthday: 9/24
BloodType: O
Sign: Libra
Shugo-Chara: Ran,
            Miki, Su

Yeah...We'll have to look first thing after school...

What am I gonna do? We have to go look for it...

After school...

No...

You Guardian Characters...

. . . . . .

Amu-chan...?

That's not what we...

That's not what I want...

You change my character without asking and then make me do things...

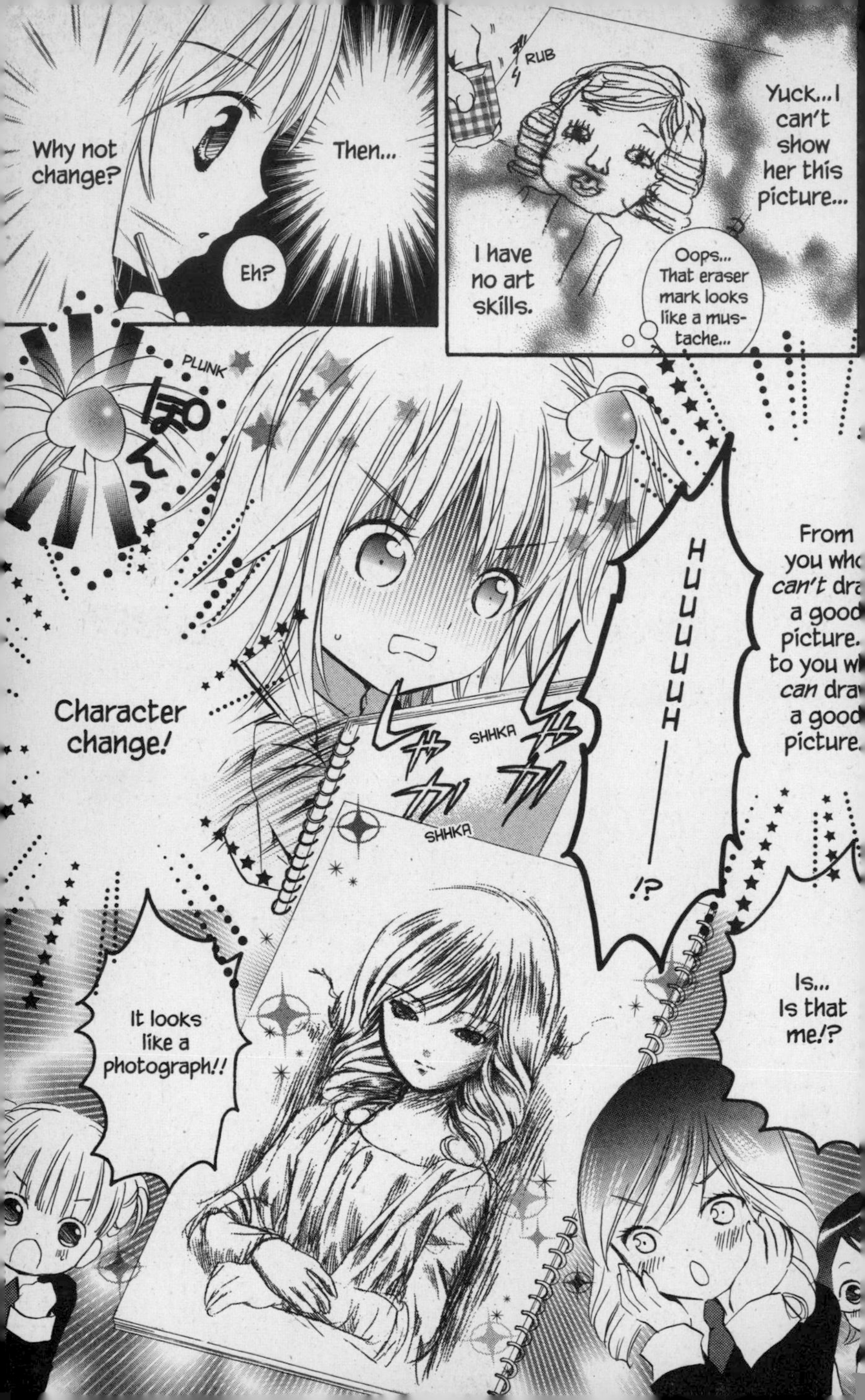
RUB
Yuck...I can't show her this picture...
I have no art skills.
Oops... That eraser mark looks like a mus-tache...
Then...
Eh?
Why not change?
From you wh can't dra a good picture. to you w can dra a good picture.
HUUUUUUH—!?
SHHKA
SHHKA
PLUNK
ぽんっ
Character change!
Is... Is that me!?
It looks like a photograph!!

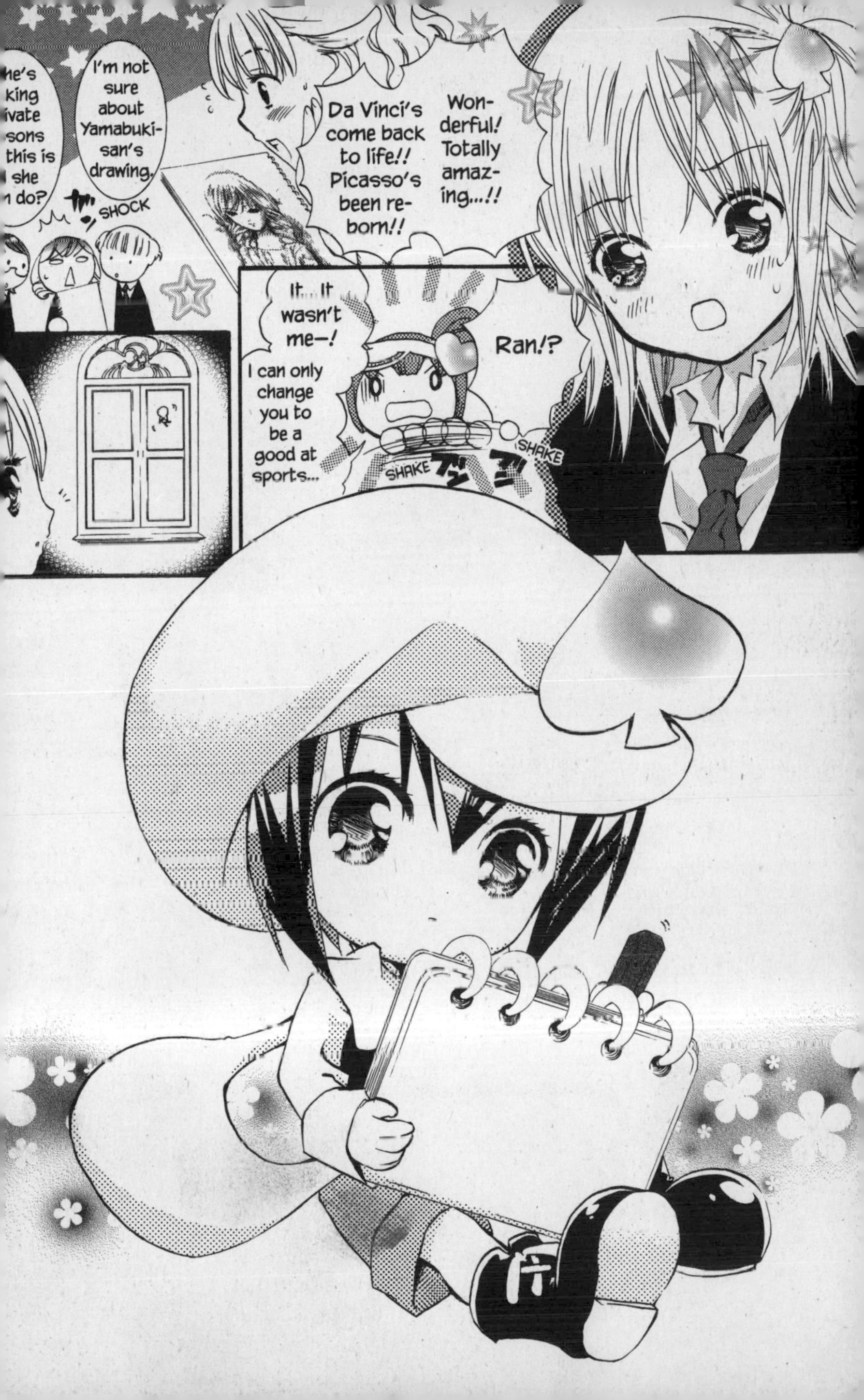
Won-derful! Totally amaz-ing...!!
Da Vinci's come back to life!! Picasso's been re-born!!
I'm not sure about Yamabuki-san's drawing.
he's king ivate sons this is she n do?
SHOCK
Ran!?
It... It wasn't me—!
I can only change you to be a good at sports...
SHAKE
SHAKE

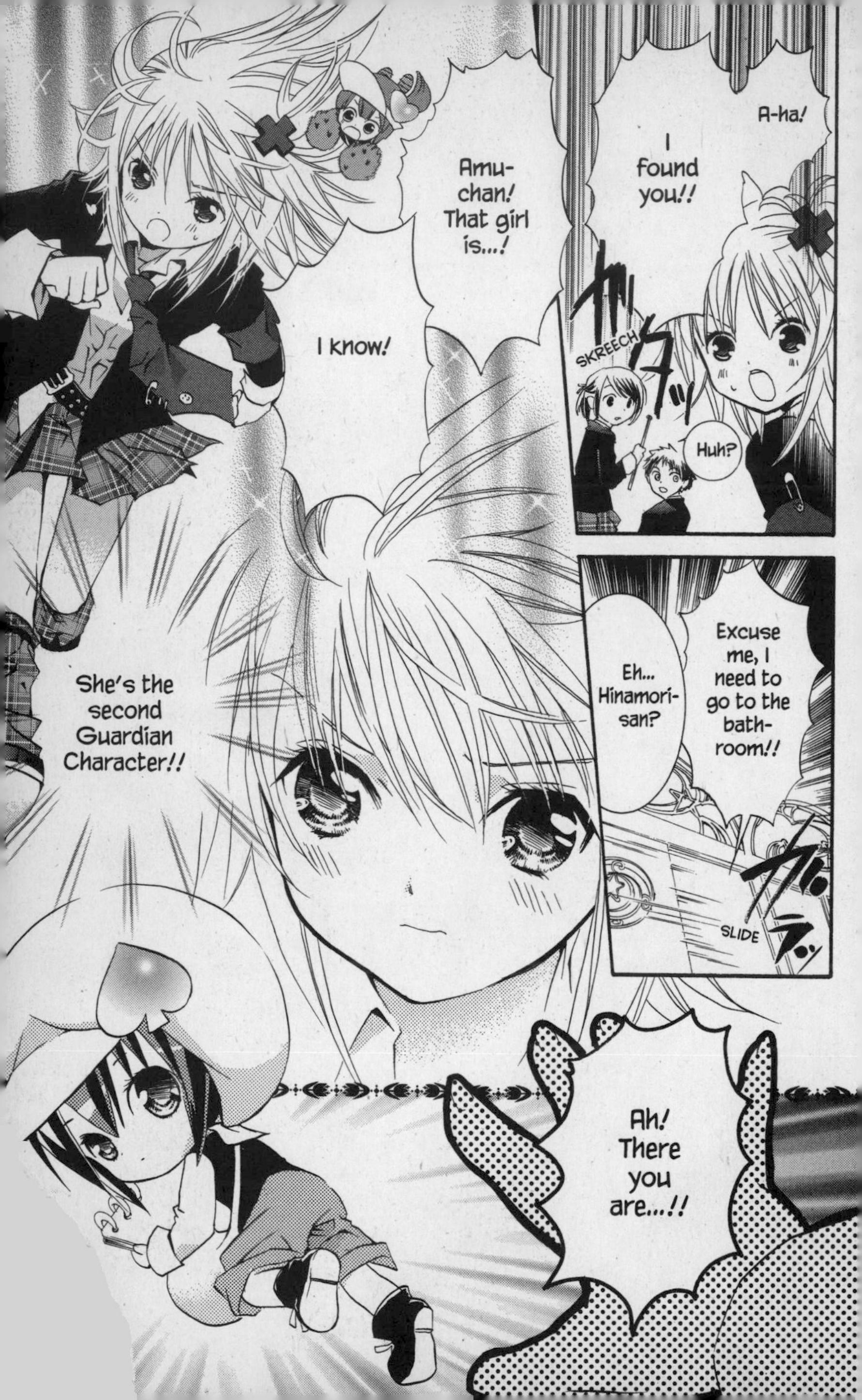
A-ha!
I found you!!
SKREECH
Huh?
Excuse me, I need to go to the bathroom!!
Eh... Hinamori-san?
SLIDE
Amu-chan! That girl is...!
I know!
She's the second Guardian Character!!
Ah! There you are...!!

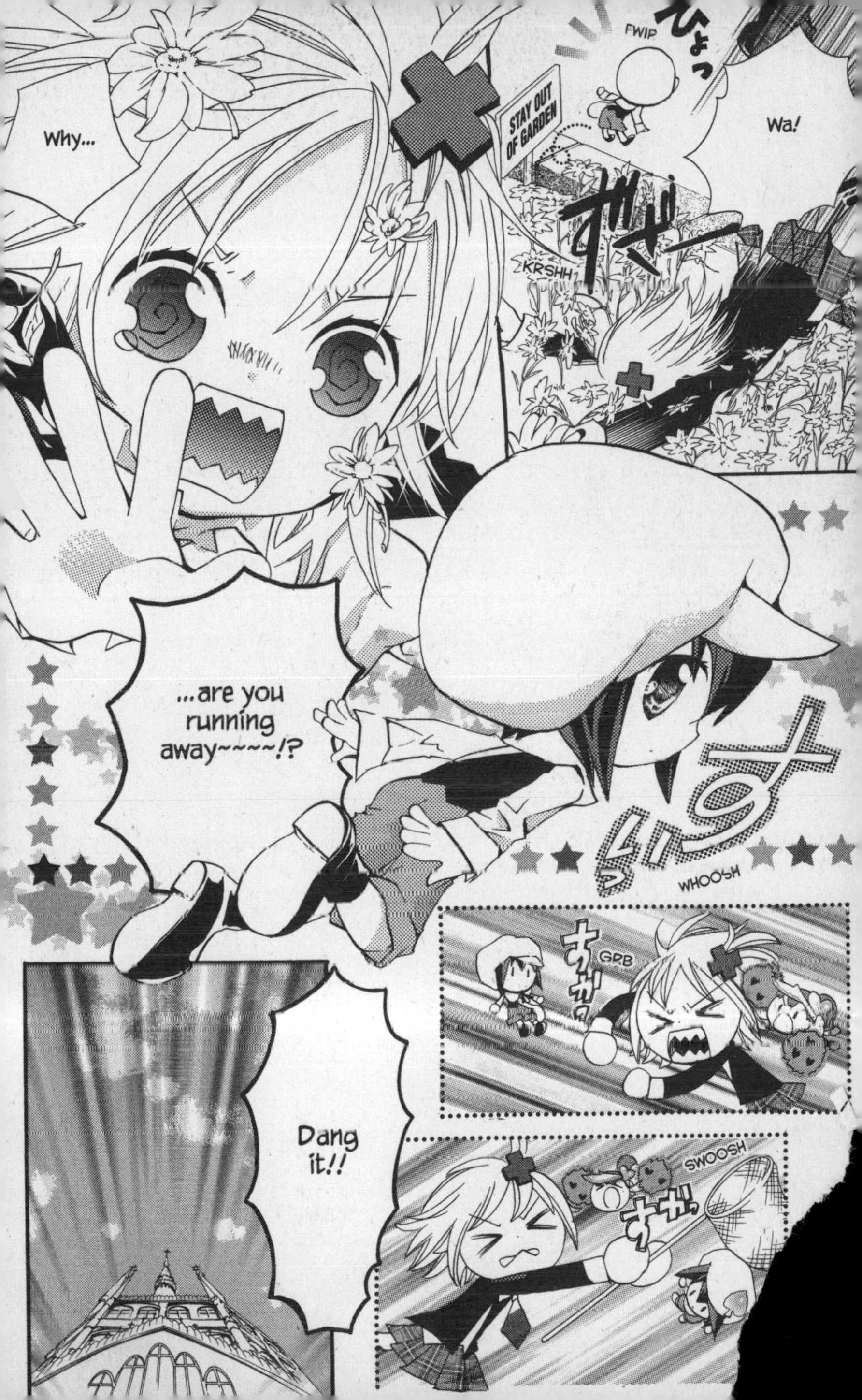
ひょっ
FWIP
Wa!
STAY OUT OF GARDEN
ずざー
KRSHH
Why...
...are you running away~~~~!?
WHOOSH
GRB
SWOOSH
Dang it!!

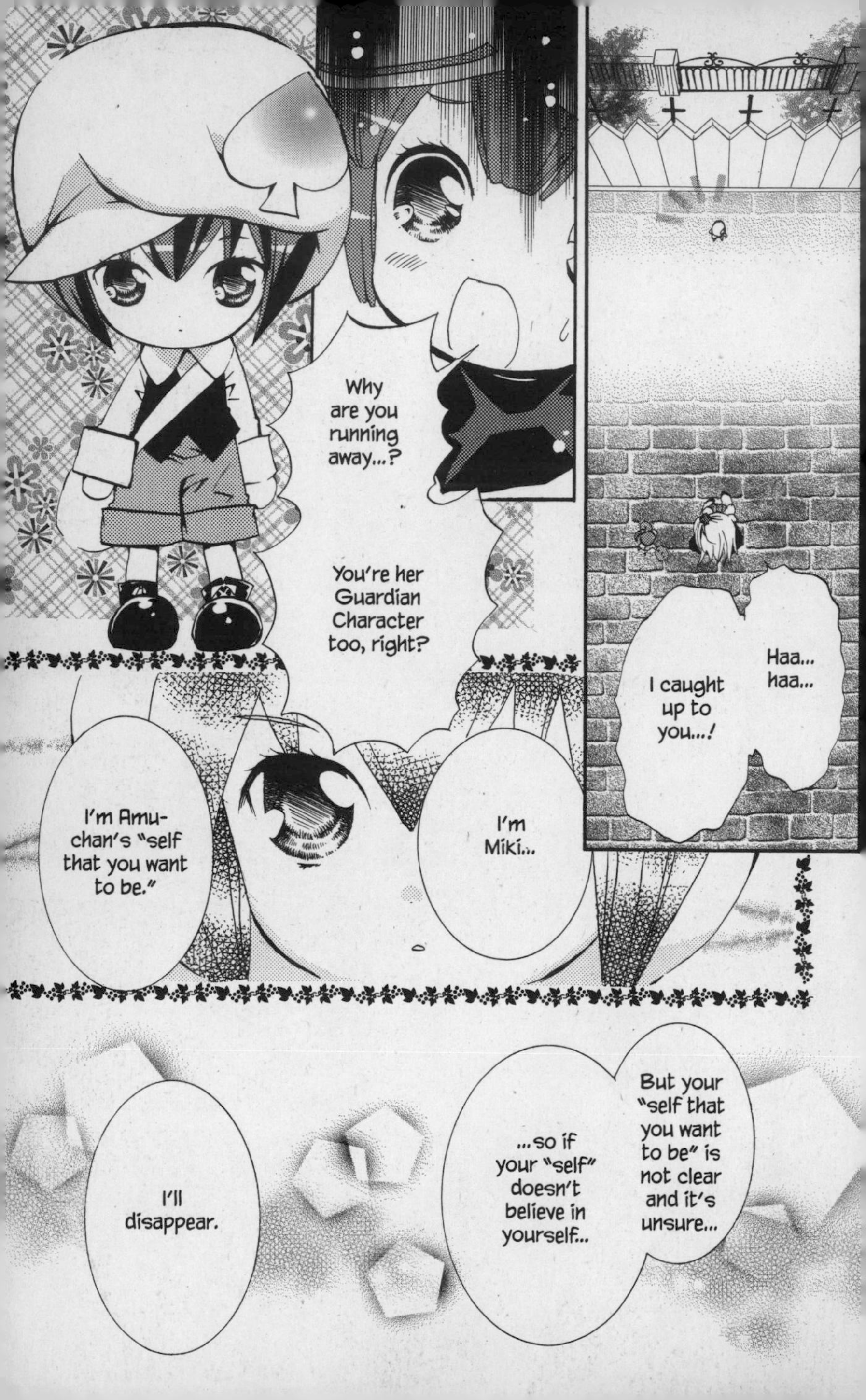
Haa... haa...
I caught up to you...!
Why are you running away...?
You're her Guardian Character too, right?
I'm Miki...
I'm Amu-chan's "self that you want to be."
But your "self that you want to be" is not clear and it's unsure...
...so if your "self" doesn't believe in yourself...
I'll disappear.

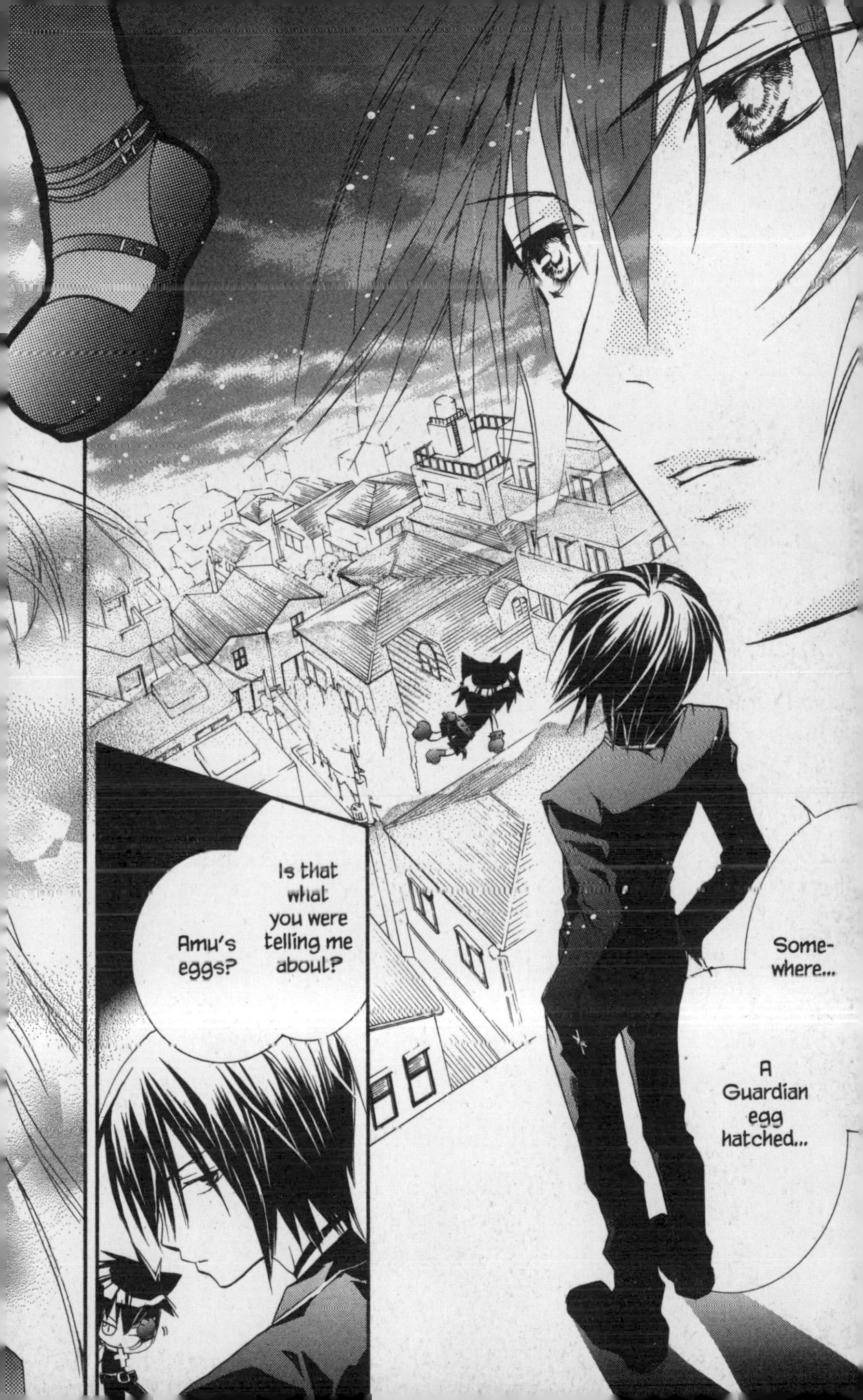
Somewhere...
A Guardian egg hatched...
Is that what you were telling me about? Amu's eggs?

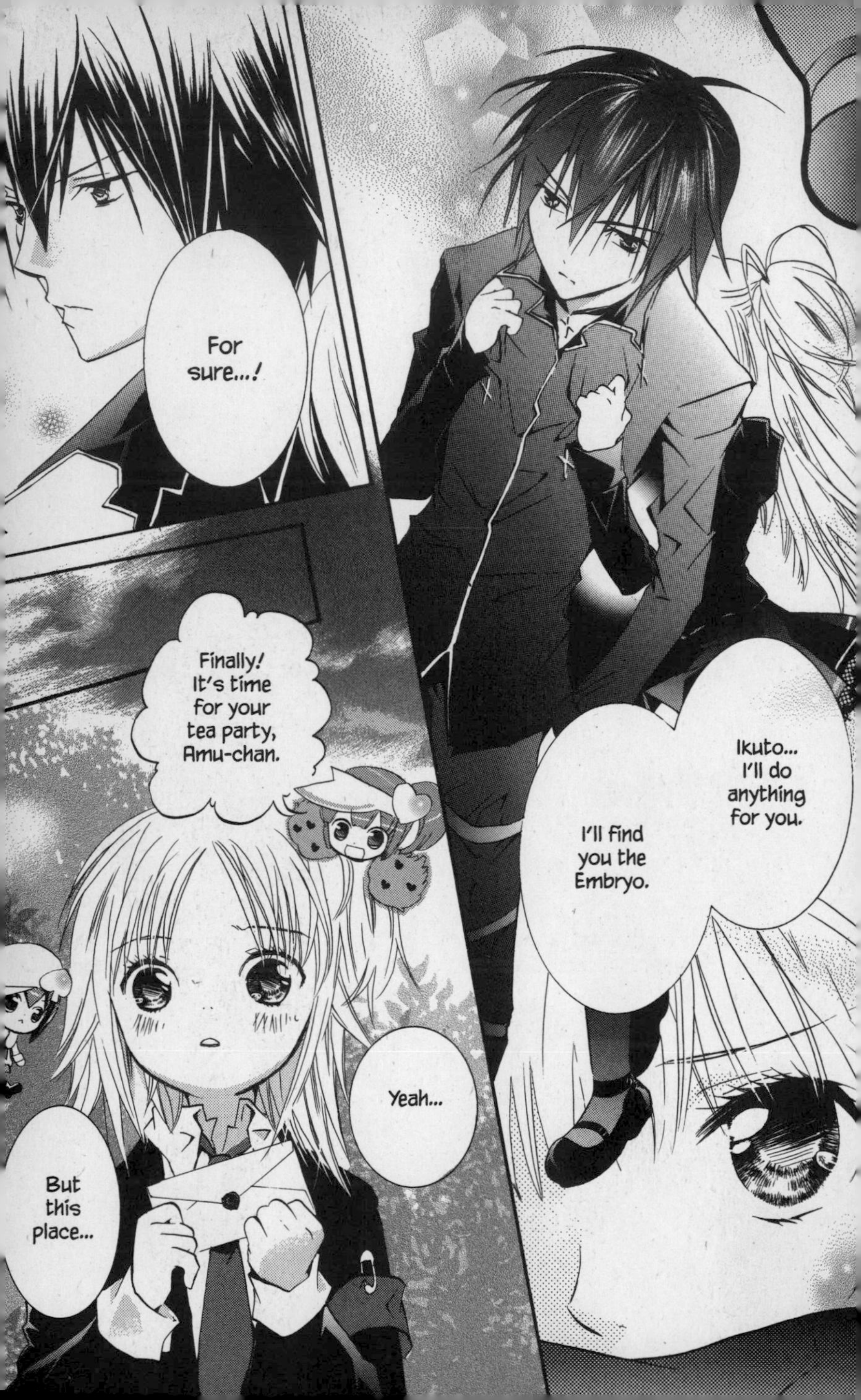
Ikuto... I'll do anything for you.
I'll find you the Embryo.
For sure...!
Finally! It's time for your tea party, Amu-chan.
Yeah...
But this place...

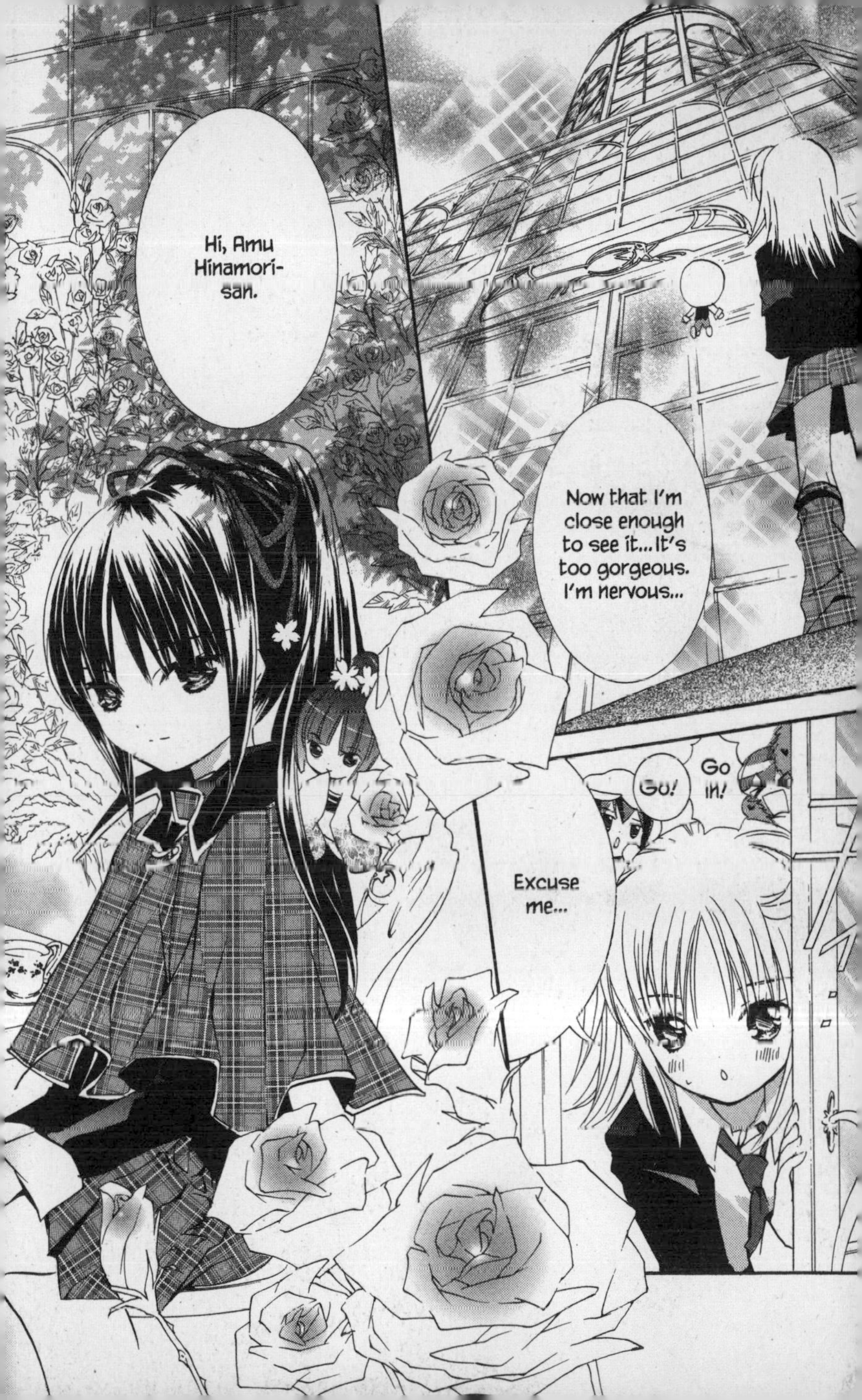
Now that I'm close enough to see it... It's too gorgeous. I'm nervous...
Go in!
Go!
Excuse me...
Hi, Amu Hinamori-san.

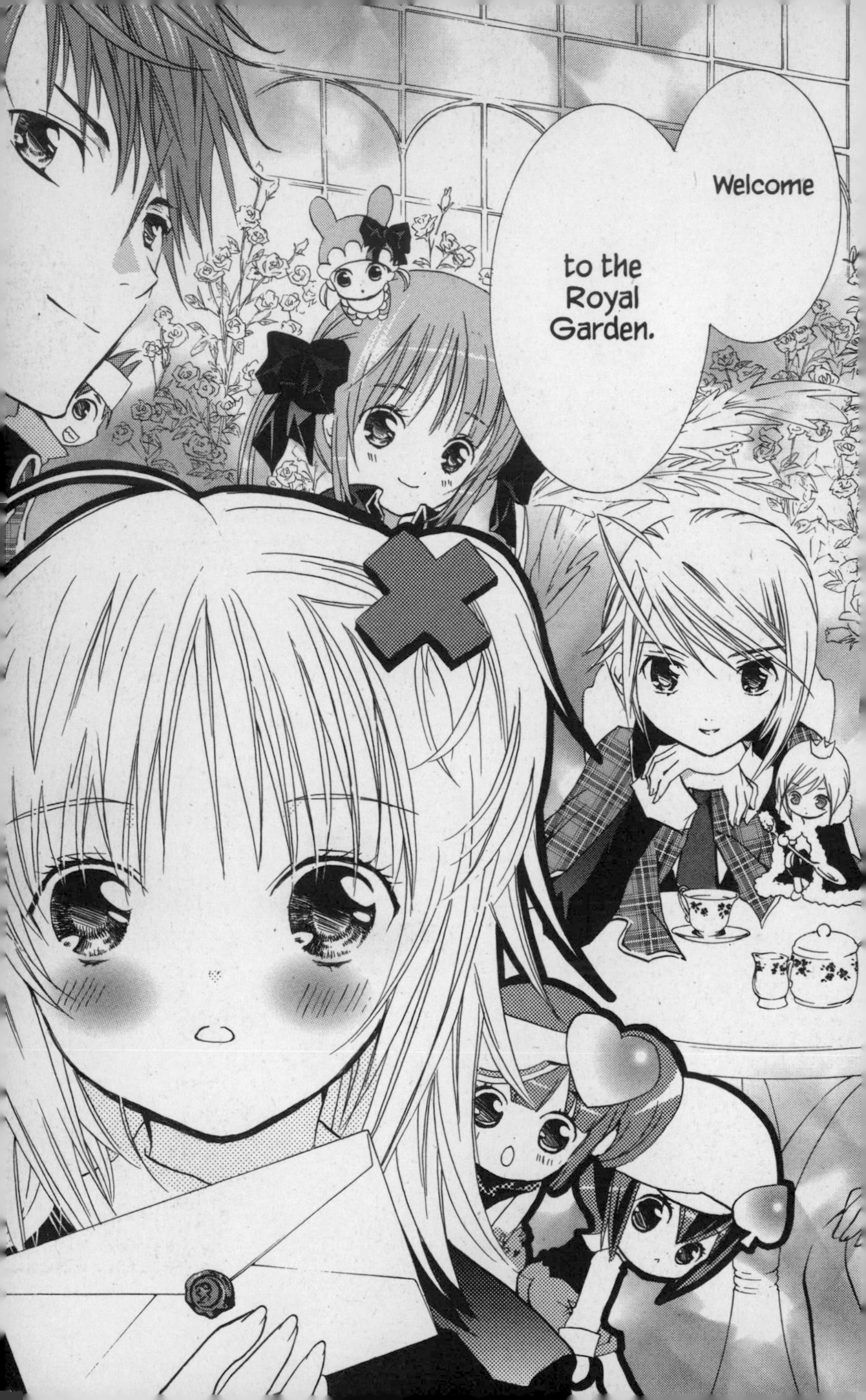
Welcome
to the Royal Garden.

Shugo Chara!

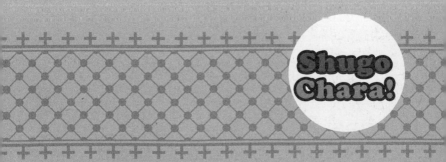

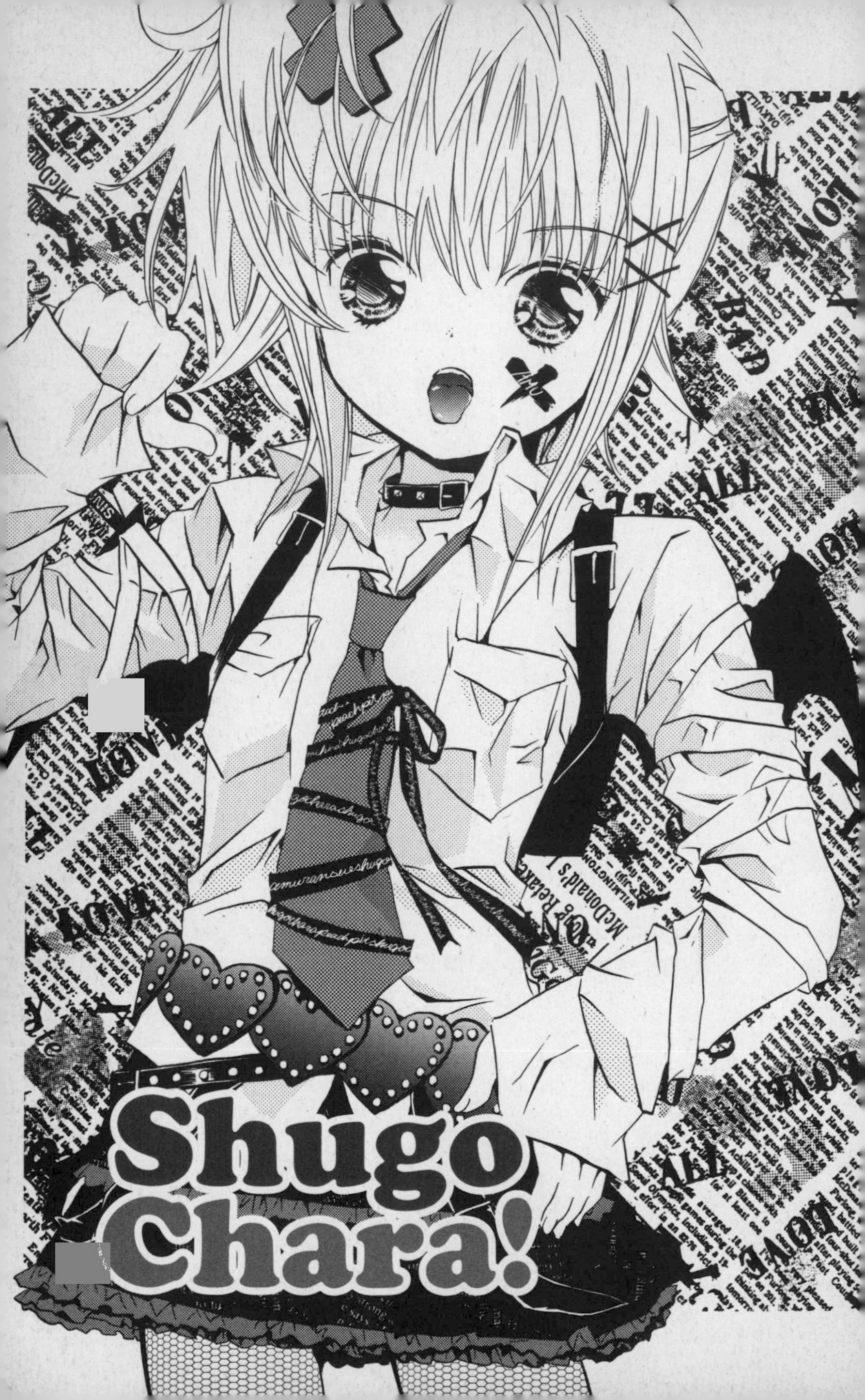
Shugo
Chara!

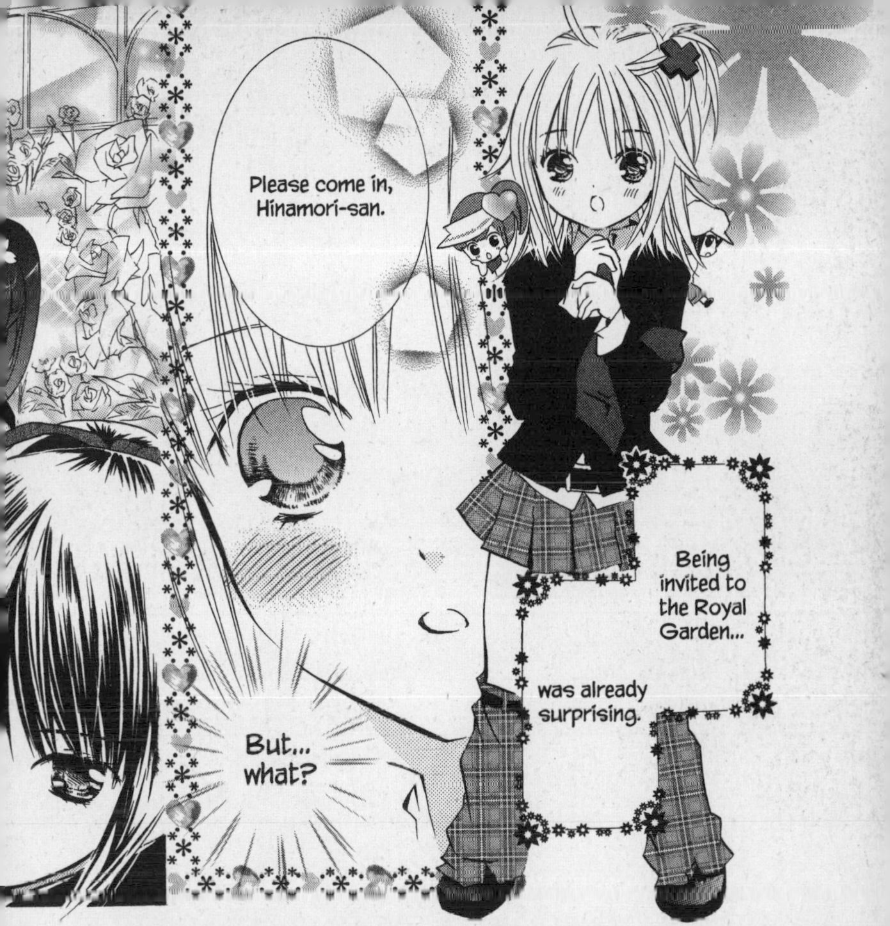
Please come in, Hinamori-san.
Being invited to the Royal Garden...
was already surprising.
But... what?

I'll answer your questions!

This is Ebara answering:

Q 1: Is PEACH-PIT-sensei a man or a woman?
A 1: Uhh...I...guess you can call us women. Yeah, biologically speaking, we're...probably women. Both of us.
Q 2: How do you draw manga together?
A 2: Banri-san creates the story, then we both draw our assigned characters.
Amu, Nadeshiko, Yaya, Ami, Guardian Characters...Shibuko Ebara
Tadase, Ikuto, Utau, Kukai...Banri Sendou
Can you tell the difference in our drawing styles?

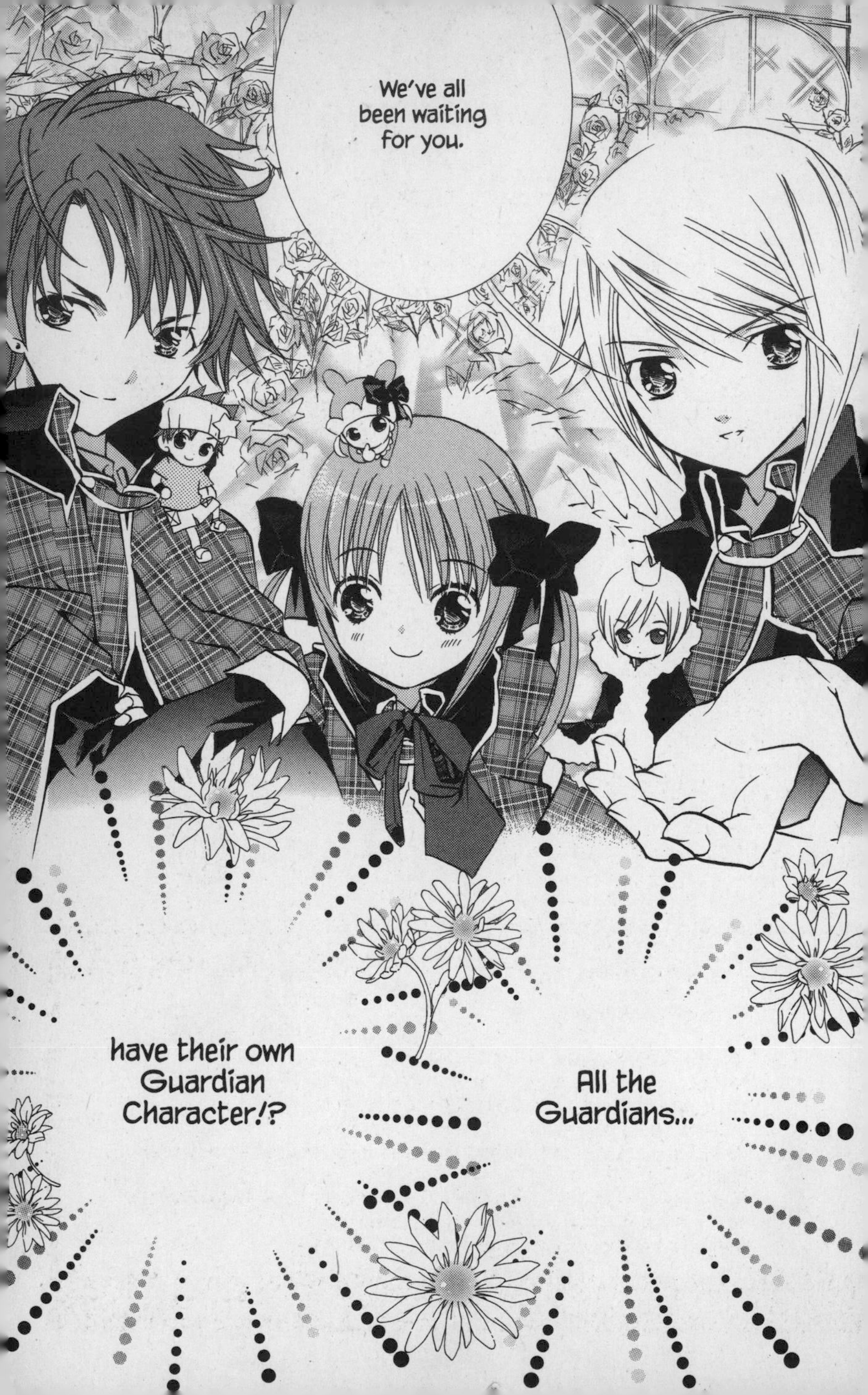
We've all been waiting for you.
All the Guardians...
have their own Guardian Character!?

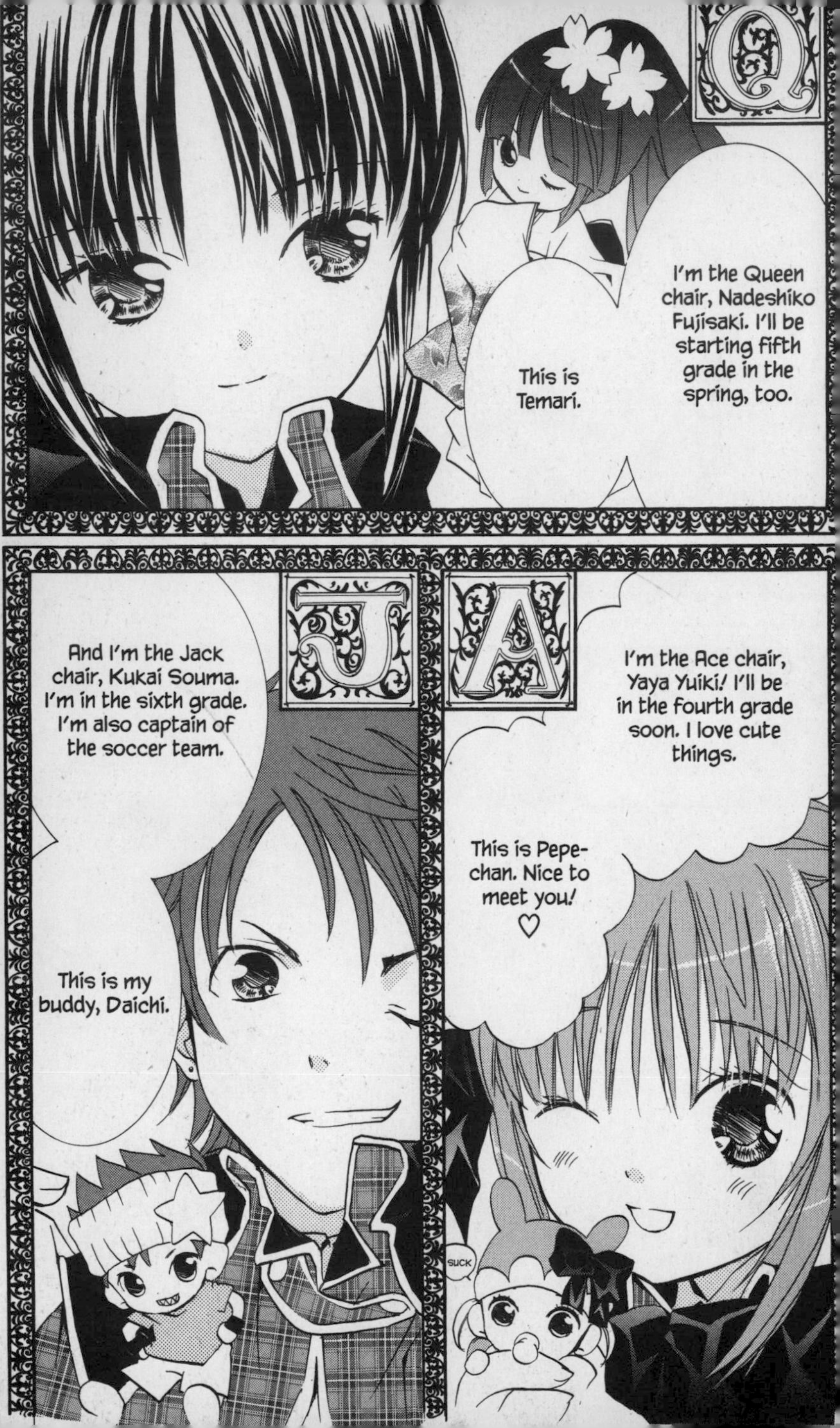
Q
I'm the Queen chair, Nadeshiko Fujisaki. I'll be starting fifth grade in the spring, too.
This is Temari.
A
I'm the Ace chair, Yaya Yuiki! I'll be in the fourth grade soon. I love cute things.
This is Pepe-chan. Nice to meet you! ♡
SUCK
J
And I'm the Jack chair, Kukai Souma. I'm in the sixth grade. I'm also captain of the soccer team.
This is my buddy, Daichi.

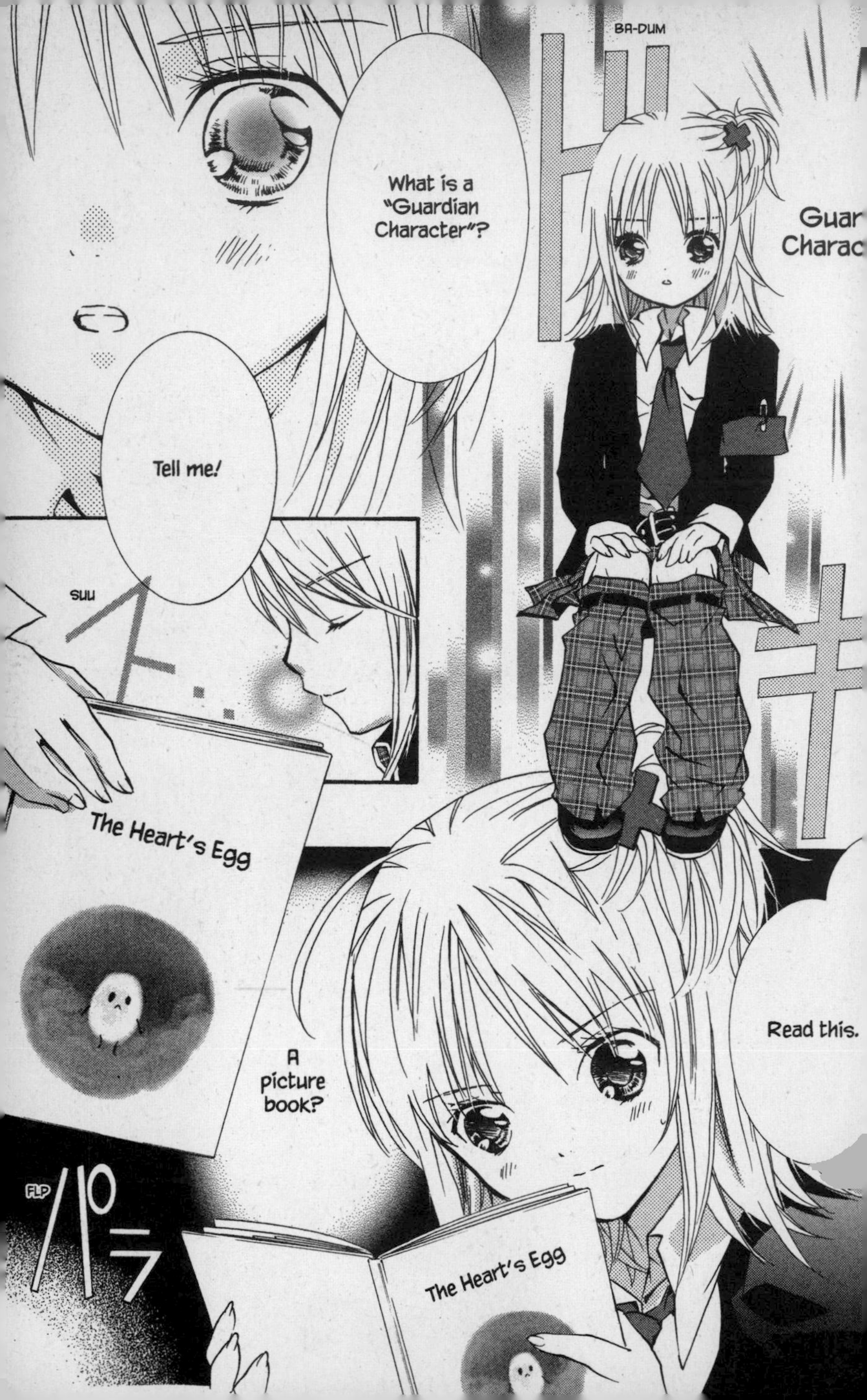
BA-DUM
Guar
Charac
What is a "Guardian Character"?
Tell me!
SUU
The Heart's Egg
Read this.
A picture book?
The Heart's Egg
FLIP

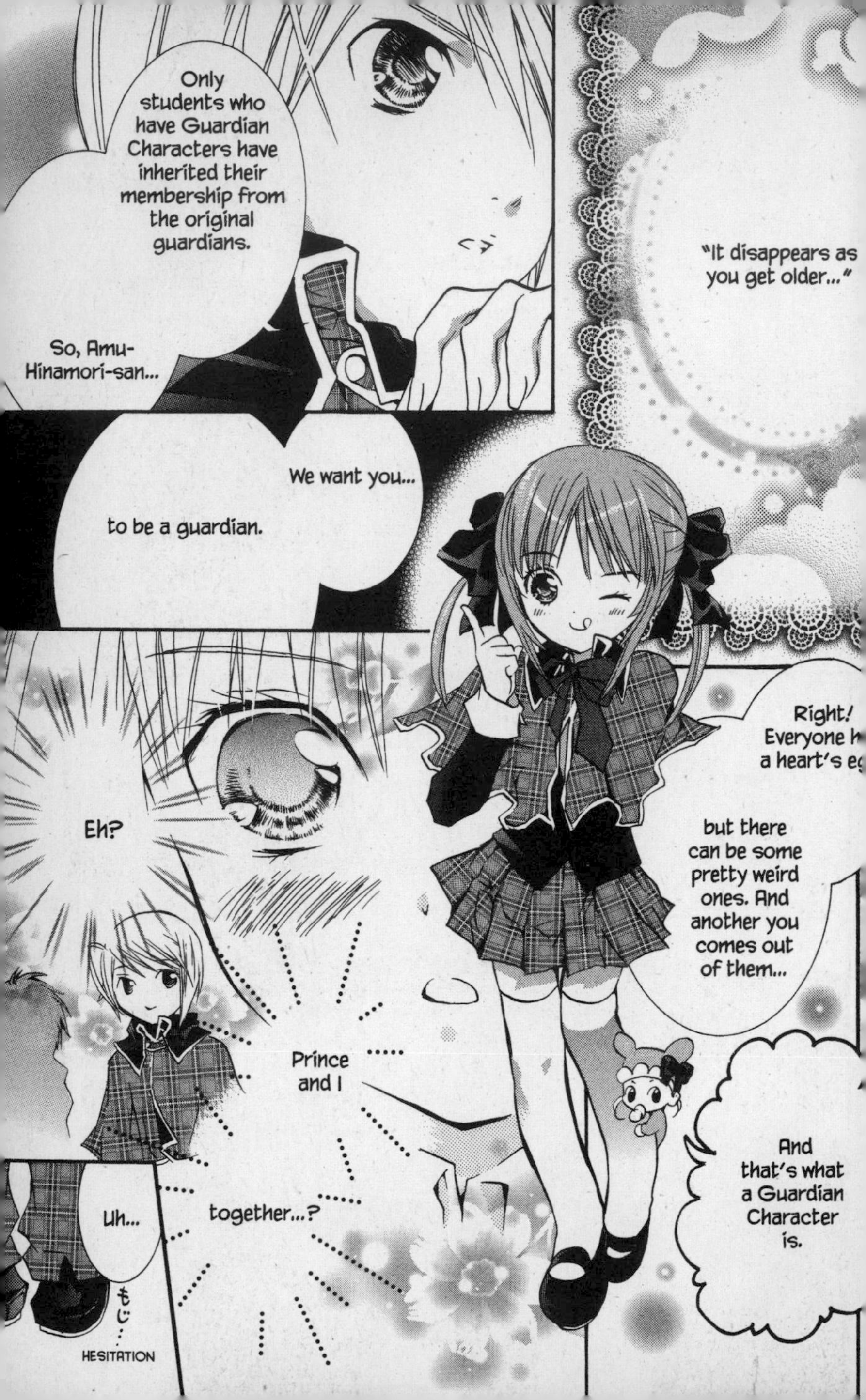
"It disappears as you get older..."
Only students who have Guardian Characters have inherited their membership from the original guardians.
So, Amu-Hinamori-san...
We want you...
to be a guardian.
Right! Everyone h a heart's eg
but there can be some pretty weird ones. And another you comes out of them...
And that's what a Guardian Character is.
Eh?
Prince and I
together...?
Uh...
もじ...
HESITATION

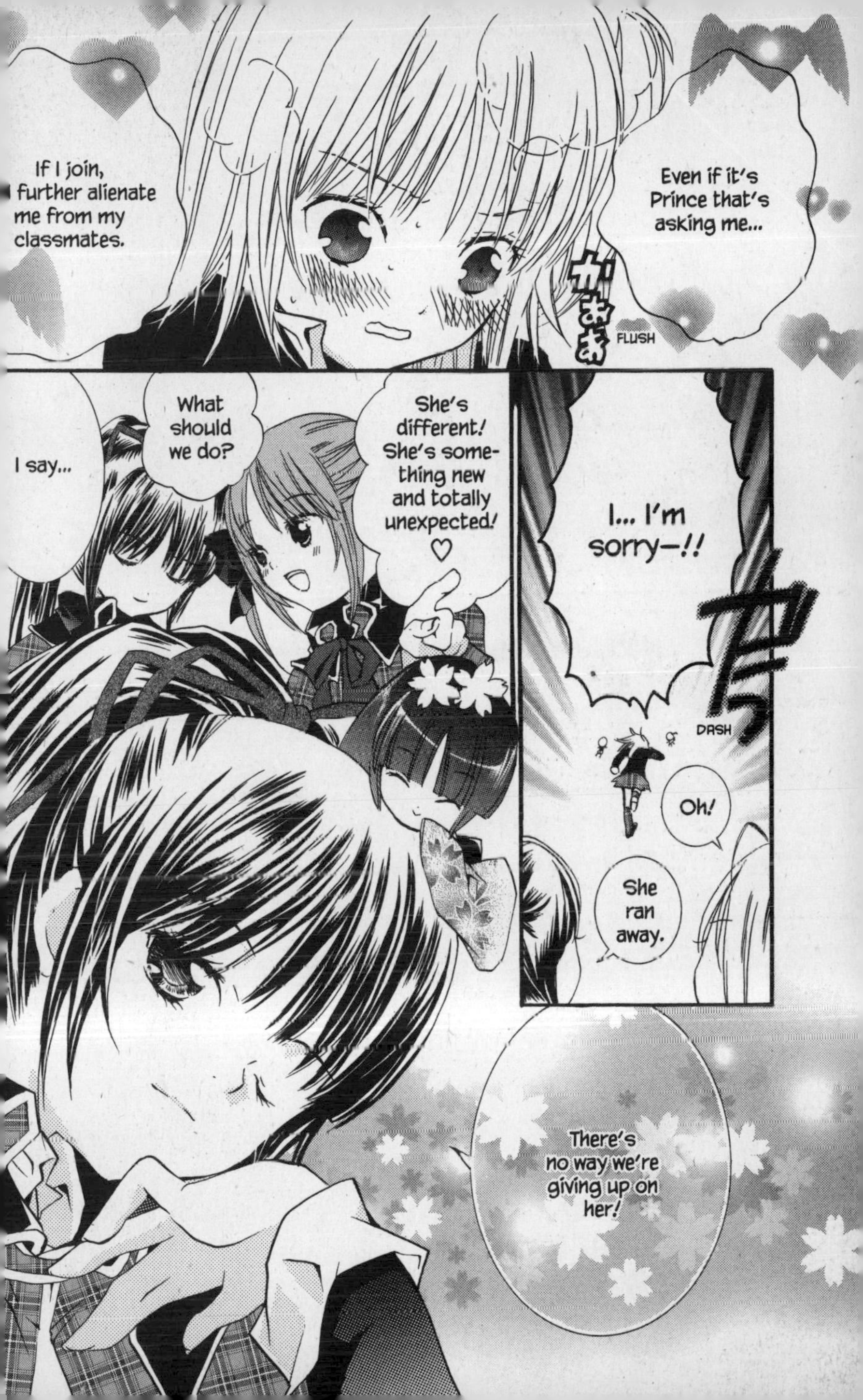
Even if it's Prince that's asking me...
FLUSH
If I join, further alienate me from my classmates.
I... I'm sorry—!!
DASH
Oh!
She ran away.
She's different! She's something new and totally unexpected! ♡
What should we do?
I say...
There's no way we're giving up on her!

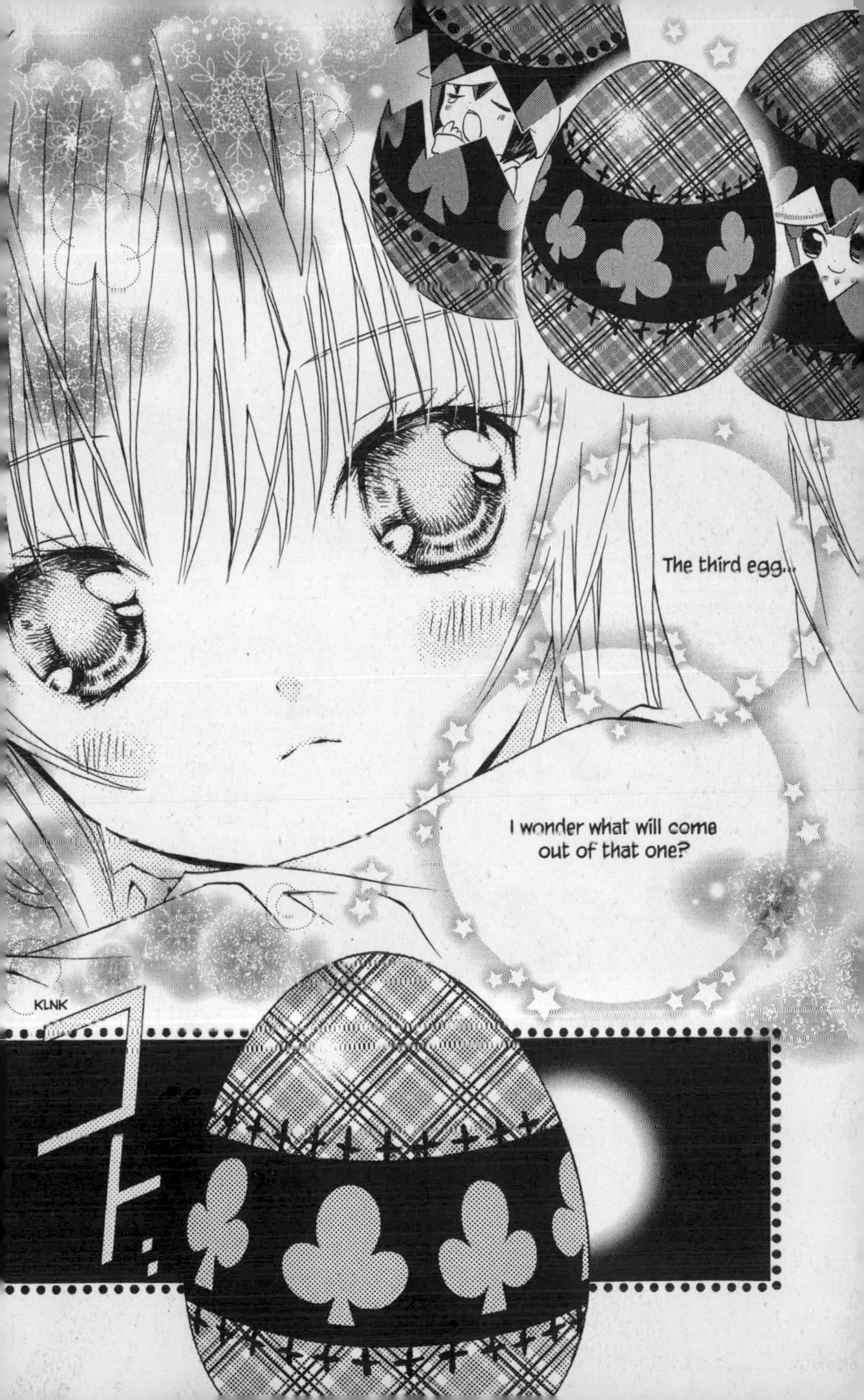
The third egg...
I wonder what will come out of that one?
KLNK
コト

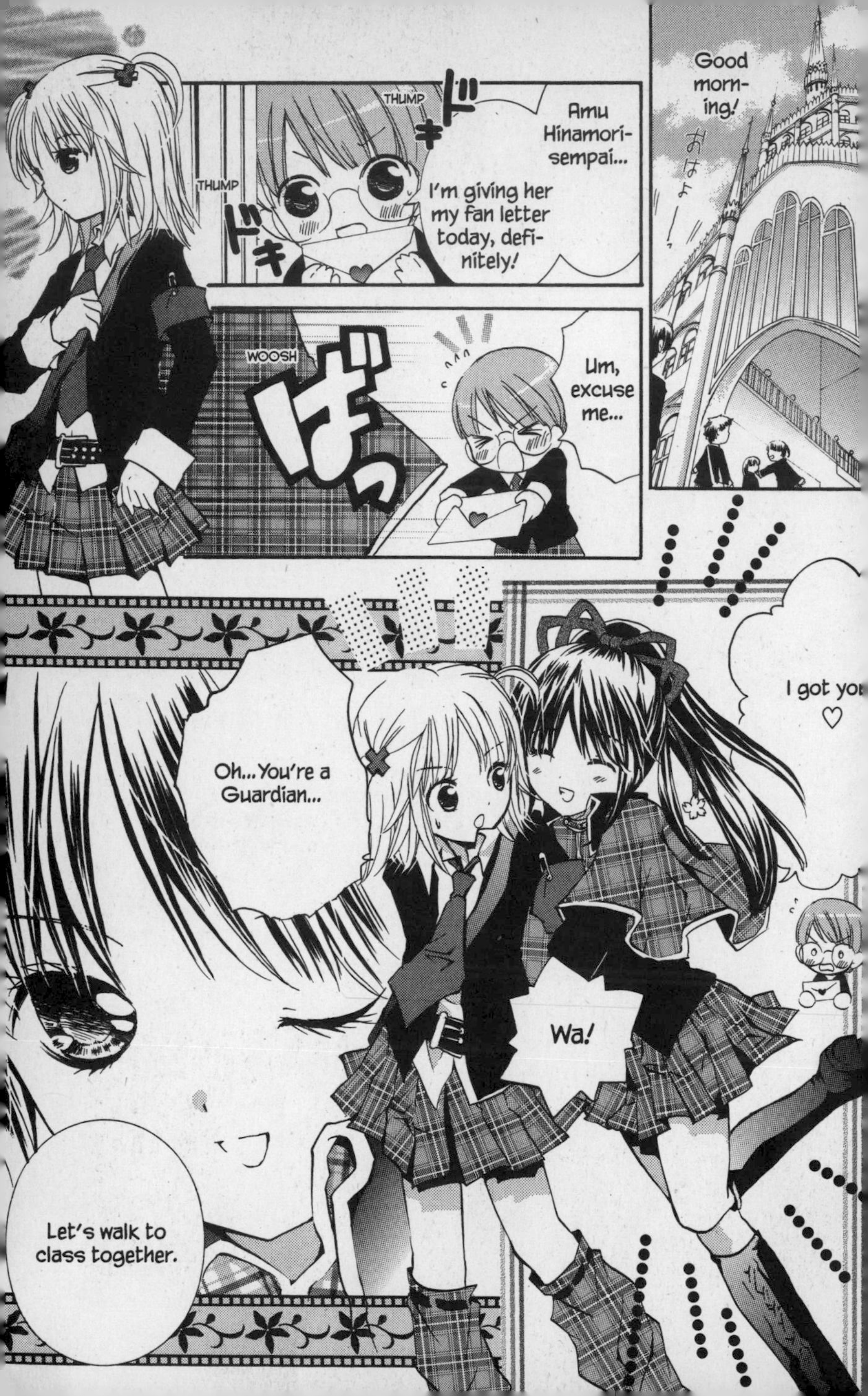
Good morning!
おはよ～！
THUMP
ドキ
THUMP
ドキ
Amu Hinamori-sempai...
I'm giving her my fan letter today, definitely!
WOOSH
ぱっ
Um, excuse me...
I got yo
♡
Oh... You're a Guardian...
Wa!
Let's walk to class together.

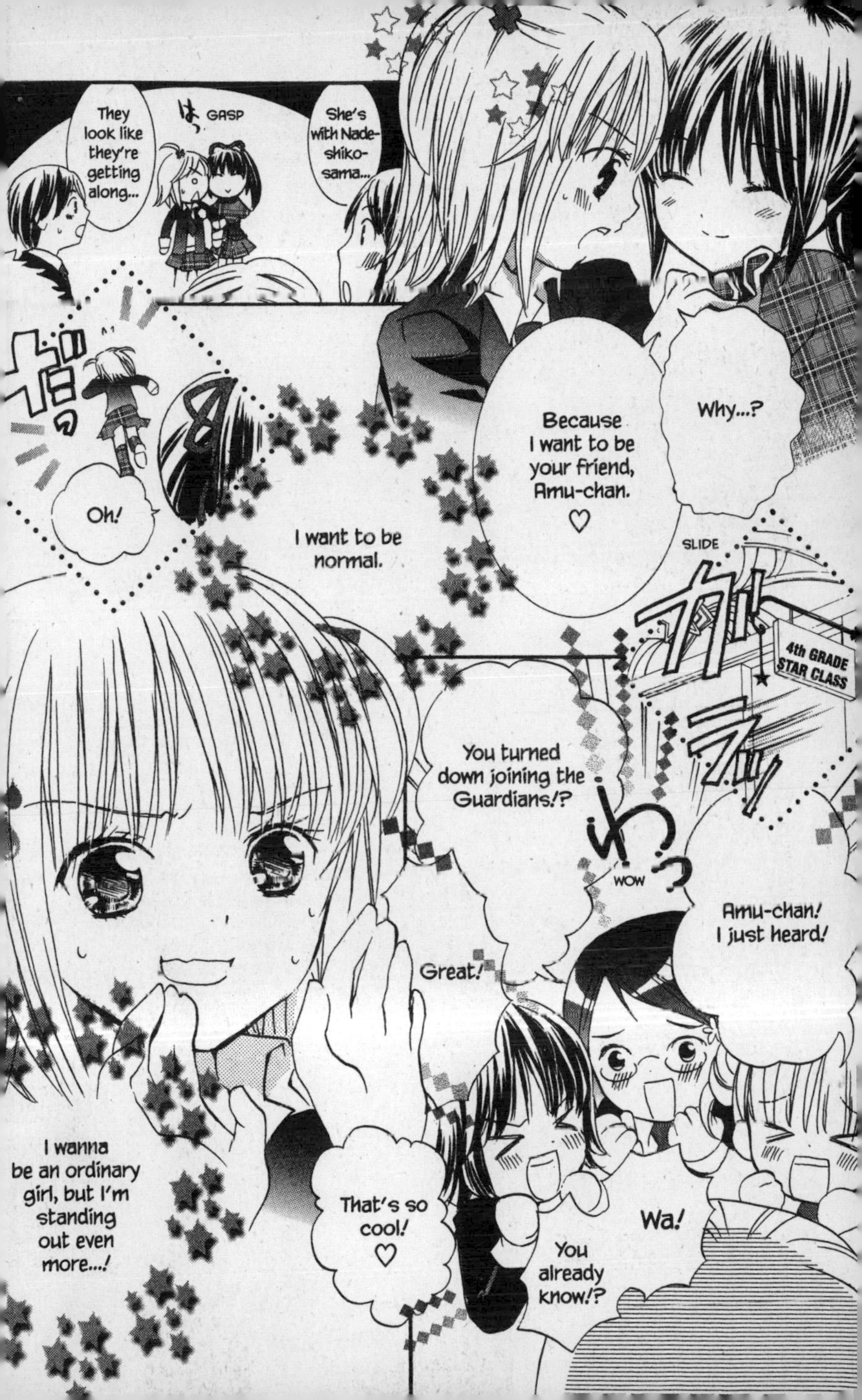
Why...?
Because I want to be your friend, Amu-chan. ♡
She's with Nade-shiko-sama...
GASP
They look like they're getting along...
Oh!
I want to be normal.
SLIDE
4th GRADE STAR CLASS
Amu-chan! I just heard!
WOW
You turned down joining the Guardians!?
Great!
Wa!
You already know!?
That's so cool! ♡
I wanna be an ordinary girl, but I'm standing out even more...!

OKAY!

I'm tired today...

And that was just the closing ceremony.

And don't forget, even though you don't have homework, don't play around too much and forget to come to next semester's opening ceremony.

In April, you'll all be in the fifth grade.

So, spring vacation starts tomorrow...

DING DONG

I'm finally getting along with Amu-chan...

Darn it. I don't want my classmates to change.

I wish I could be in the same class as you.

Yeah.

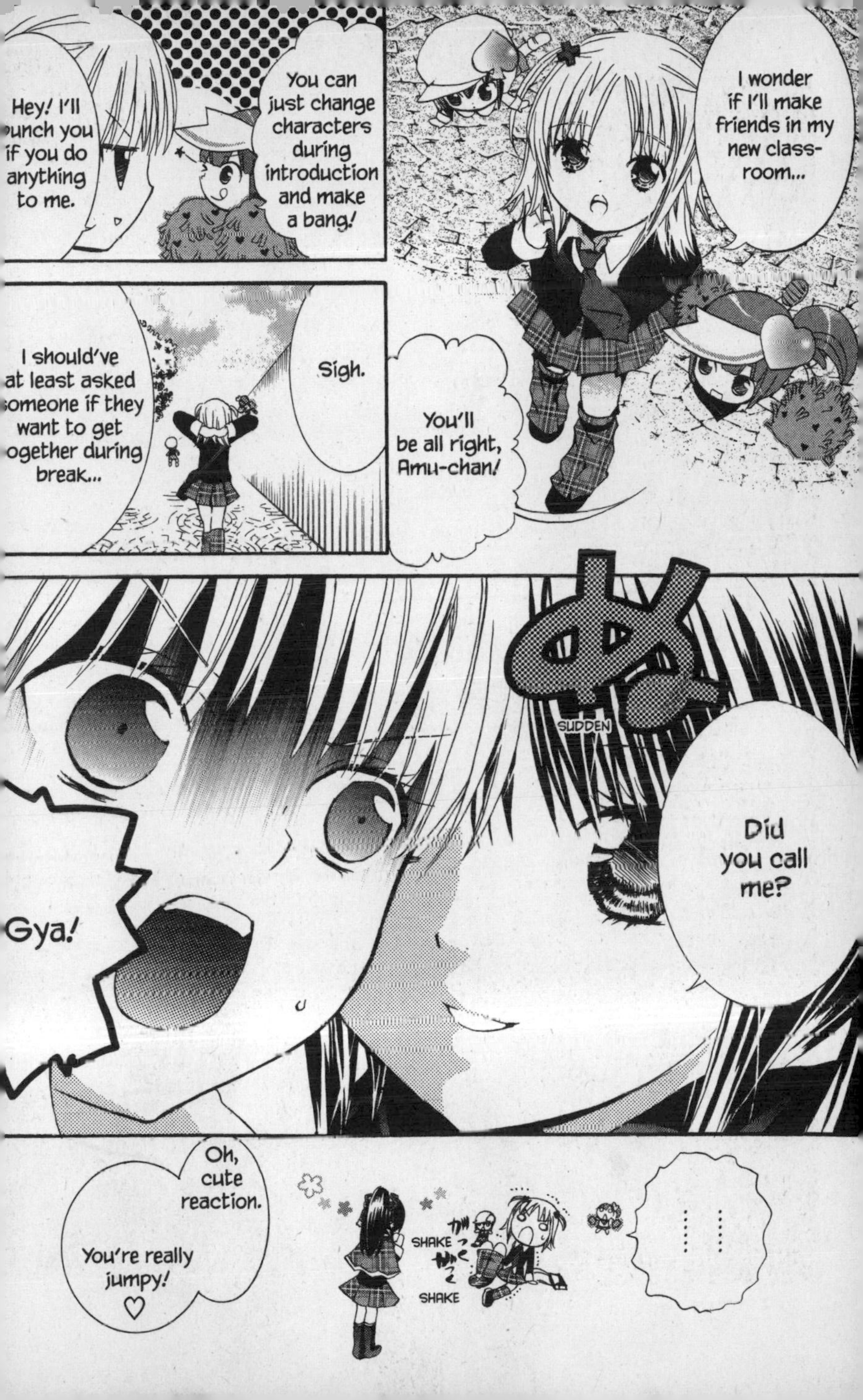
I wonder if I'll make friends in my new class-room...
You'll be all right, Amu-chan!
You can just change characters during introduction and make a bang!
Hey! I'll unch you if you do anything to me.
Sigh.
I should've at least asked omeone if they want to get ogether during break...
SUDDEN
Did you call me?
Gya!
......
SHAKE
SHAKE
Oh, cute reaction.
You're really jumpy! ♡

You're just saying that to...

You c[...] hang o[...] with m[...]

Let's get together a l[...] and be bes[...] friends. ♡

...get me to join the Guardians. Right!?

I thought so!

You can tell?

Okay—!

Nadeshiko, you should bring out the...

I'm gonna use a secret weapon on Amu-chan...

suu

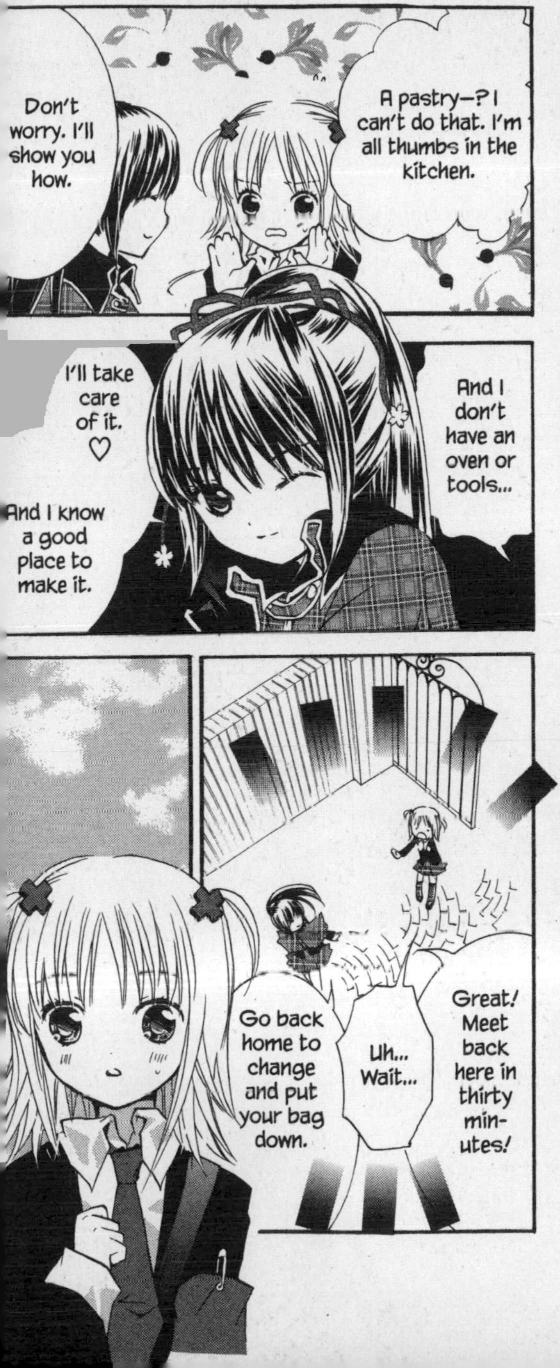
A pastry—? I can't do that. I'm all thumbs in the kitchen.
Don't worry. I'll show you how.
And I don't have an oven or tools...
I'll take care of it. ♡
And I know a good place to make it.
Great! Meet back here in thirty min-utes!
Uh... Wait...
Go back home to change and put your bag down.

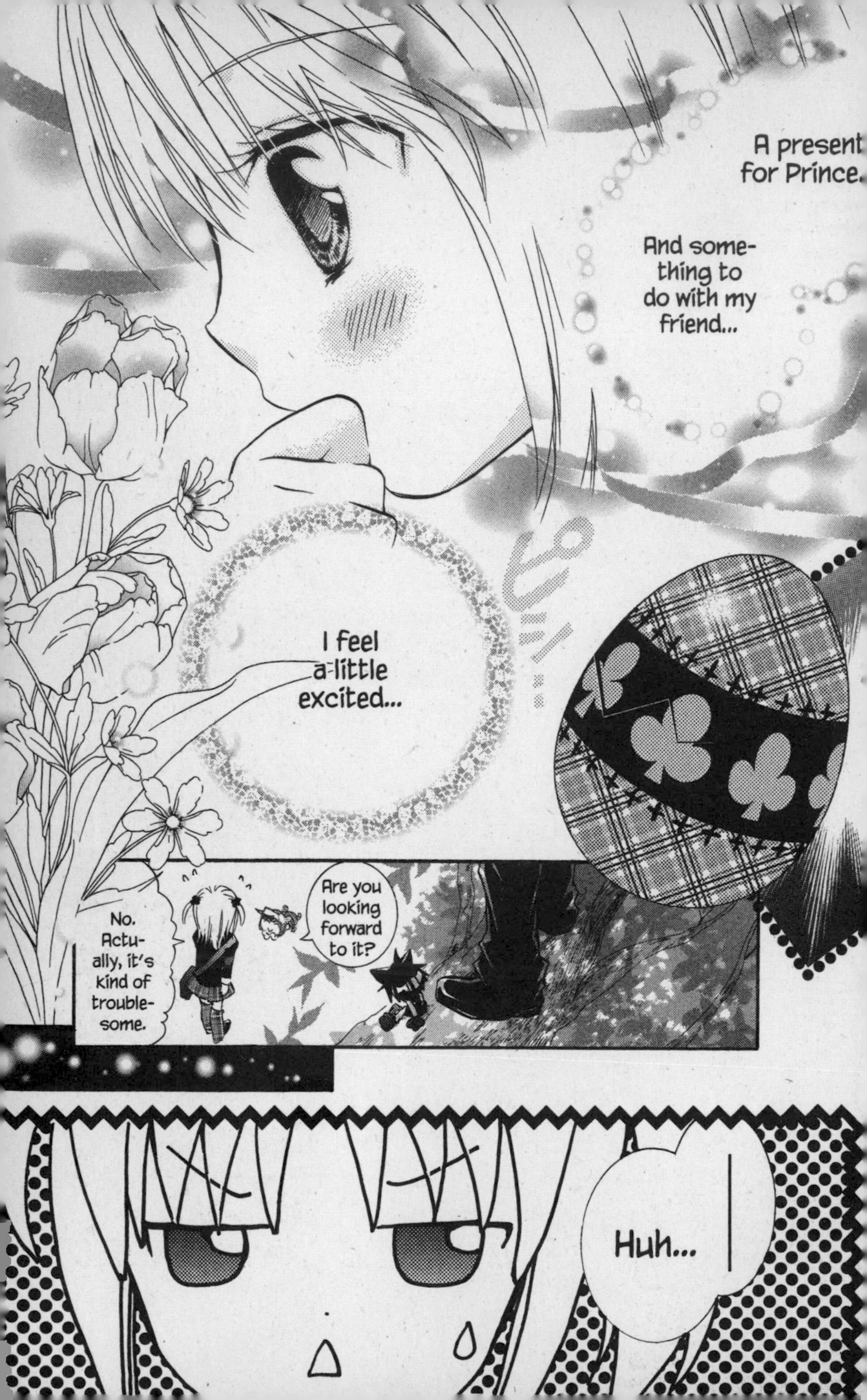
A present for Prince.
And something to do with my friend...
I feel a little excited...
Are you looking forward to it?
No. Actually, it's kind of troublesome.
Huh...

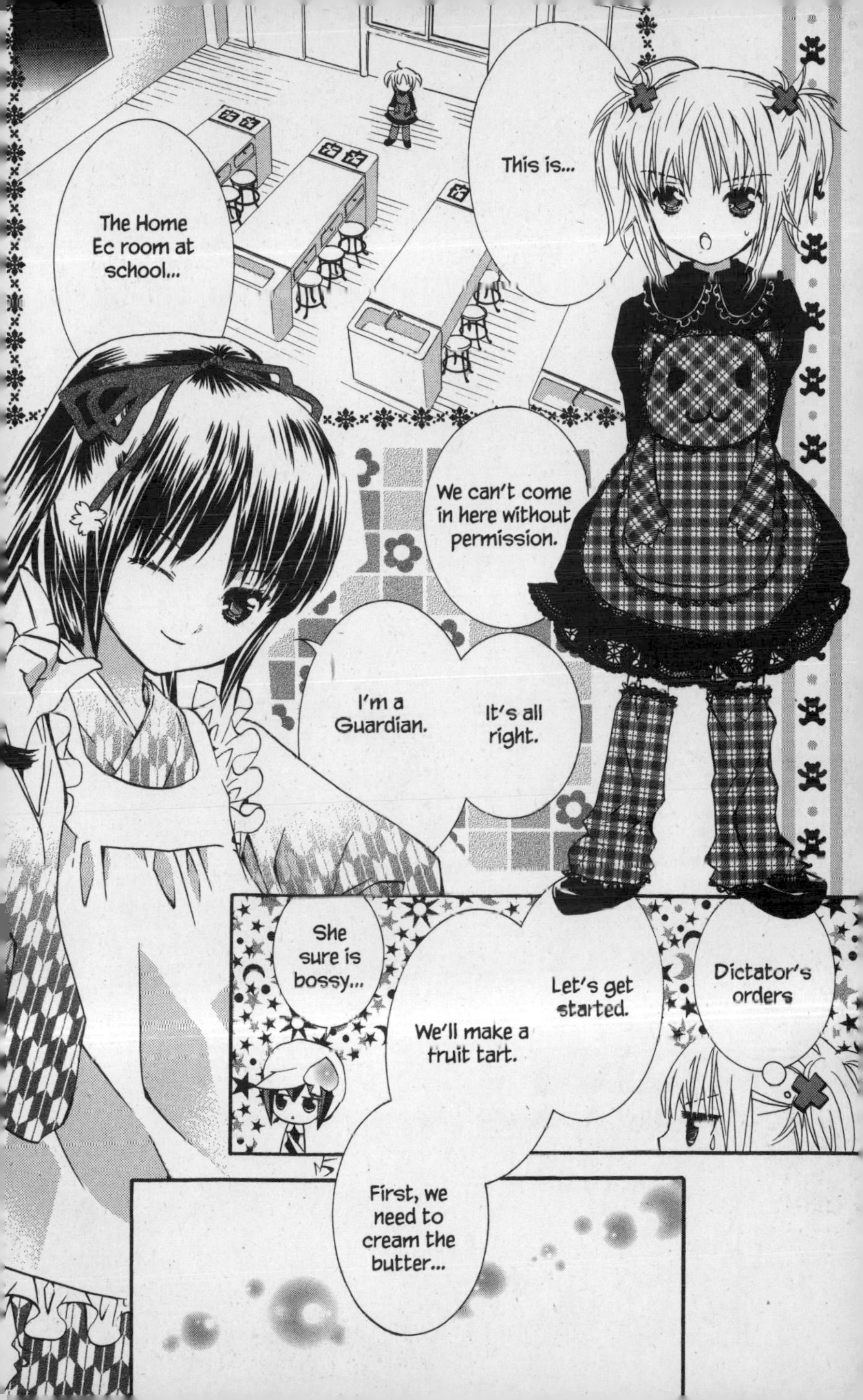
This is...
The Home Ec room at school...
We can't come in here without permission.
It's all right.
I'm a Guardian.
Dictator's orders
Let's get started.
We'll make a fruit tart.
She sure is bossy...
First, we need to cream the butter...

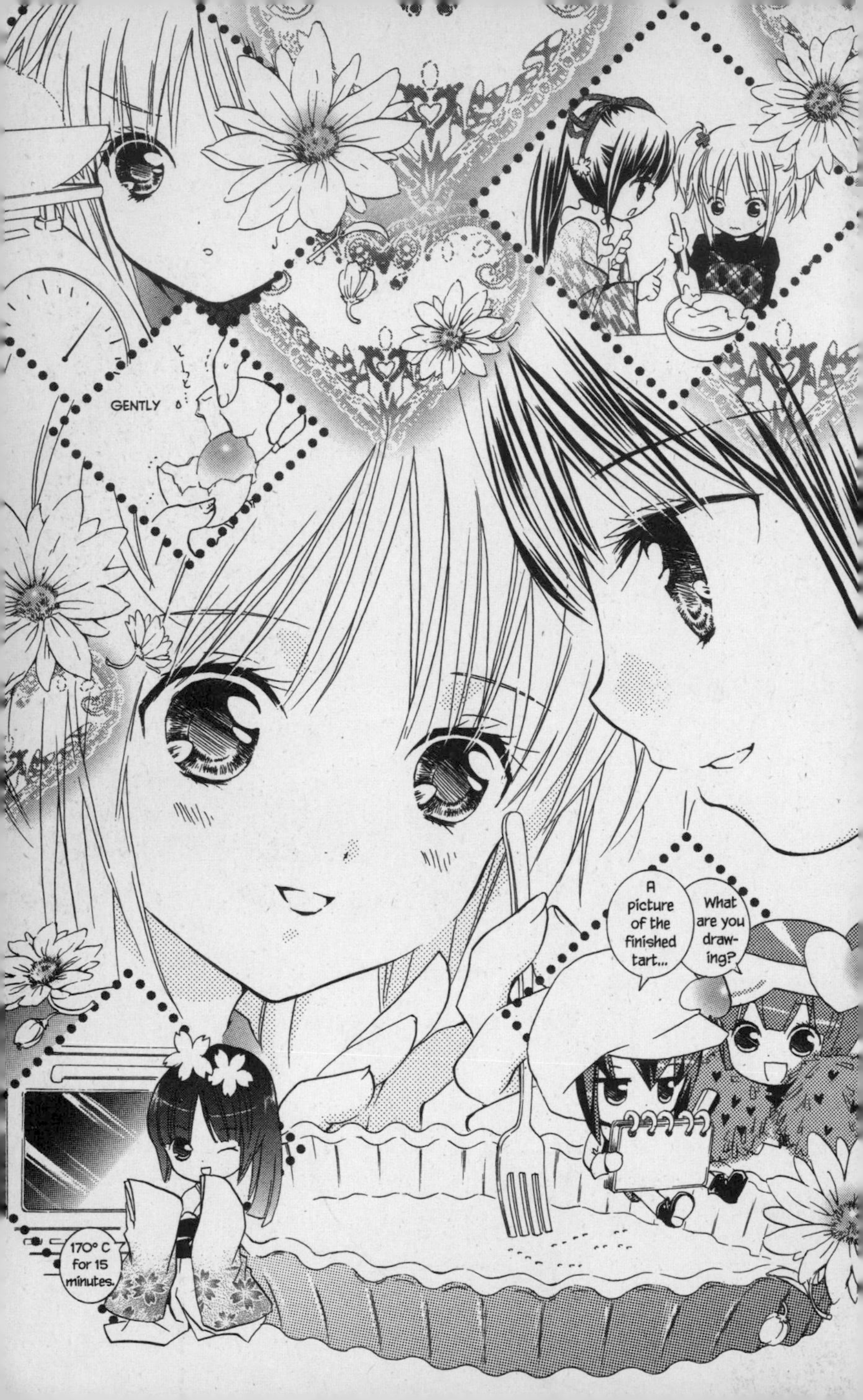
GENTLY
What are you draw-ing?
A picture of the finished tart...
170° C for 15 minutes.

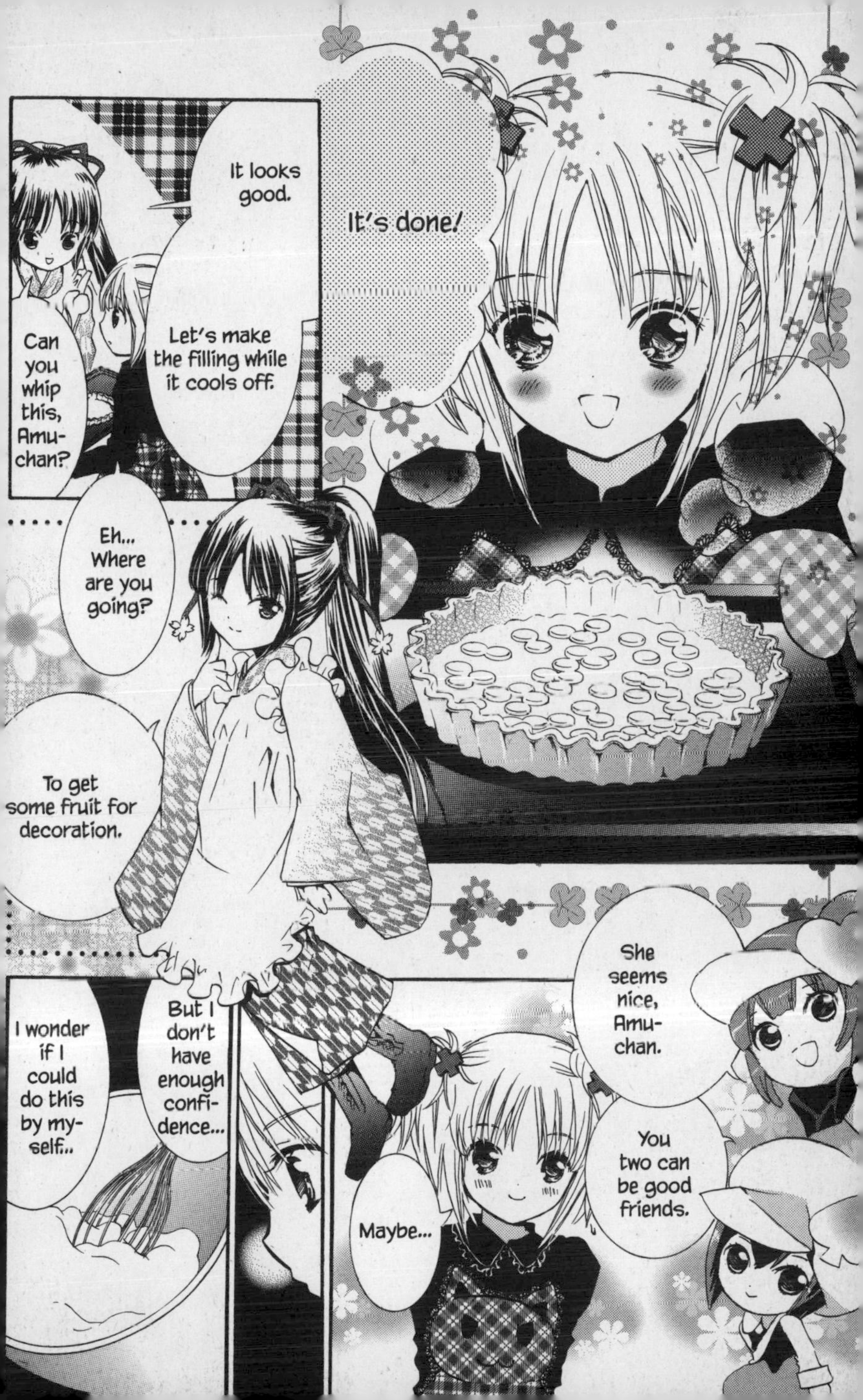
It's done!
It looks good.
Let's make the filling while it cools off.
Can you whip this, Amu-chan?
Eh... Where are you going?
To get some fruit for decoration.
She seems nice, Amu-chan.
You two can be good friends.
Maybe...
But I don't have enough confidence...
I wonder if I could do this by myself...

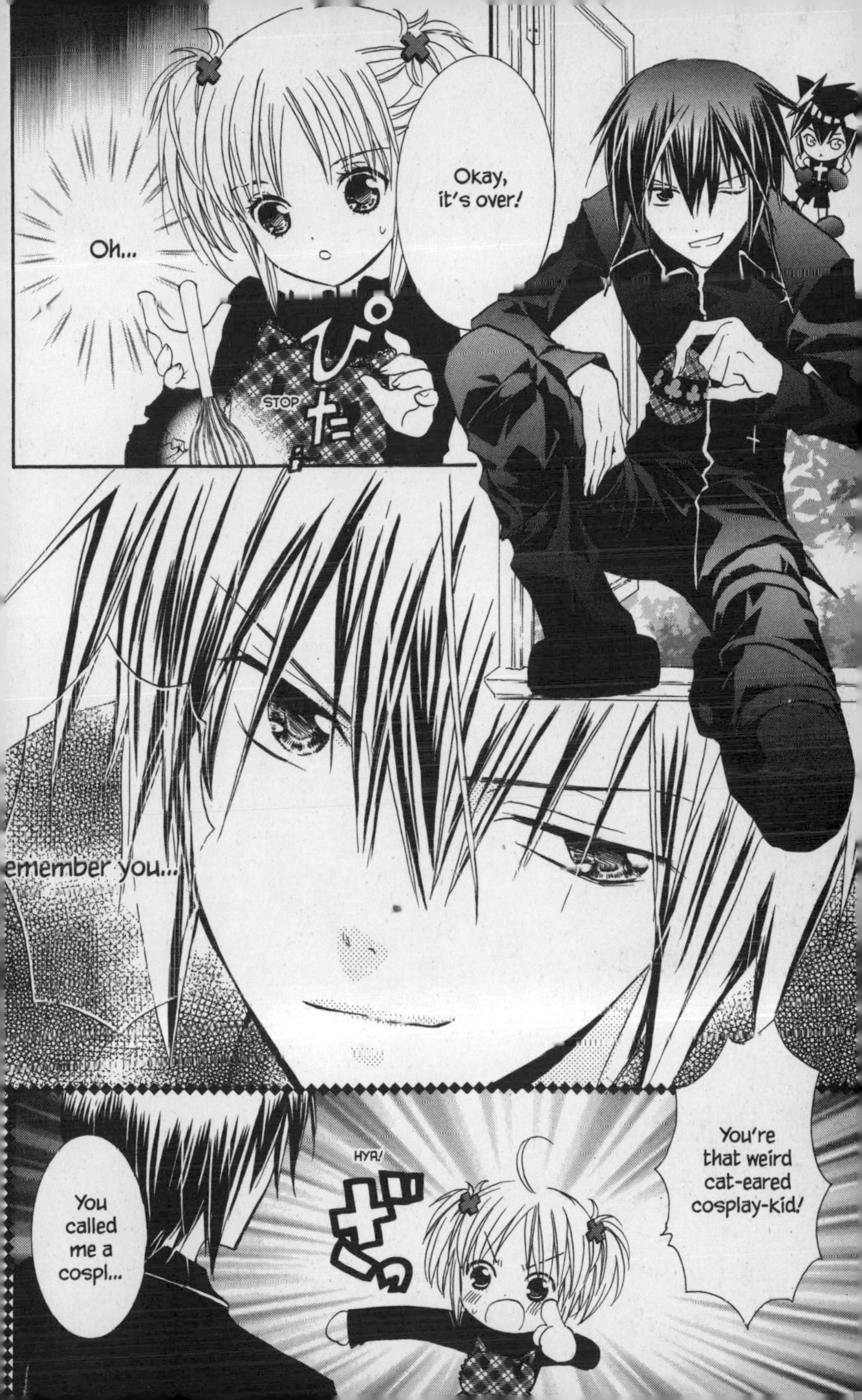
Okay, it's over!
Oh...
ぴた
STOP
emember you...
You're that weird cat-eared cosplay-kid!
HYA!
You called me a cospl...

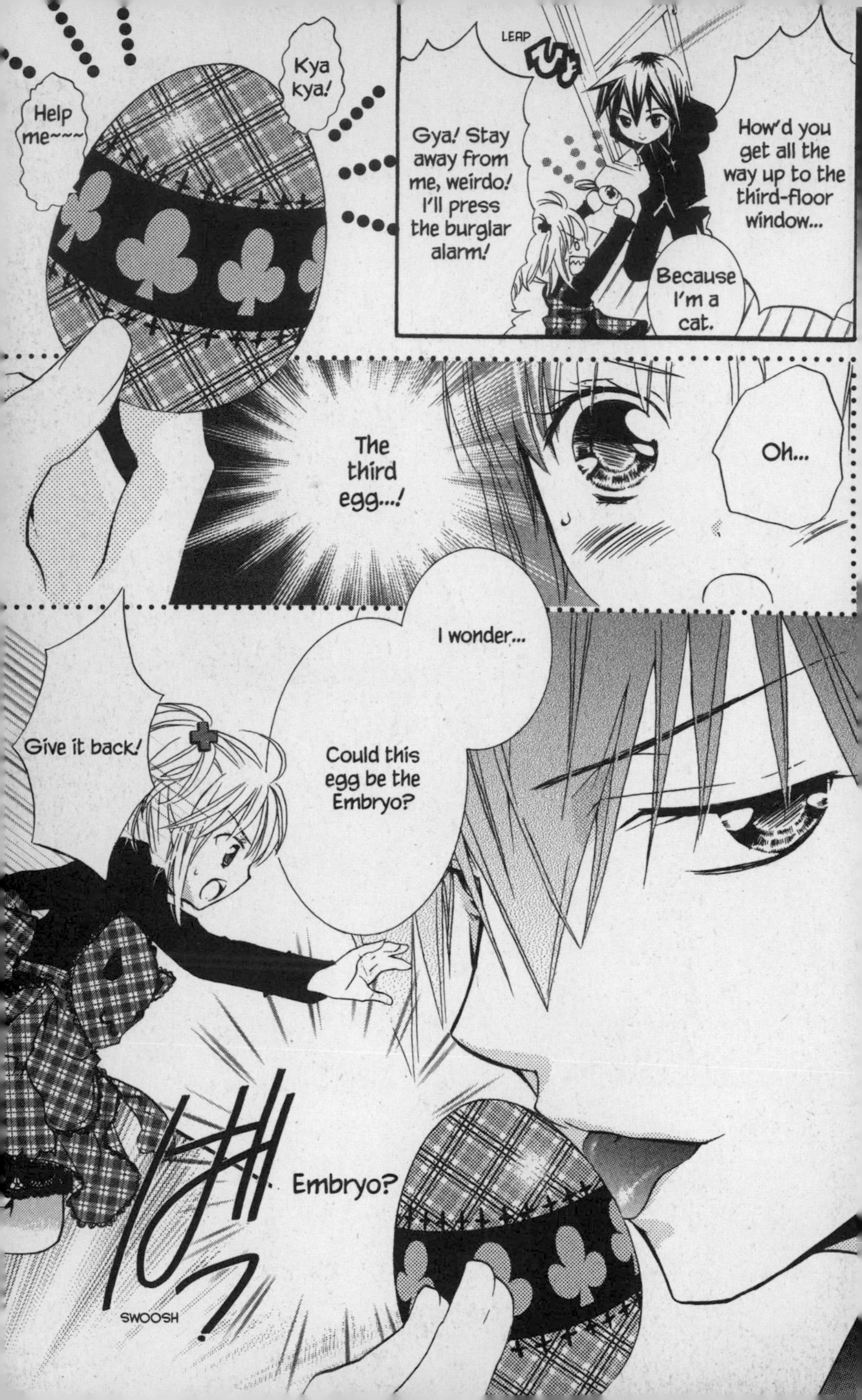
LEAP
How'd you get all the way up to the third-floor window...
Because I'm a cat.
Gya! Stay away from me, weirdo! I'll press the burglar alarm!
Kya kya!
Help me~~~
Oh...
The third egg...!
I wonder...
Could this egg be the Embryo?
Give it back!
Embryo?
SWOOSH

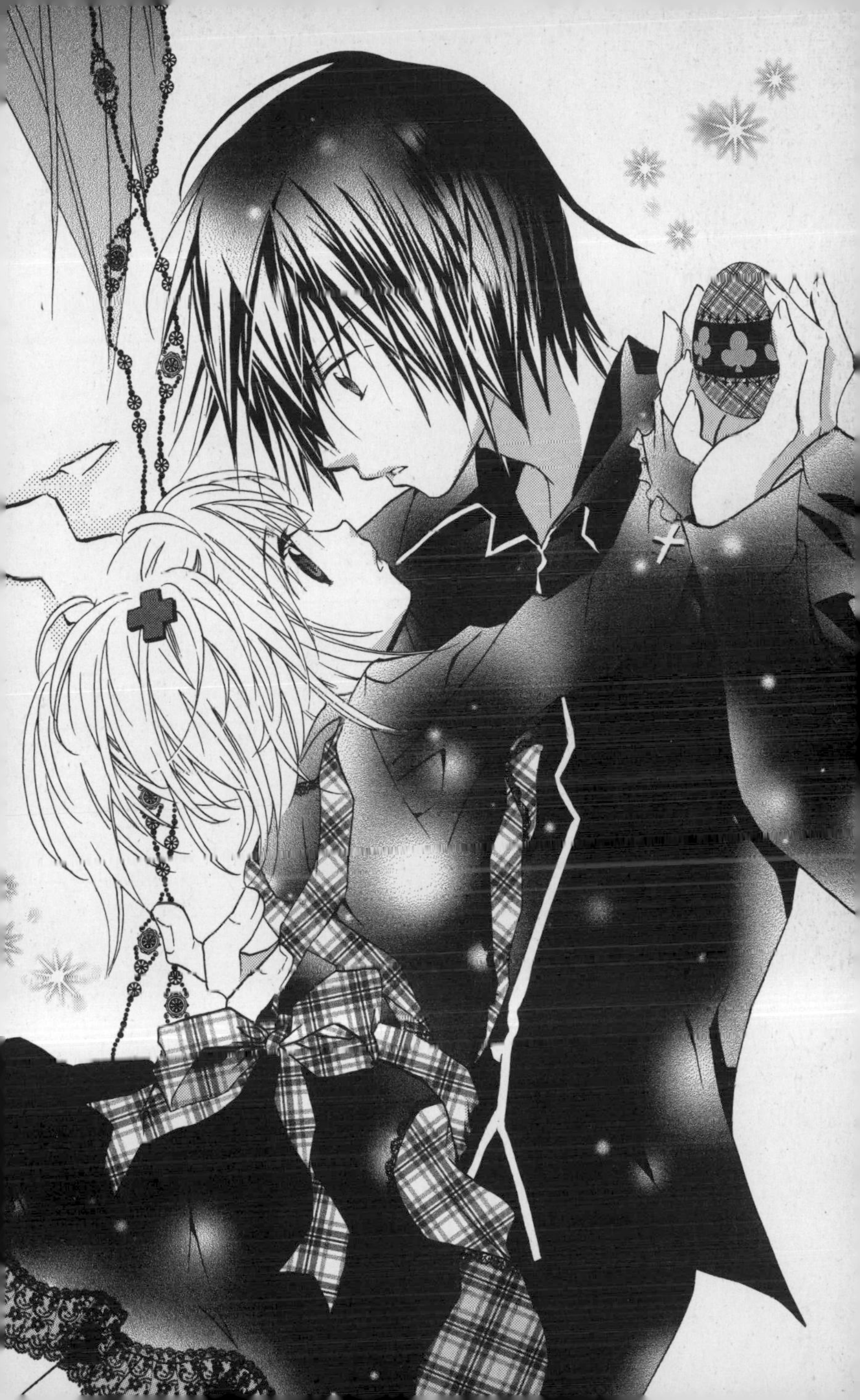

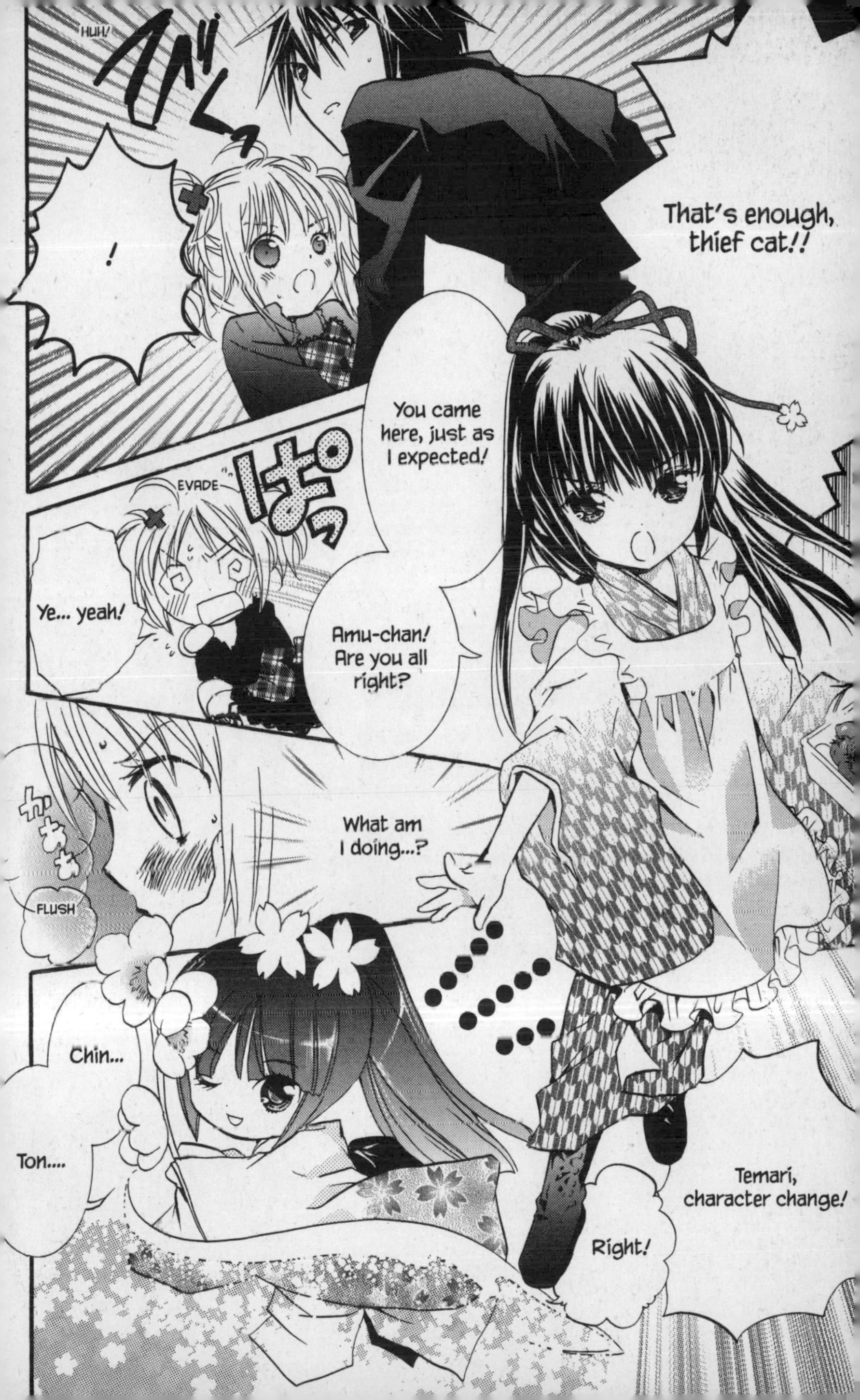
That's enough, thief cat!!
You came here, just as I expected!
Amu-chan! Are you all right?
HUH!
!
EVADE
Ye... yeah!
What am I doing...?
FLUSH
Temari, character change!
Right!
Chin...
Ton....

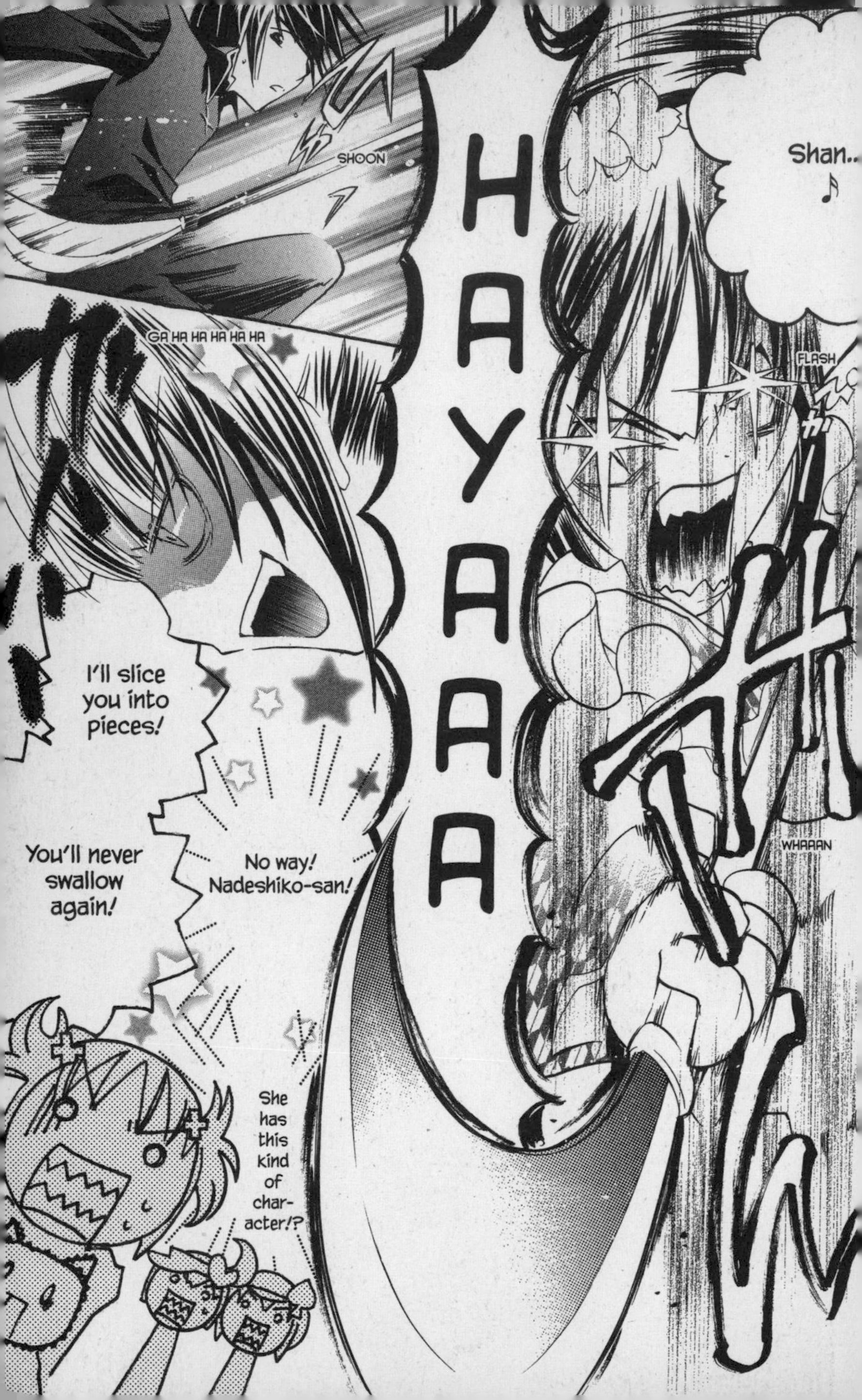
Shan..♪
FLASH
HAYAAAA
WHAAAN
SHOON
GA HA HA HA HA HA
I'll slice you into pieces!
You'll never swallow again!
No way! Nadeshiko-san!
She has this kind of character!?

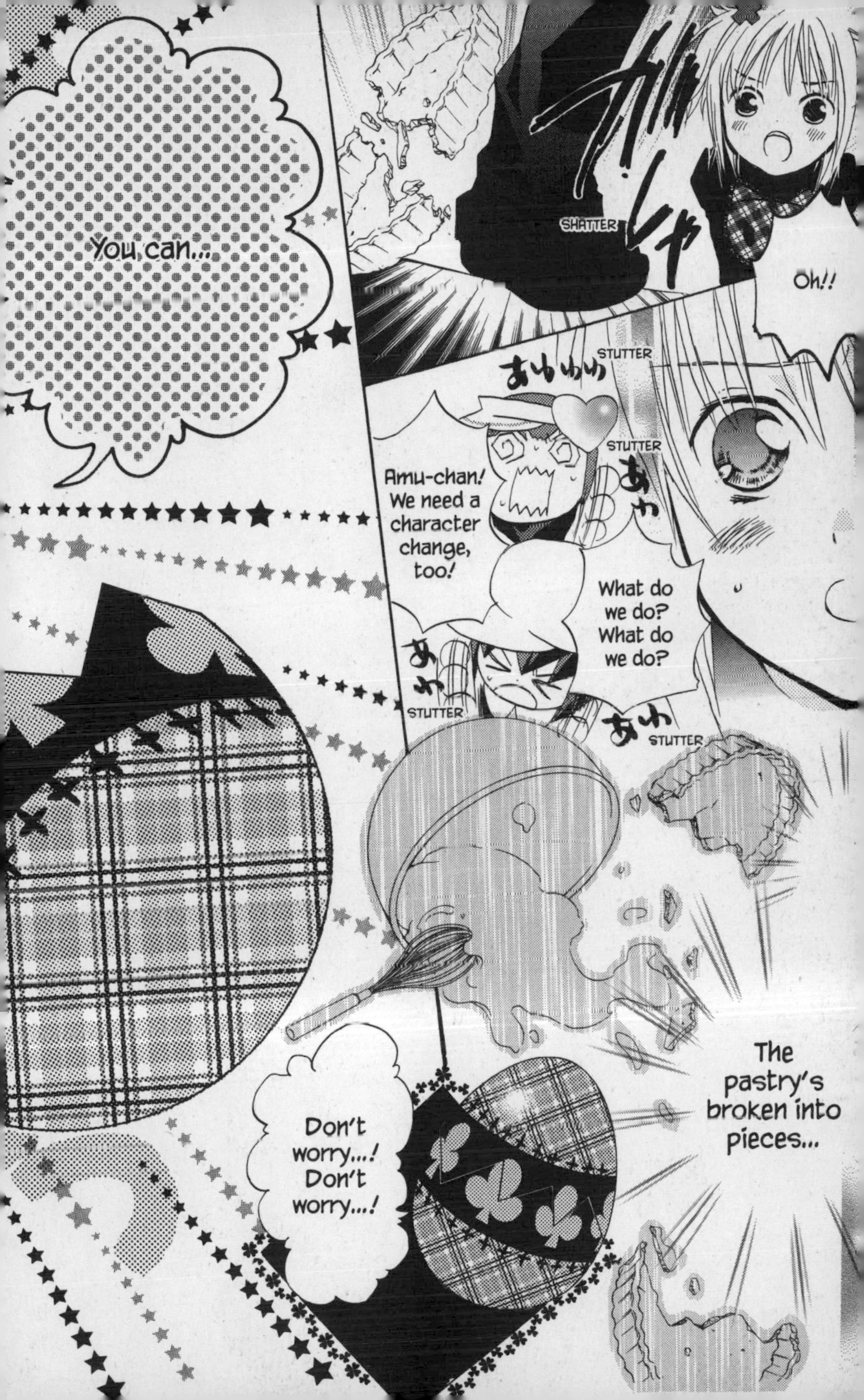
SHATTER
Oh!!
STUTTER
STUTTER
Amu-chan! We need a character change, too!
What do we do? What do we do?
STUTTER
STUTTER
The pastry's broken into pieces...
You can...
Don't worry...! Don't worry...!

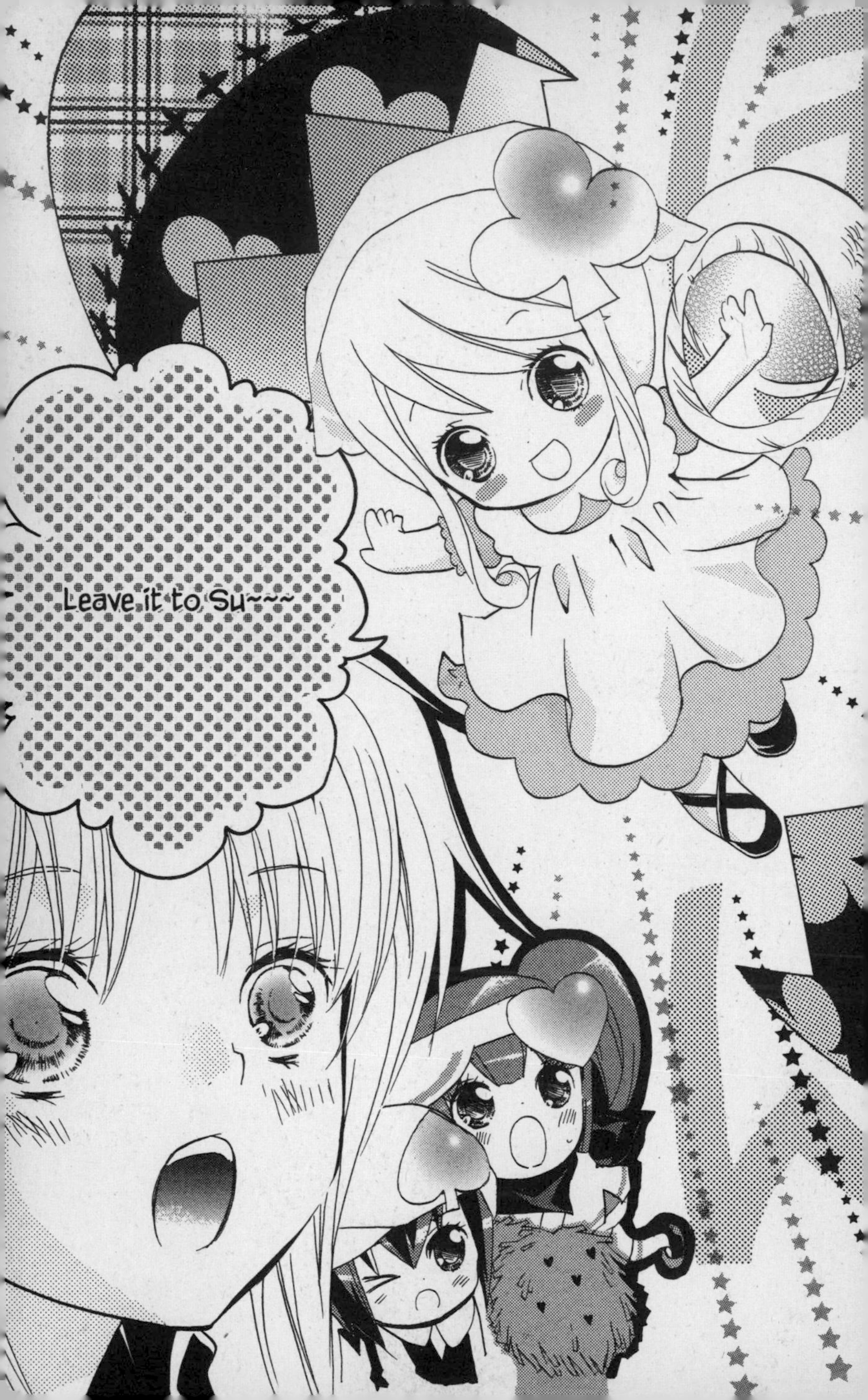
Leave it to Su~~~

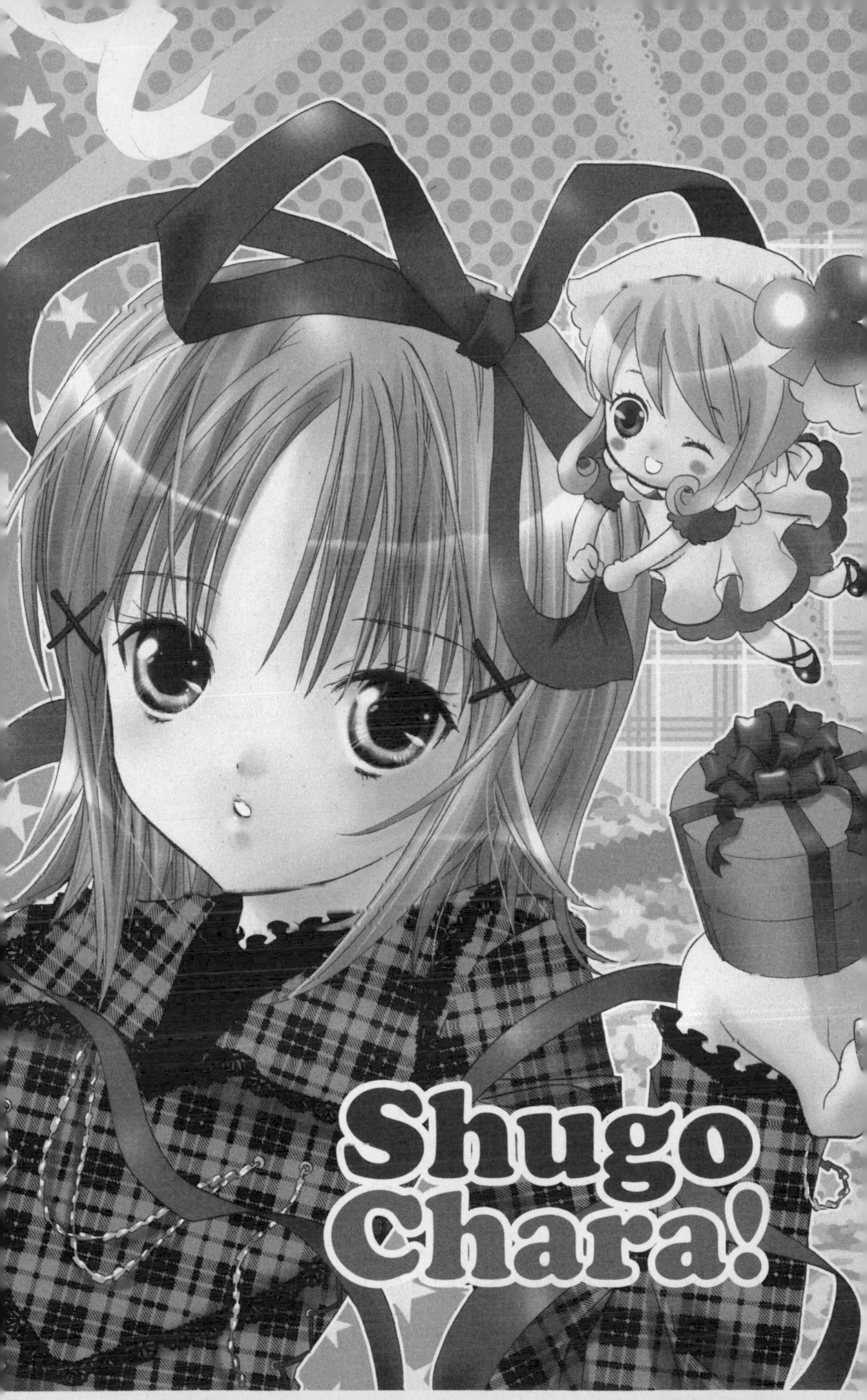
Shugo
Chara!

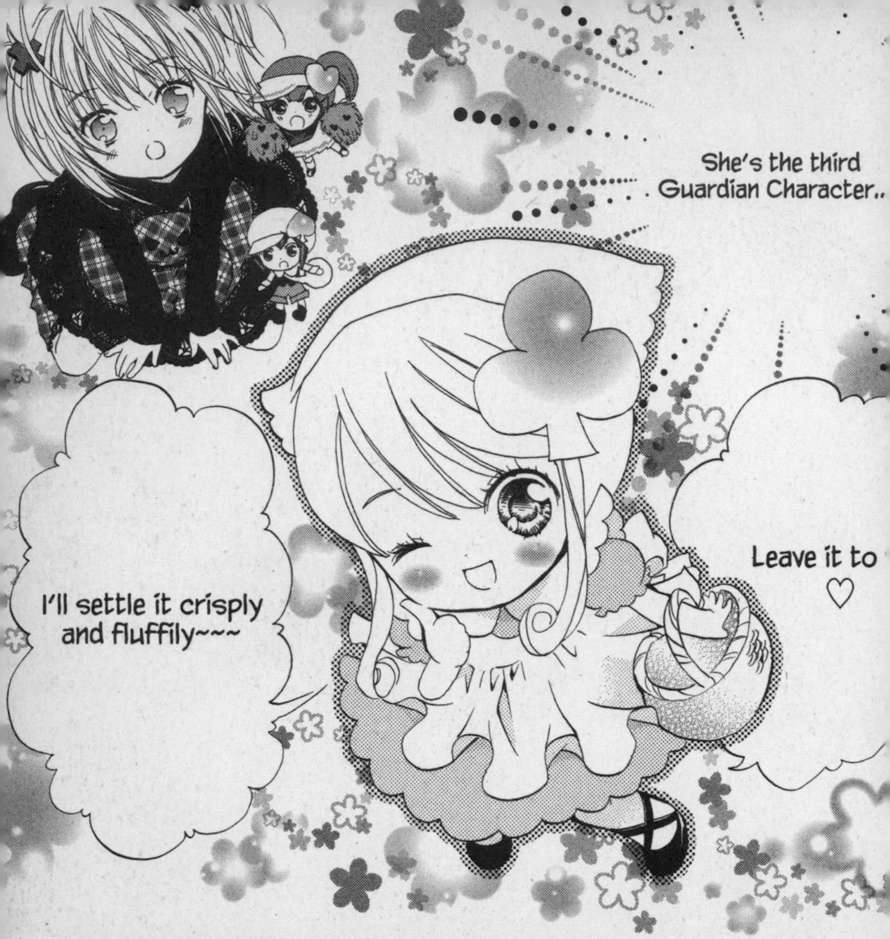
She's the third Guardian Character..
Leave it to ♡
I'll settle it crisply and fluffily~~~

Q 3. I want to be a manga artist. Do you have any suggestions?
A 3. Well...If you like manga and keep drawing it, maybe some day you might just naturally become a manga artist. But there's a lot more to it than just drawing pictures. So I suggest that for now, you hang out with your friends, fall in love with someone, and study hard. (I envy your youth!)
Q 4. Are you more of a Kamenashi-san fan or an Akanishi-kun fan?
A 4. Hm....Ebara is a fan of Kamenishi-kun and Banri-san is a fan of Yamapi. Akanishi-kun...?

That's all for now. See you in volume 2! ♡

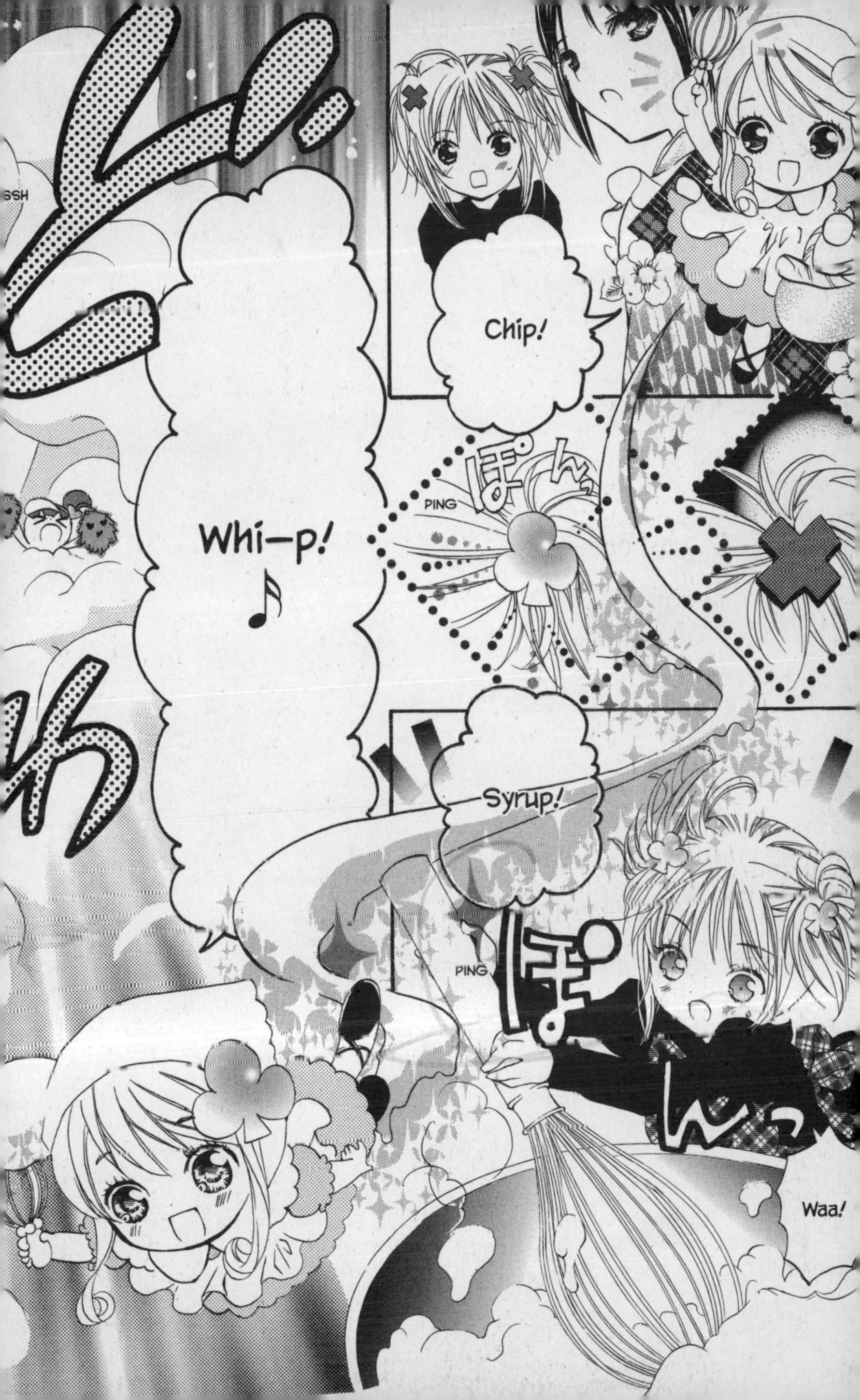
Chip!
PING
Syrup!
PING
Waa!
SSH
Whi-p! ♪

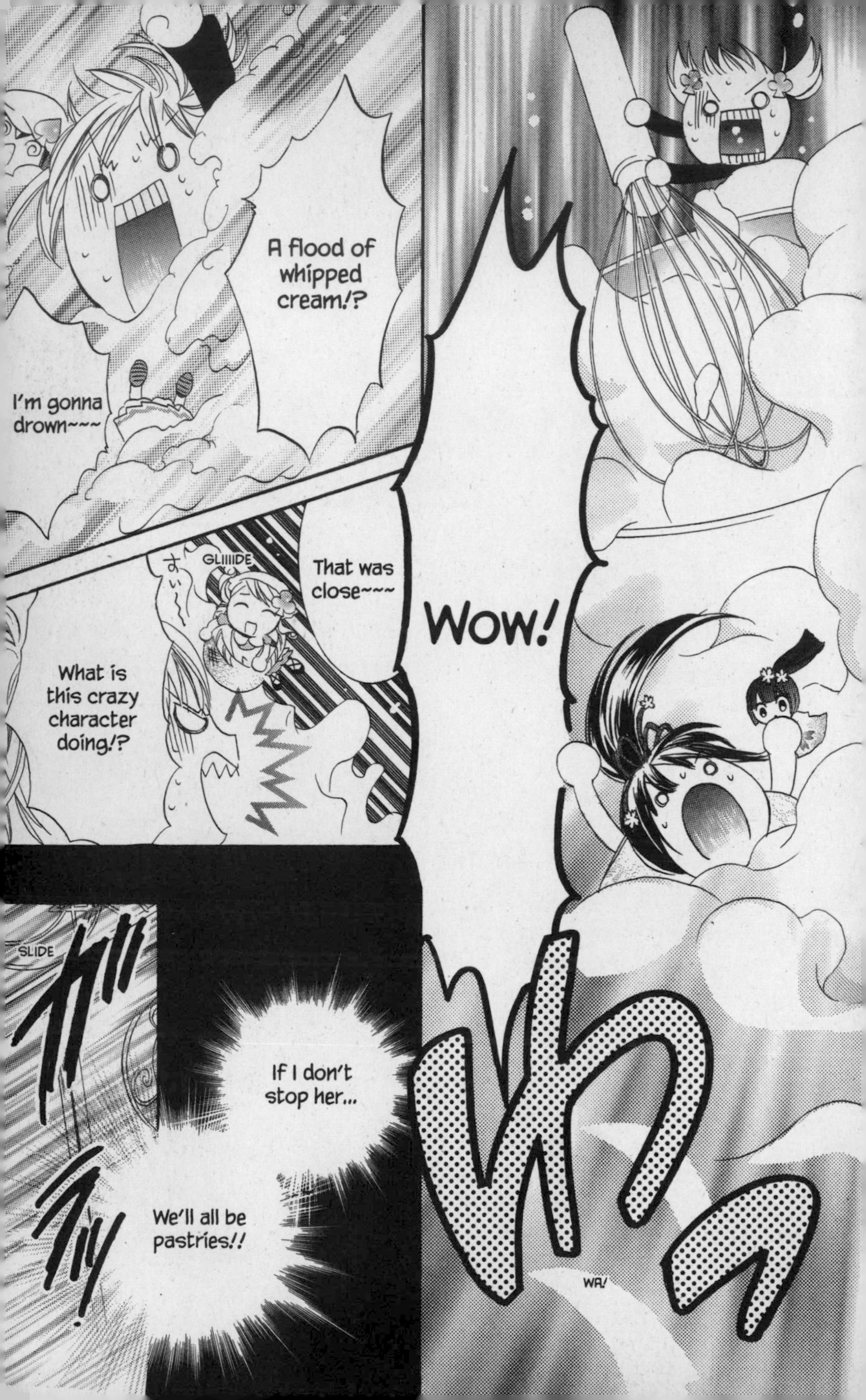
WOW!
WA!
A flood of whipped cream!?
I'm gonna drown~~~
That was close~~~
GLIIIIDE
What is this crazy character doing!?
If I don't stop her...
We'll all be pastries!!
SLIDE

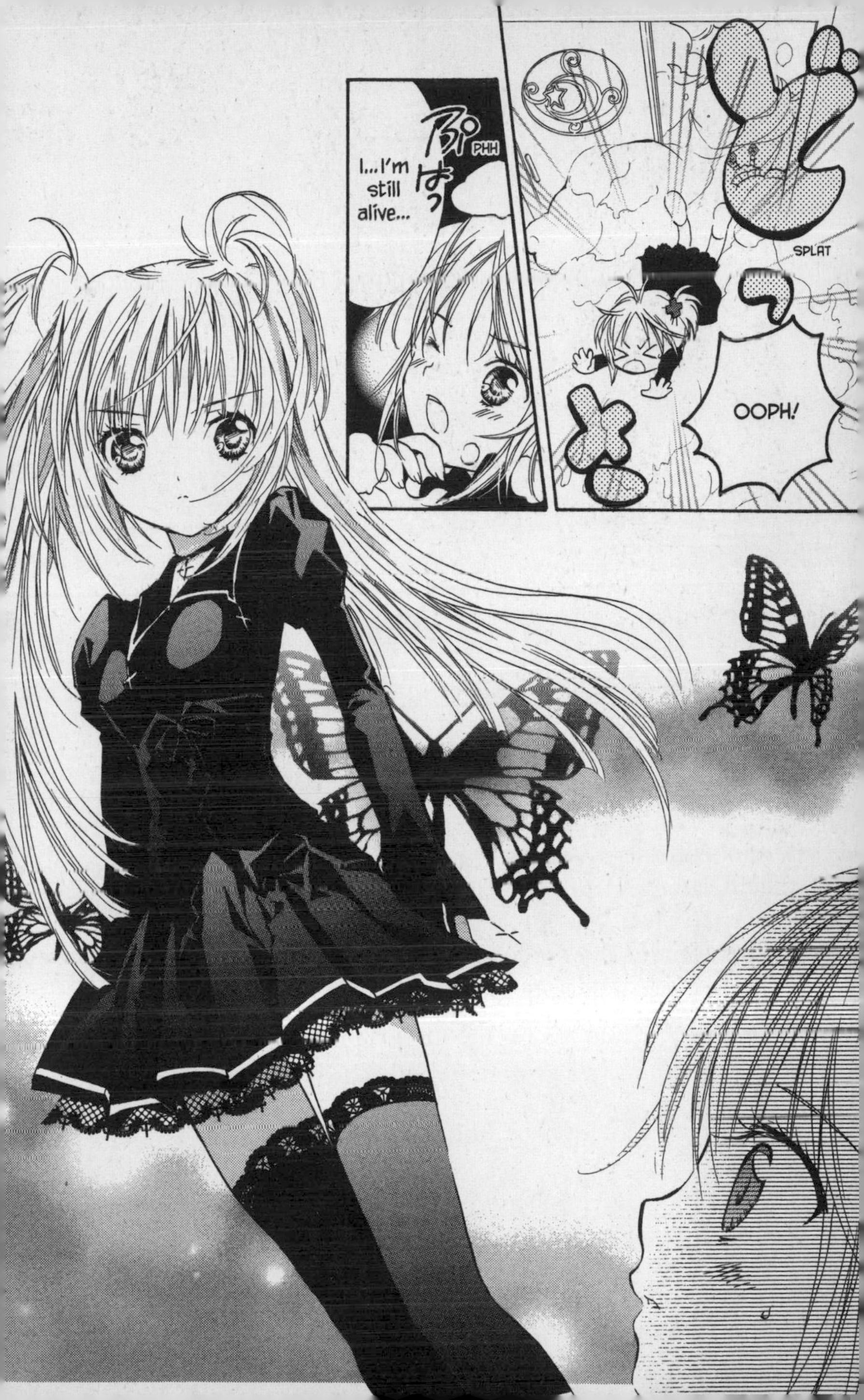
SPLAT
OOPH!
ぷはっ
PHH
I...I'm still alive...

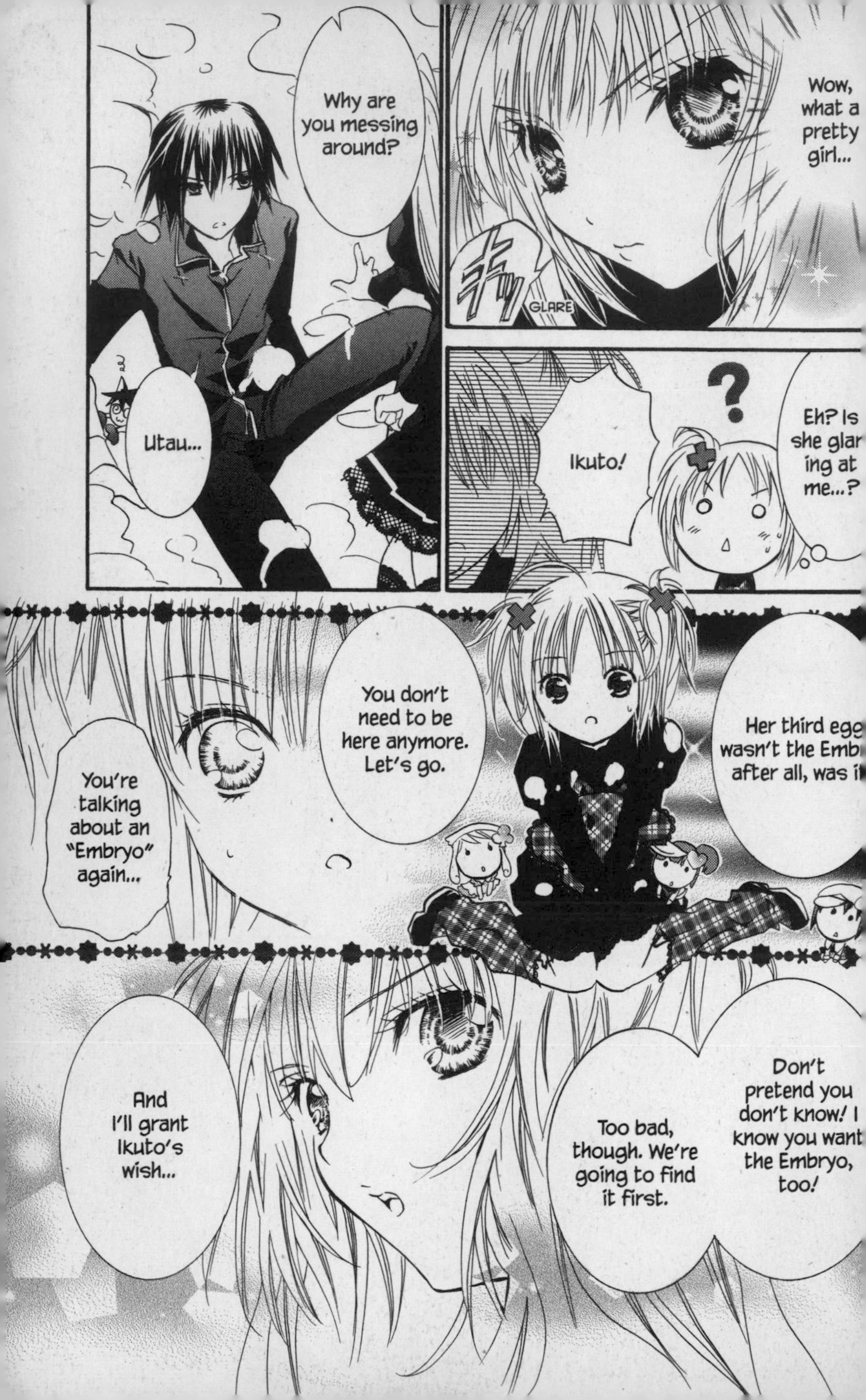

Wow, what a pretty girl...
キッ
GLARE
Eh? Is she glar ing at me...?
Ikuto!
Why are you messing around?
Utau...
Her third egg wasn't the Emb after all, was i
You don't need to be here anymore. Let's go.
You're talking about an "Embryo" again...
Don't pretend you don't know! I know you want the Embryo, too!
Too bad, though. We're going to find it first.
And I'll grant Ikuto's wish...

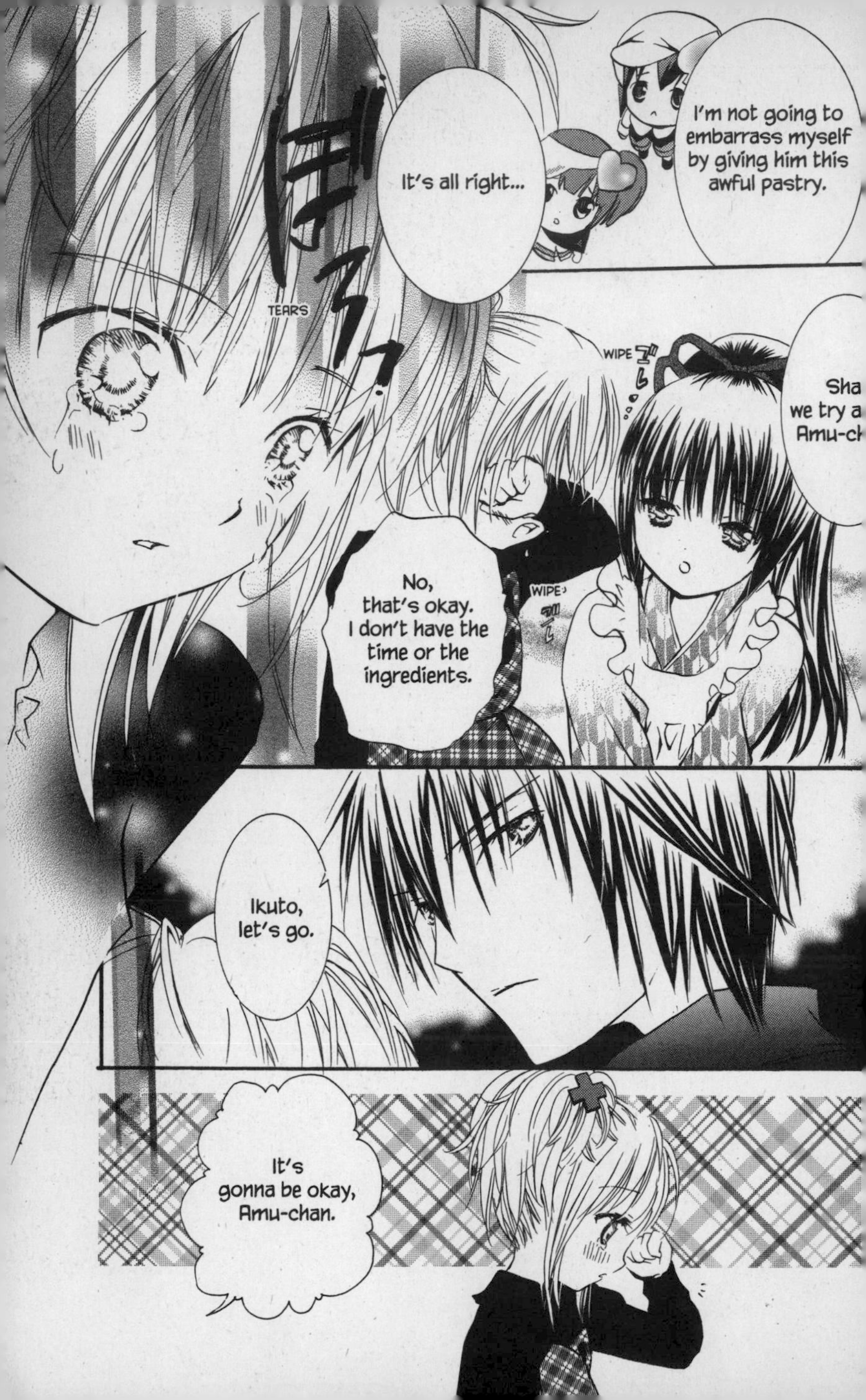
I'm not going to embarrass myself by giving him this awful pastry.
It's all right...
Sha
we try a
Amu-c
WIPE
No, that's okay. I don't have the time or the ingredients.
WIPE
TEARS
Ikuto, let's go.
It's gonna be okay, Amu-chan.

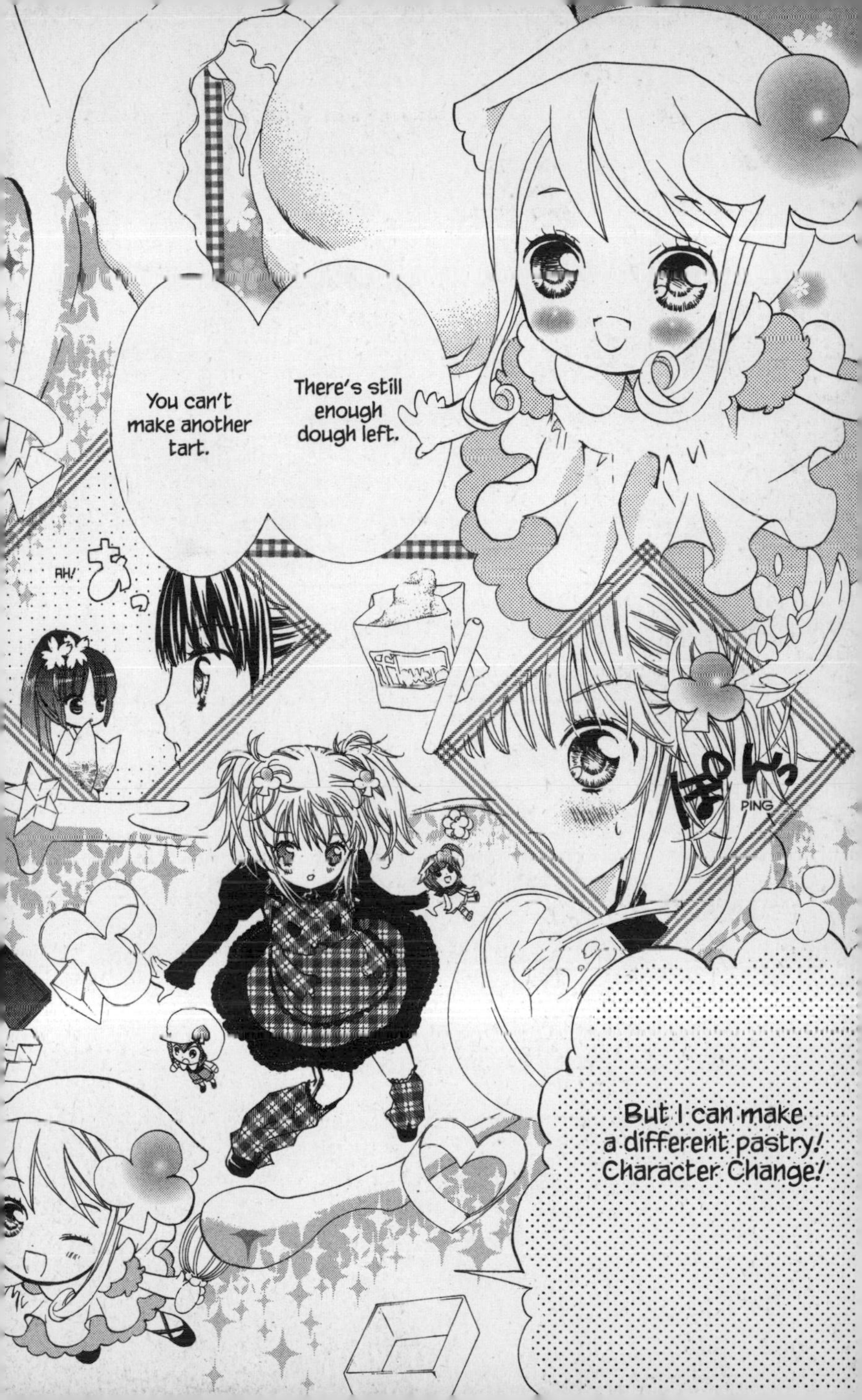
There's still enough dough left.
You can't make another tart.
AH!
PING
But I can make a different pastry! Character Change!

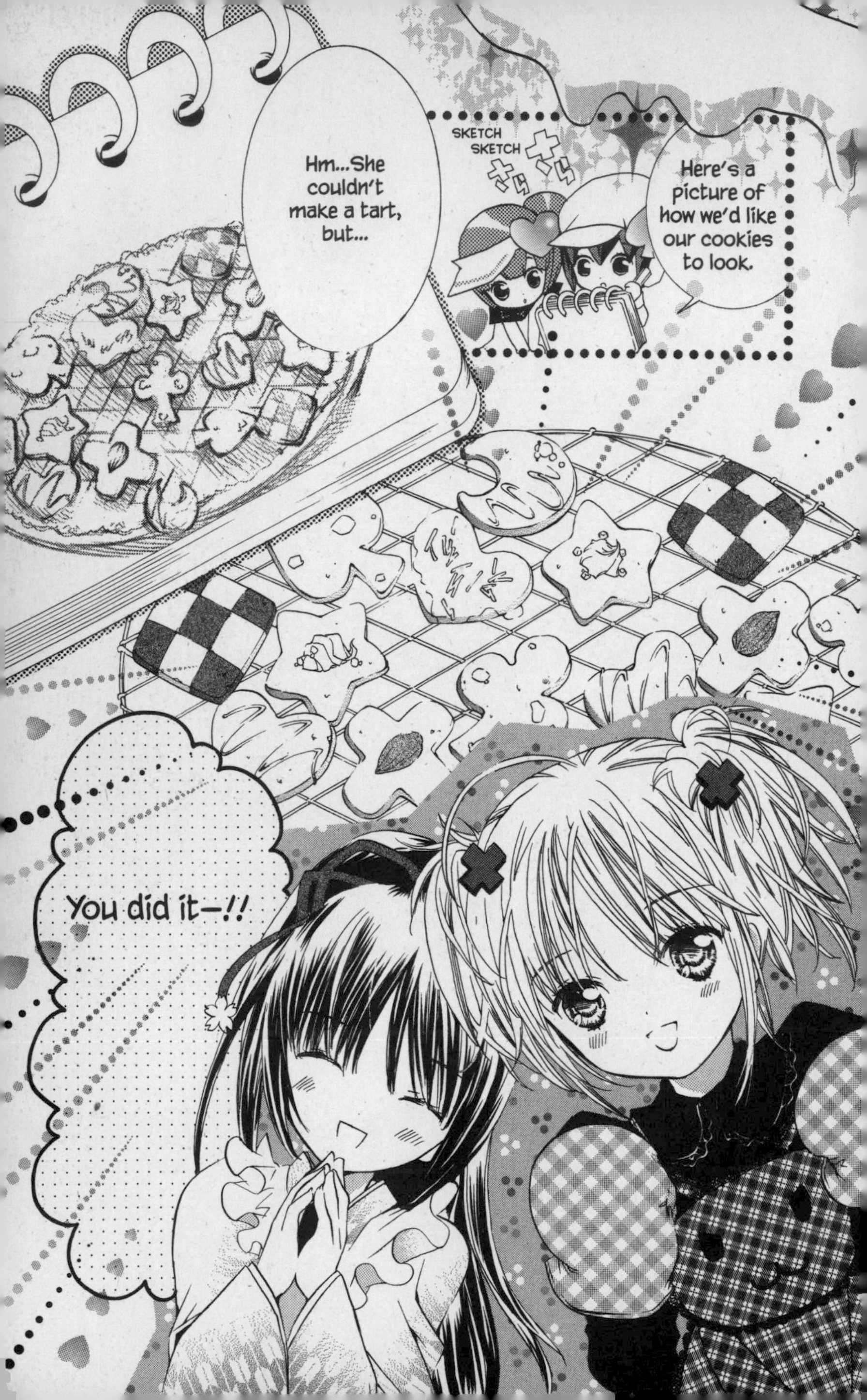
SKETCH SKETCH
Here's a picture of how we'd like our cookies to look.
Hm...She couldn't make a tart, but...
You did it—!!

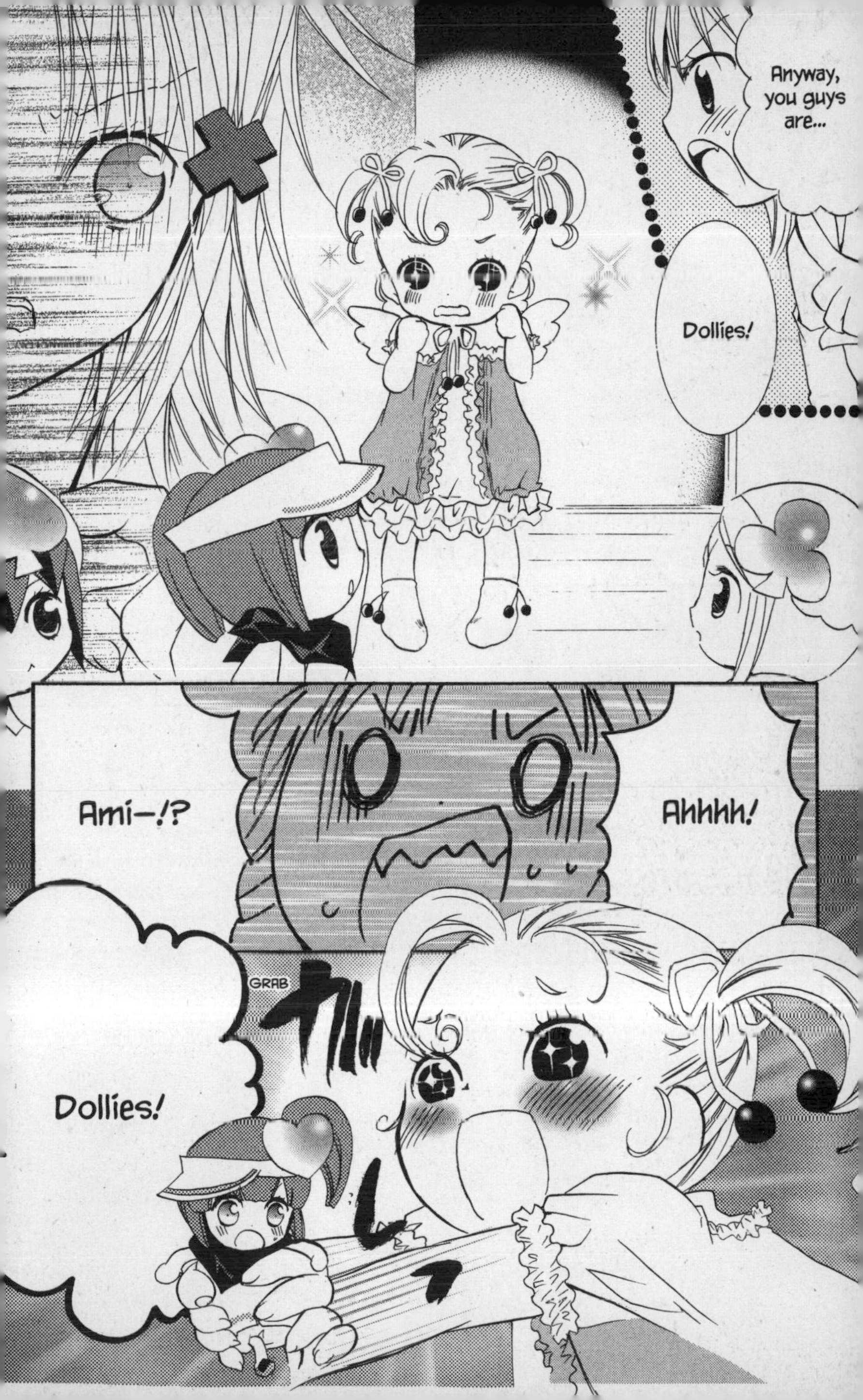
Anyway, you guys are...
Dollies!
Ahhhh!
Ami-!?
GRAB
Dollies!

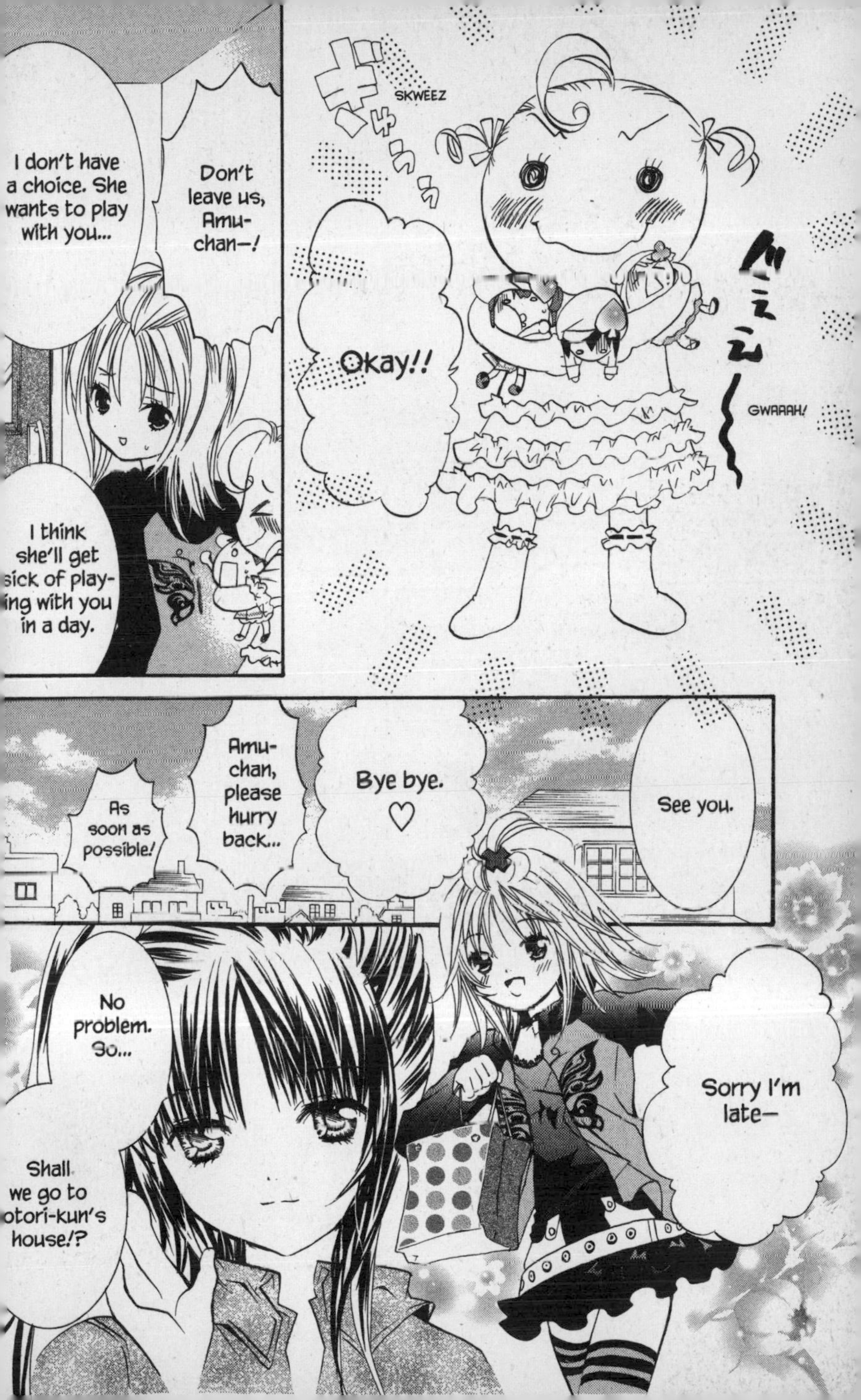
SKWEEZ
GWAAAH!
Okay!!
Don't leave us, Amu-chan—!
I don't have a choice. She wants to play with you...
I think she'll get sick of play-ing with you in a day.
See you.
Bye bye. ♡
Amu-chan, please hurry back...
As soon as possible!
Sorry I'm late—
No problem. So...
Shall we go to otori-kun's house!?

LOOK AROUND

GASP

Amu-chan, this isn't right. You should give it to him in person.

This is okay! I can't do that.

You're too shy.

Then... Thank you, Nadeshiko.

We're friends now, aren't we? You can call me just Nade-shiko.

You're welcome.

Thank you for coming here with me today.

Na...Nade-shiko-san...

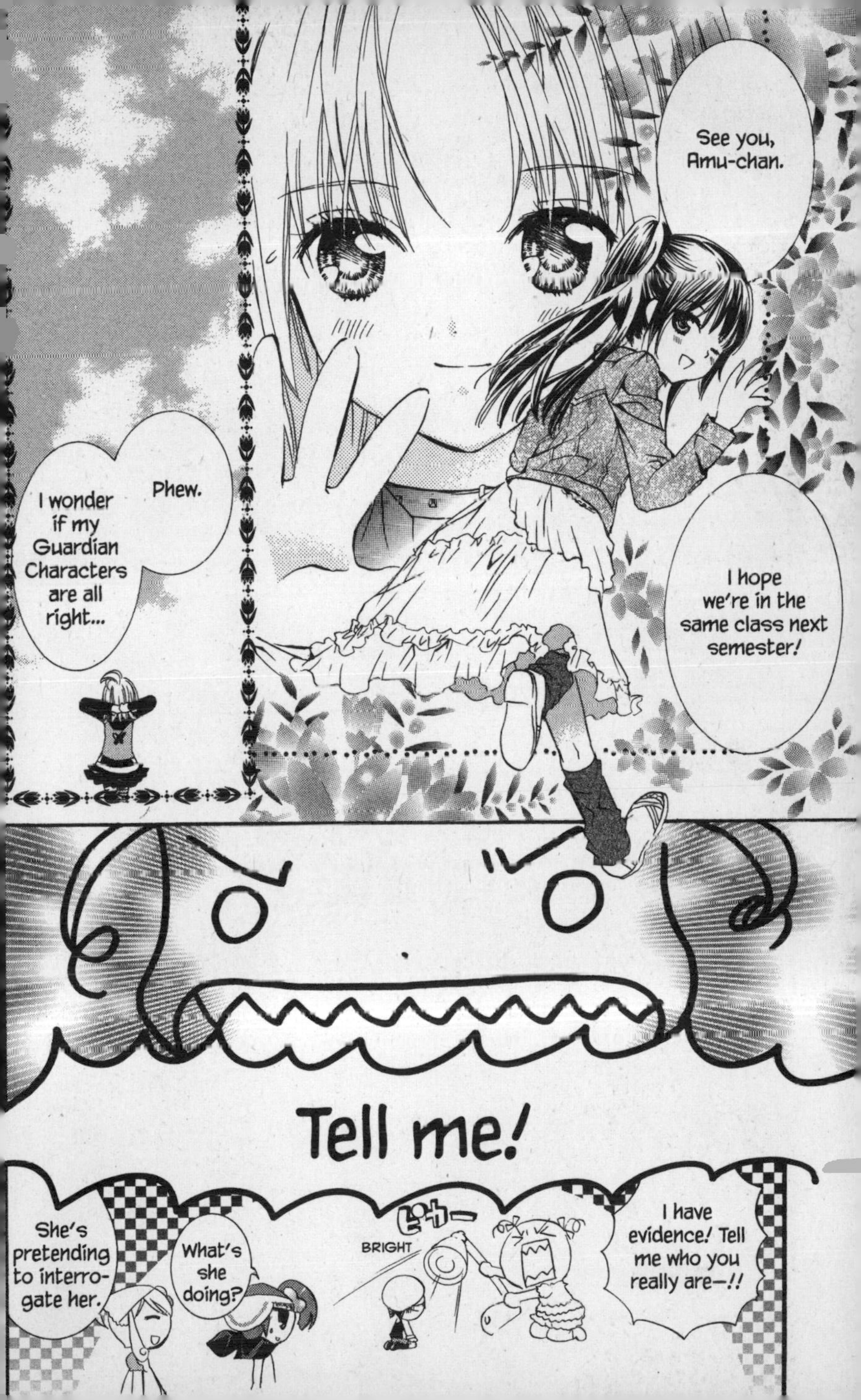
See you, Amu-chan.
I hope we're in the same class next semester!
Phew.
I wonder if my Guardian Characters are all right...
Tell me!
I have evidence! Tell me who you really are—!!
ピカー
BRIGHT
What's she doing?
She's pretending to interrogate her.

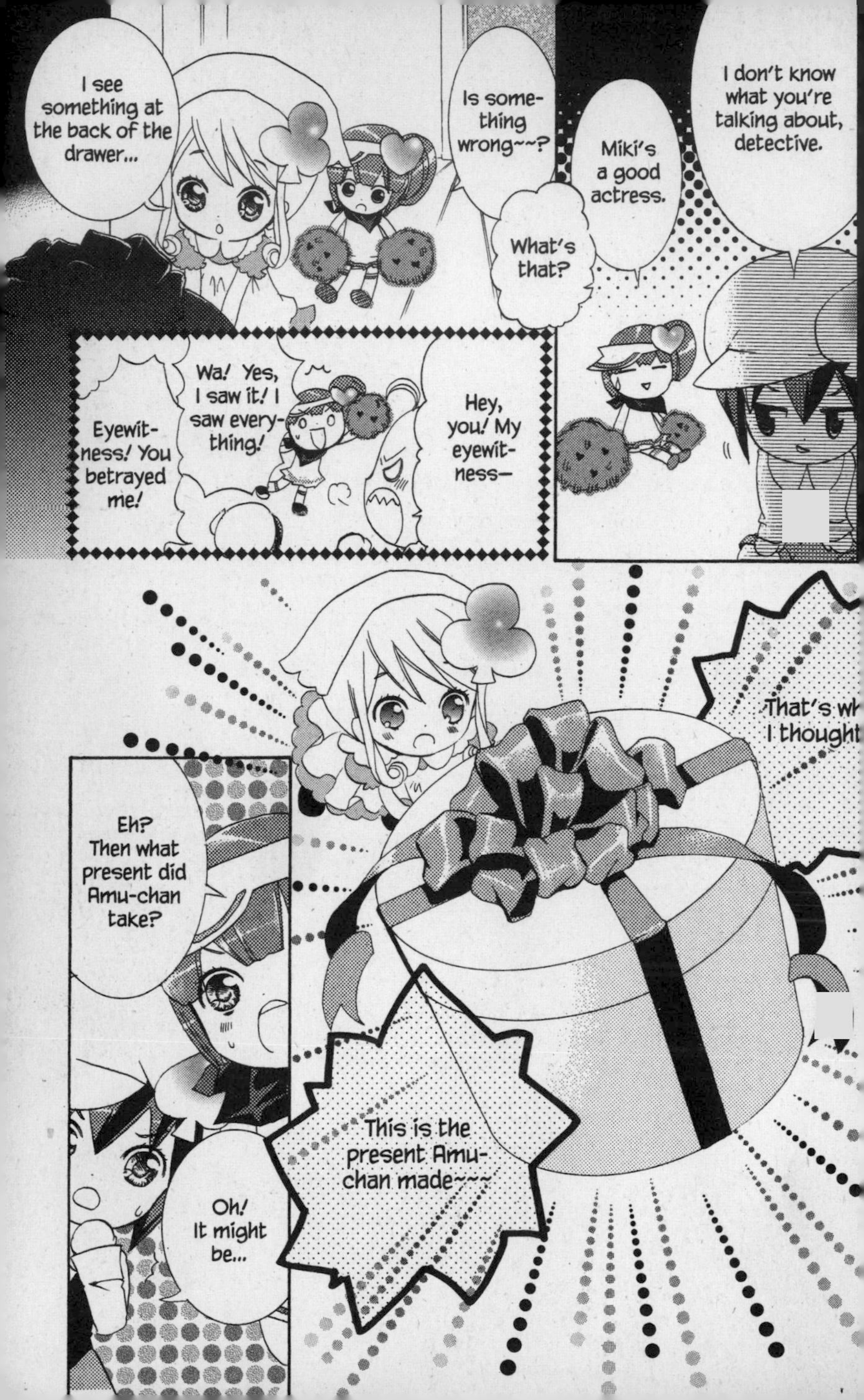
I don't know what you're talking about, detective.
Miki's a good actress.
What's that?
Is something wrong~~?
I see something at the back of the drawer...
Hey, you! My eyewitness—
Wa! Yes, I saw it! I saw everything!
Eyewitness! You betrayed me!
That's wh I thought
This is the present Amu-chan made~~~
Eh? Then what present did Amu-chan take?
Oh! It might be...

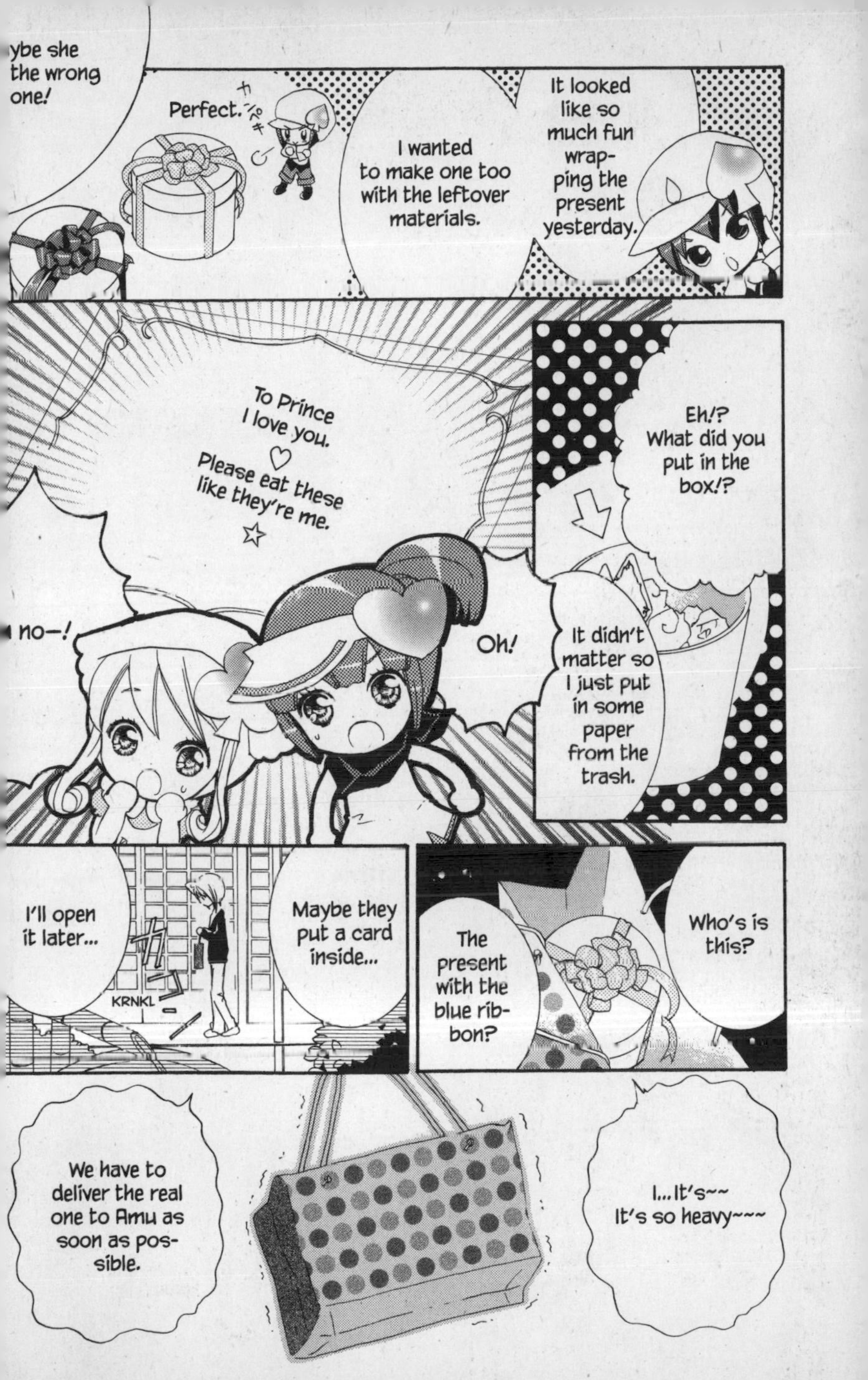
It looked like so much fun wrap-ping the present yesterday.
I wanted to make one too with the leftover materials.
Perfect.
ybe she the wrong one!
Eh!? What did you put in the box!?
It didn't matter so I just put in some paper from the trash.
Oh!
To Prince I love you. ♡ Please eat these like they're me. ☆
n no–!
Who's is this?
The present with the blue rib-bon?
Maybe they put a card inside...
I'll open it later...
KRNKL
I...It's~~ It's so heavy~~~
We have to deliver the real one to Amu as soon as pos-sible.

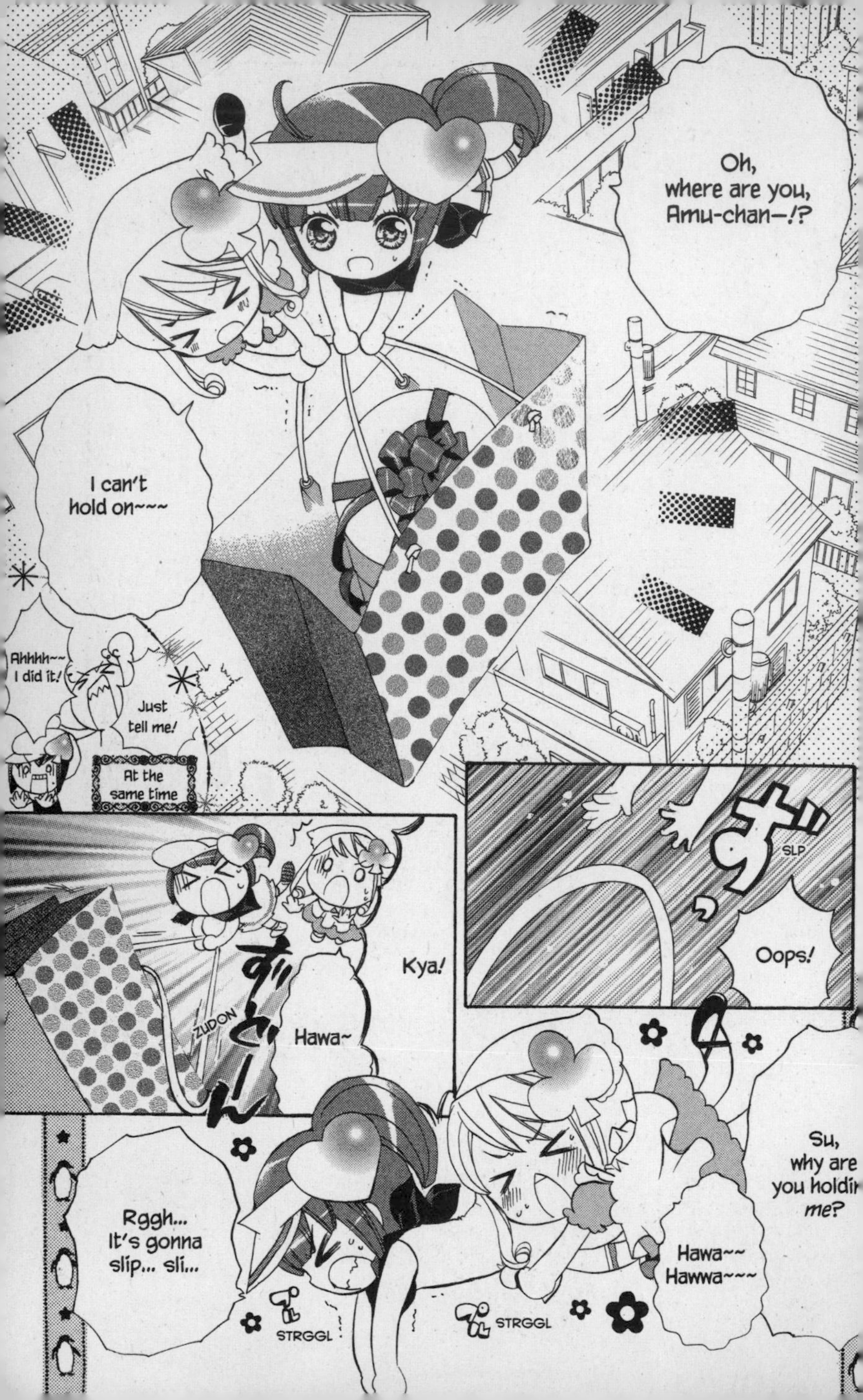
Oh, where are you, Amu-chan—!?
I can't hold on~~~
Just tell me!
Ahhhh~~ I did it!
At the same time
SLP
Oops!
Kya!
Hawa~
ZUDON
Su, why are you holdi
me?
Hawa~~ Hawwa~~~
STRGGL
Rggh... It's gonna slip... sli...
STRGGL

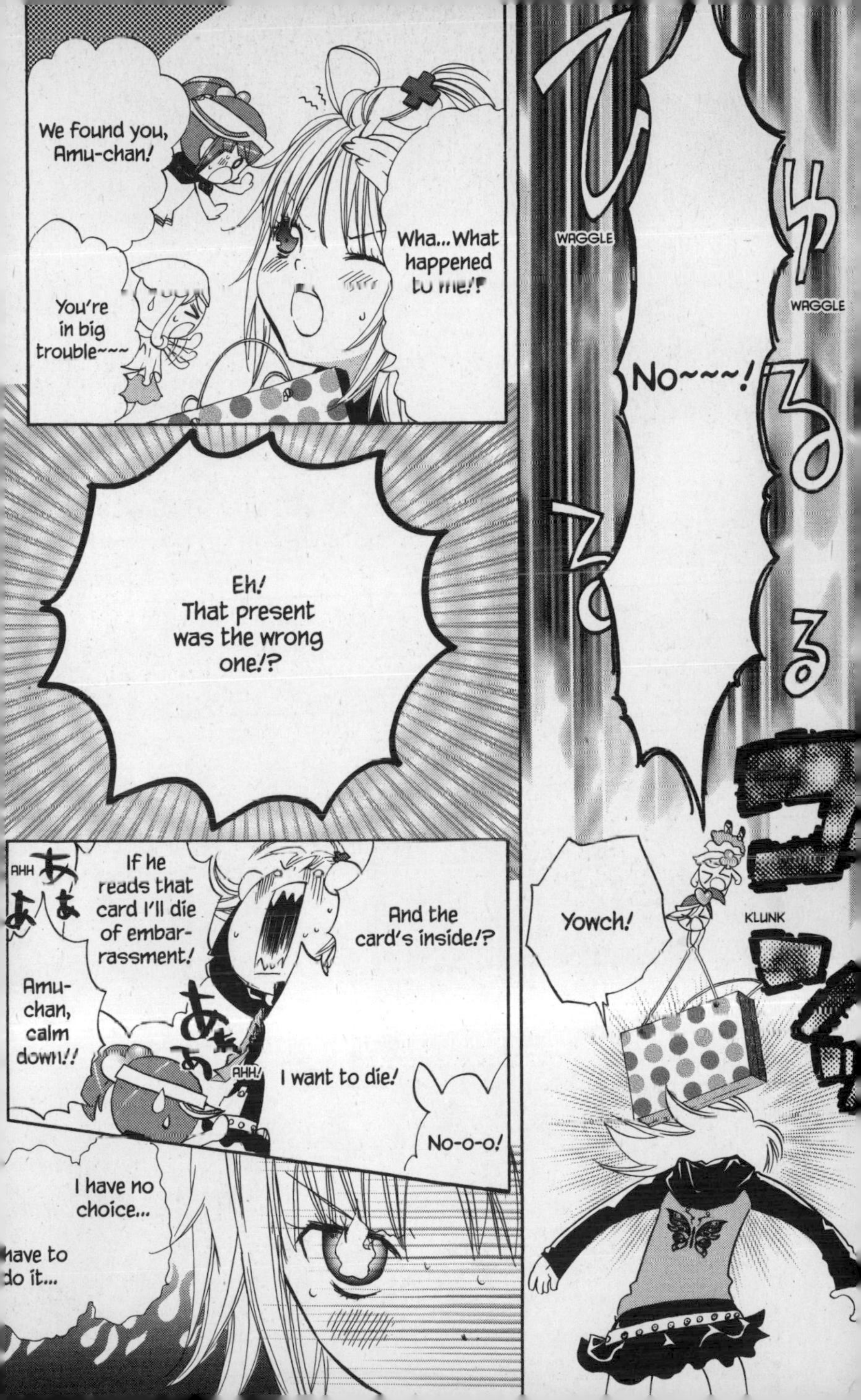
WAGGLE
WAGGLE
No~~~!
KLUNK
Yowch!
We found you, Amu-chan!
Wha...What happened to me!?
You're in big trouble~~~
Eh! That present was the wrong one!?
And the card's inside!?
If he reads that card I'll die of embarrassment!
AHH
Amu-chan, calm down!!
AHH!
I want to die!
No-o-o!
I have no choice...
have to do it...

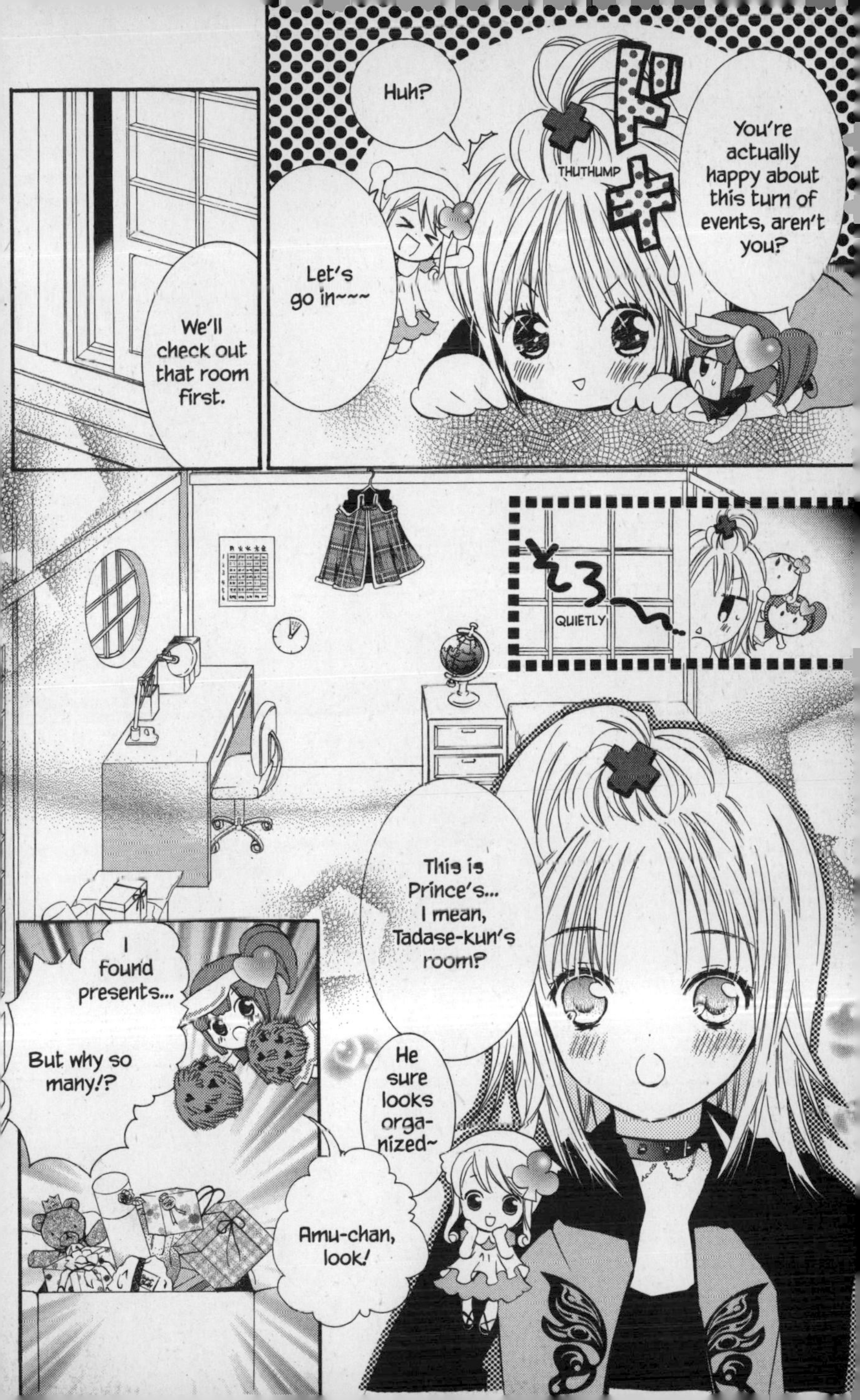

You're actually happy about this turn of events, aren't you?
THUTHUMP
Huh?
Let's go in~~~
We'll check out that room first.
そろ〜
QUIETLY
This is Prince's... I mean, Tadase-kun's room?
He sure looks orga-nized~
Amu-chan, look!
I found presents...
But why so many!?

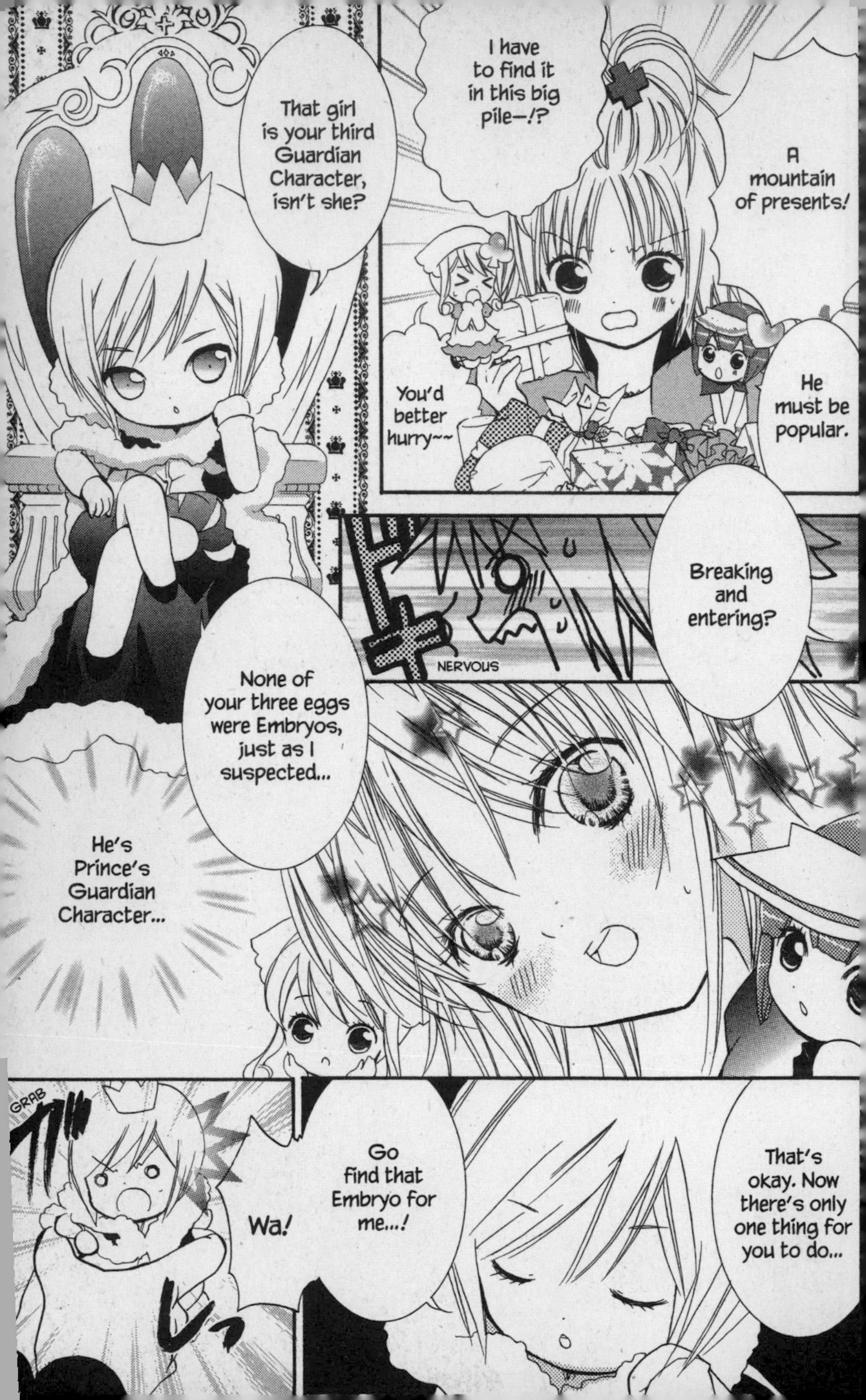
A mountain of presents!
I have to find it in this big pile—!?
He must be popular.
You'd better hurry~~
Breaking and entering?
NERVOUS
That girl is your third Guardian Character, isn't she?
None of your three eggs were Embryos, just as I suspected...
He's Prince's Guardian Character...
That's okay. Now there's only one thing for you to do...
Go find that Embryo for me...!
Wa!
GRAB

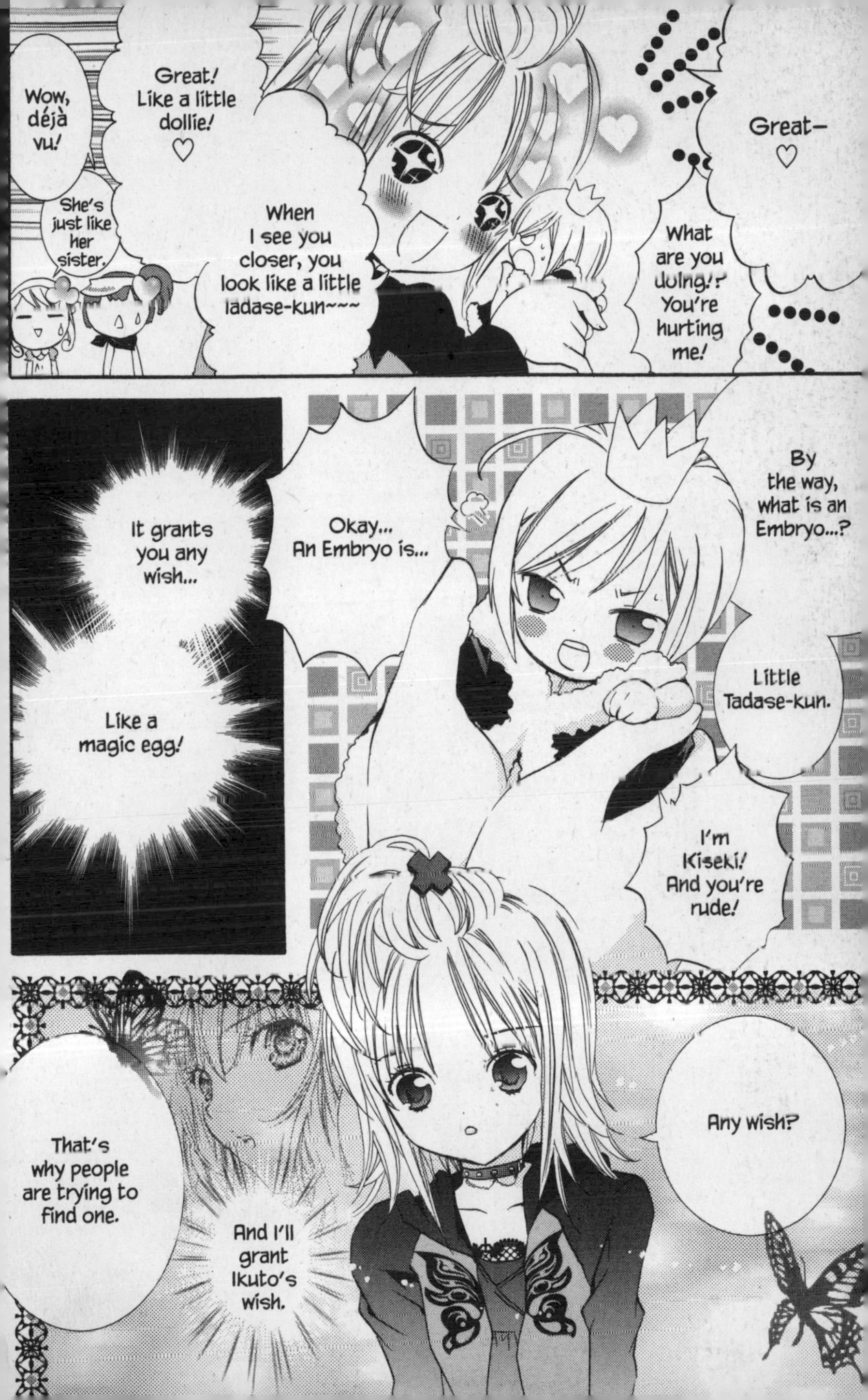
Great— ♡
What are you doing!? You're hurting me!
When I see you closer, you look like a little Tadase-kun~~~
Great! Like a little dollie! ♡
Wow, déjà vu!
She's just like her sister.
By the way, what is an Embryo...?
Okay... An Embryo is...
Little Tadase-kun.
I'm Kiseki! And you're rude!
It grants you any wish...
Like a magic egg!
Any wish?
That's why people are trying to find one.
And I'll grant Ikuto's wish.

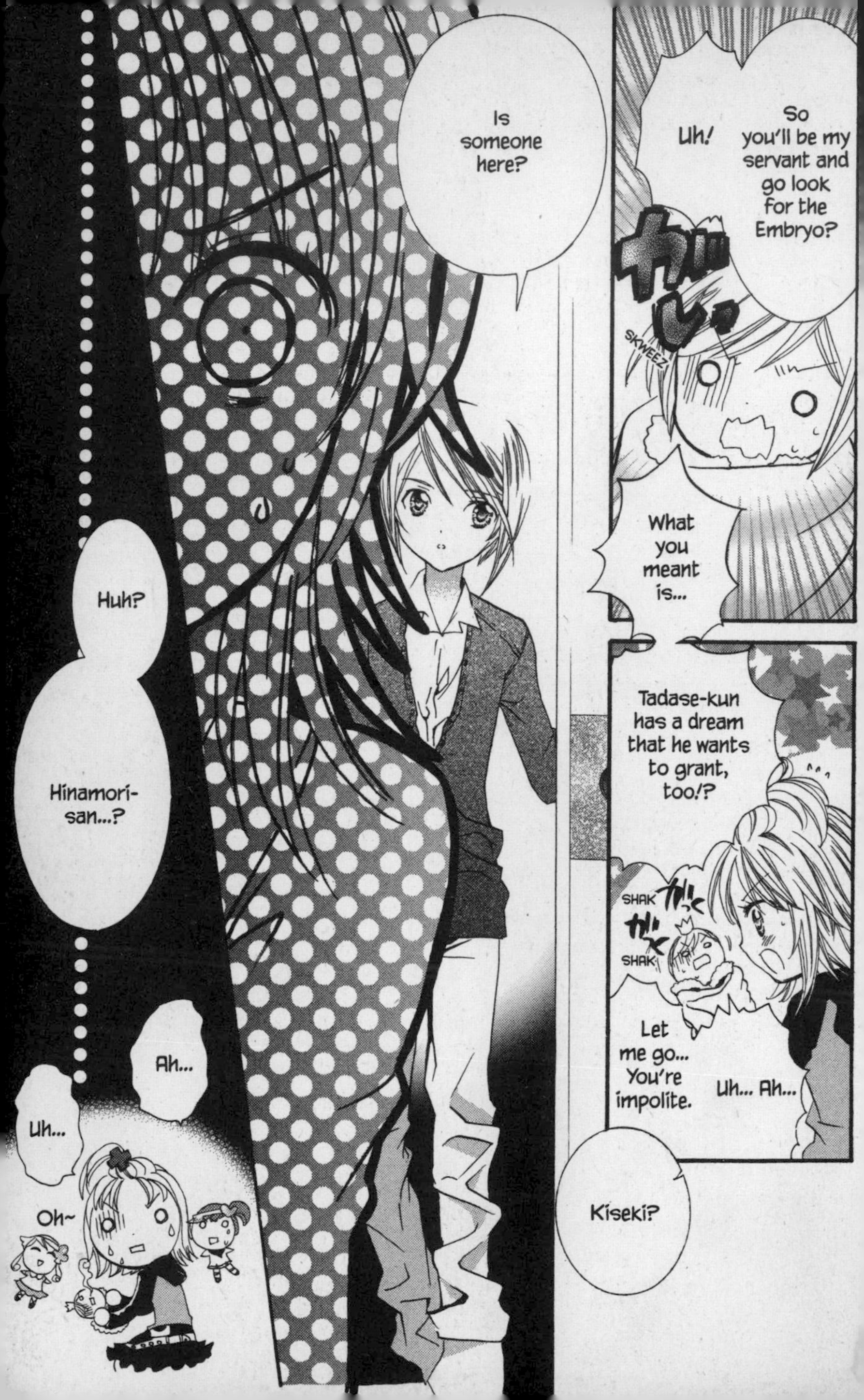

So you'll be my servant and go look for the Embryo?
Uh!
SKWEEZ
What you meant is...
Tadase-kun has a dream that he wants to grant, too!?
SHAK
SHAK
Let me go... You're impolite.
Uh... Ah...
Kiseki?
Is someone here?
Huh?
Hinamori-san...?
Ah...
Uh...
Oh~

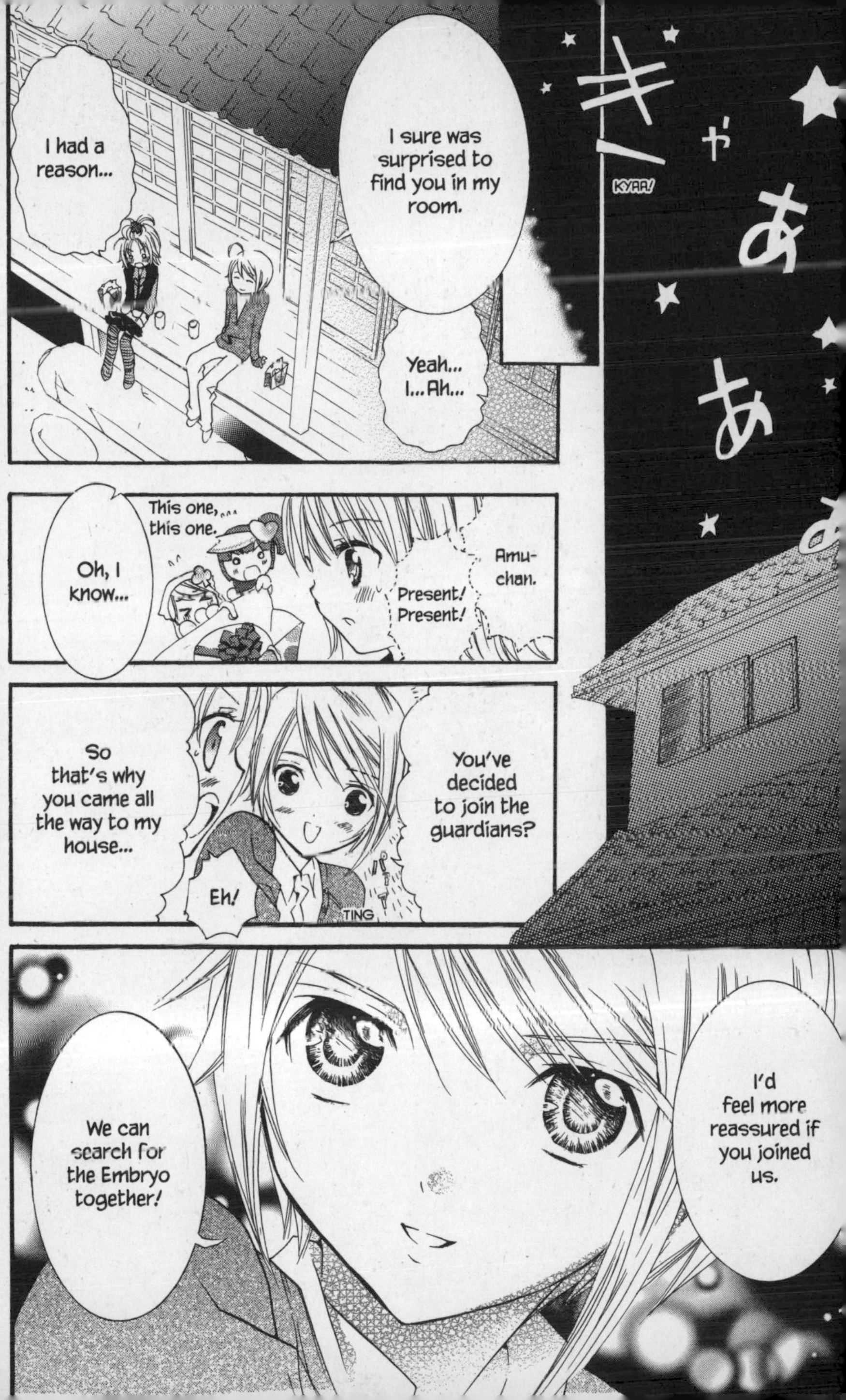
キャあああ
KYAA!
I sure was surprised to find you in my room.
Yeah... I...Ah...
I had a reason...
Amu-chan.
Present! Present!
This one, this one.
Oh, I know...
You've decided to join the guardians?
TING
Eh!
So that's why you came all the way to my house...
I'd feel more reassured if you joined us.
We can search for the Embryo together!

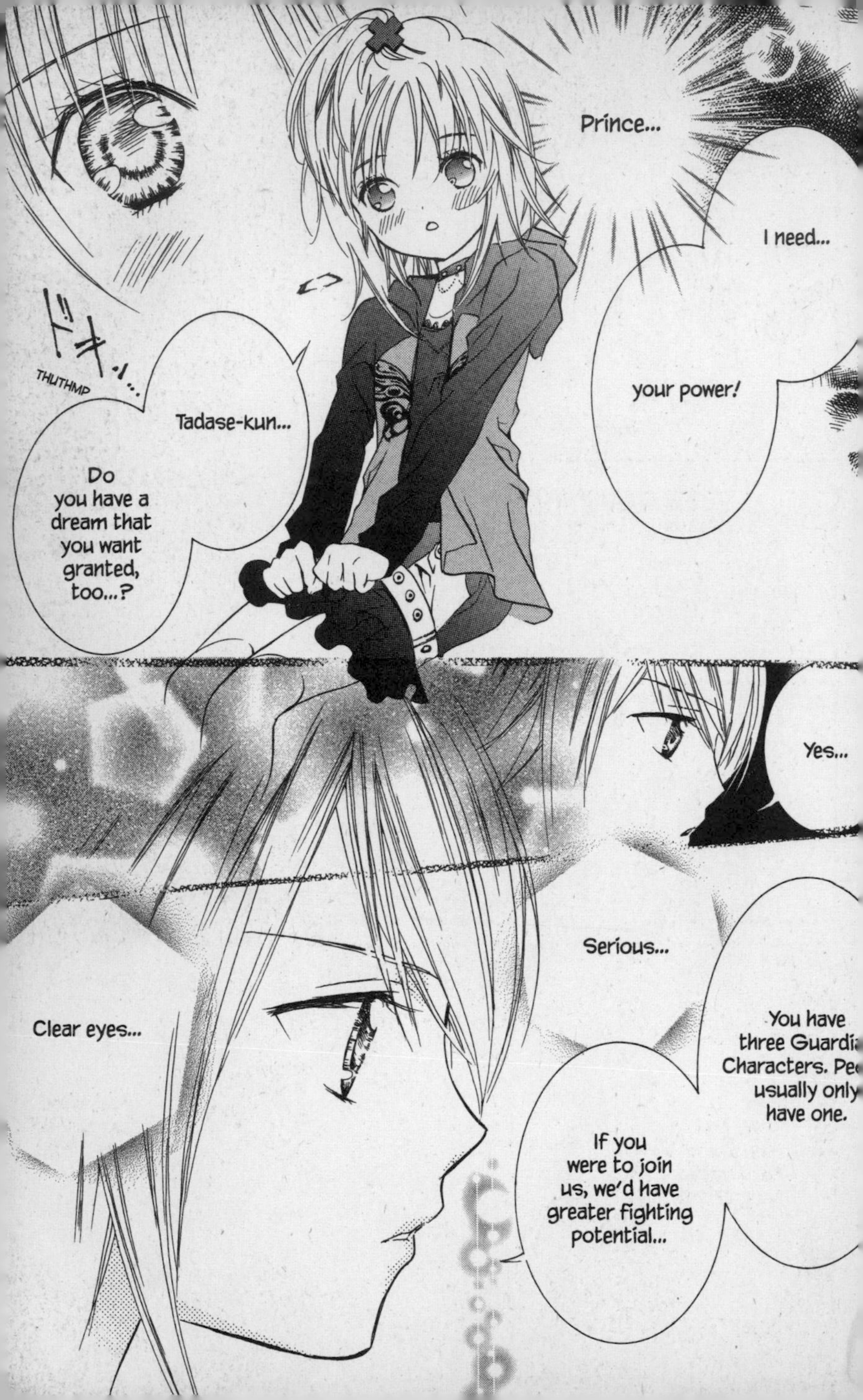

Prince...
I need...
your power!
ドキッ…
THUTHMP
Tadase-kun...
Do you have a dream that you want granted, too...?
Yes...
You have three Guardi Characters. Pe usually only have one.
If you were to join us, we'd have greater fighting potential...
Serious...
Clear eyes...

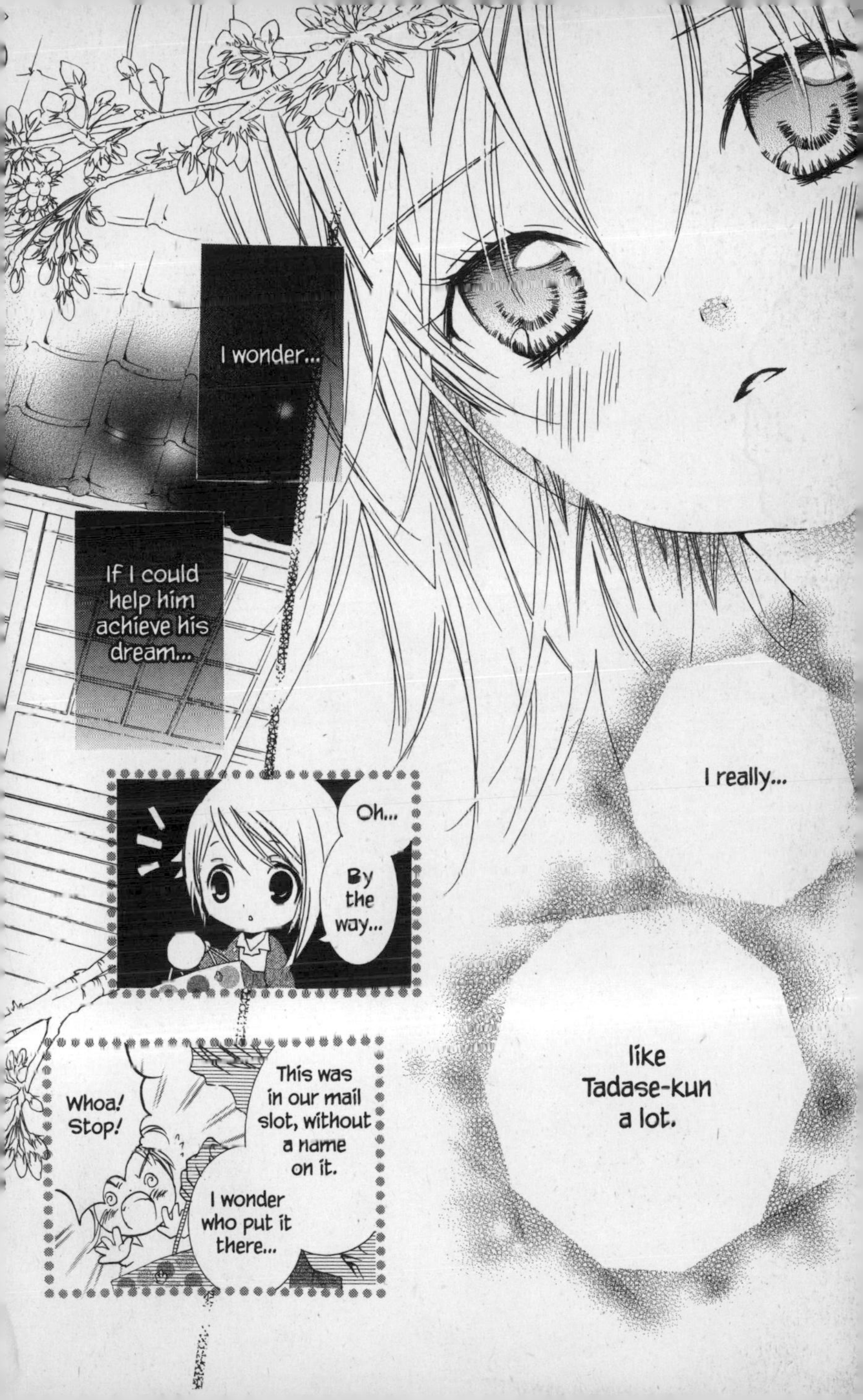

I wonder...
If I could help him achieve his dream...
I really...
like Tadase-kun a lot.
Oh...
By the way...
This was in our mail slot, without a name on it.
I wonder who put it there...
Whoa! Stop!

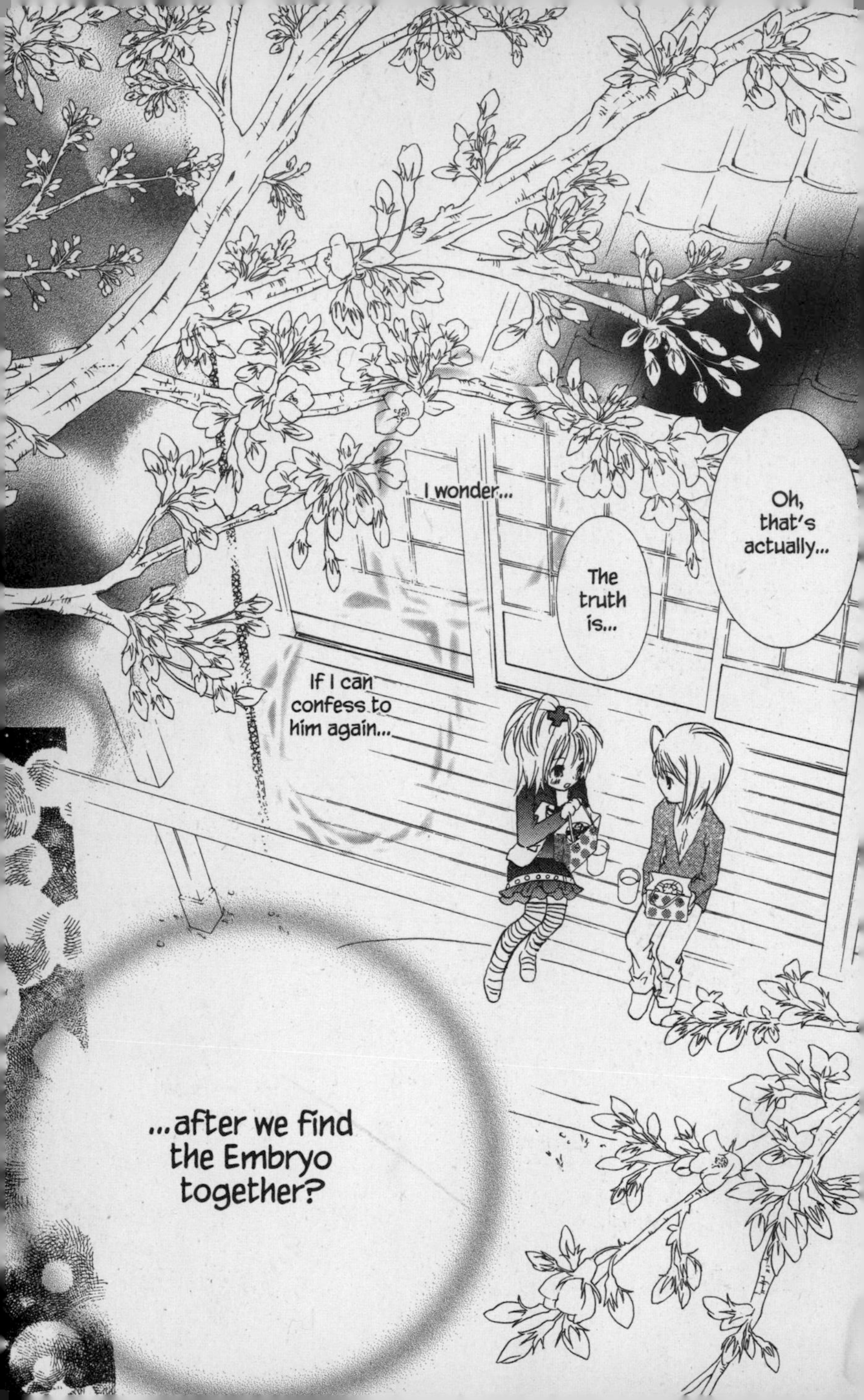

Oh, that's actually...
The truth is...
I wonder...
If I can confess to him again...
...after we find the Embryo together?

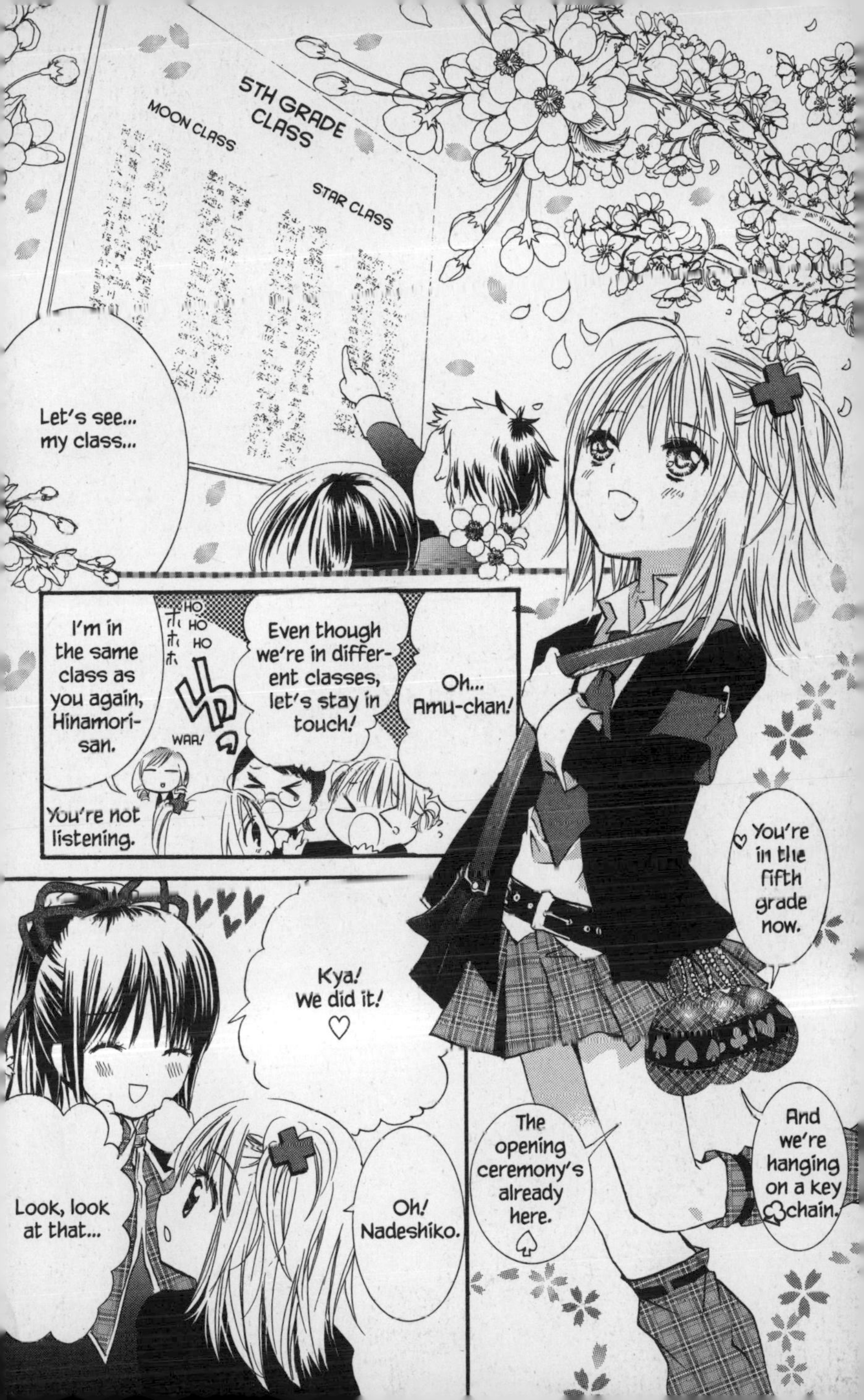
5TH GRADE CLASS
MOON CLASS
STAR CLASS
Let's see... my class...
You're in the fifth grade now.
And we're hanging on a key chain.
The opening ceremony's already here.
Oh... Amu-chan!
Even though we're in different classes, let's stay in touch!
HO HO HO
WAA!
I'm in the same class as you again, Hinamori-san.
You're not listening.
Kya! We did it!
Oh! Nadeshiko.
Look, look at that...

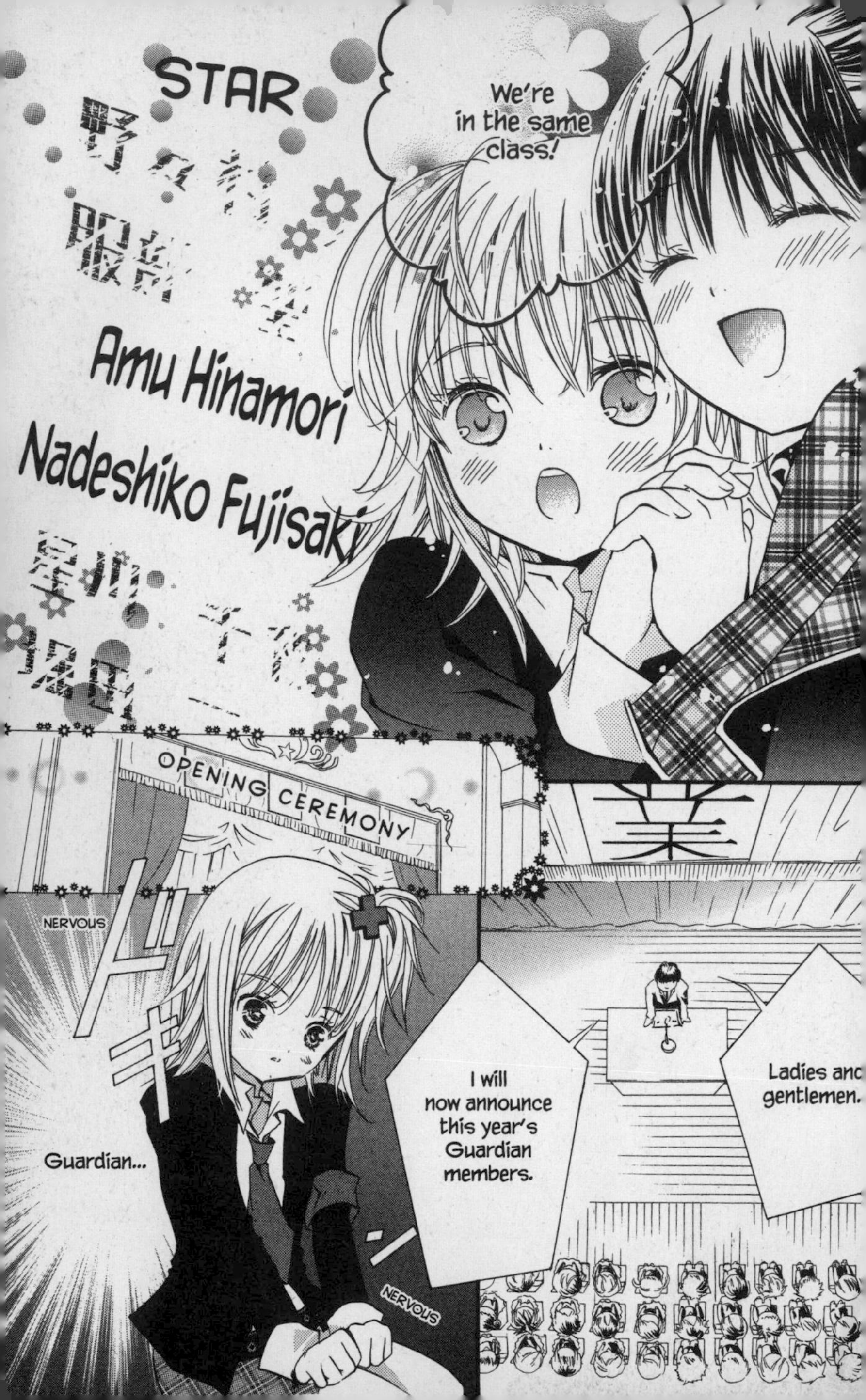
We're in the same class!
STAR
Amu Hinamori
Nadeshiko Fujisaki
OPENING CEREMONY
Ladies and gentlemen.
I will now announce this year's Guardian members.
NERVOUS
ドキ
Guardian...
NERVOUS

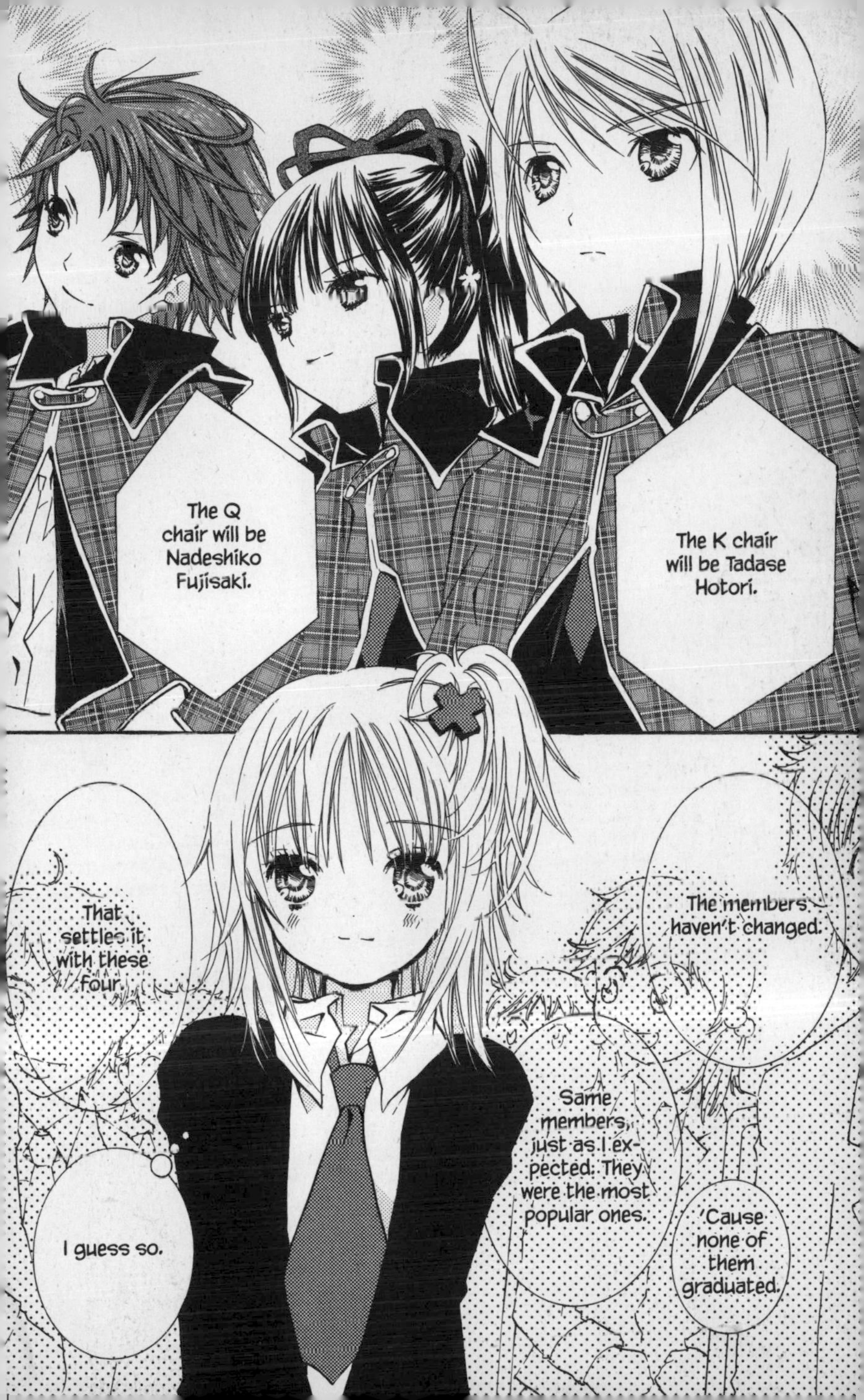
The K chair will be Tadase Hotori.
The Q chair will be Nadeshiko Fujisaki.
The members haven't changed.
Same members, just as I expected. They were the most popular ones.
'Cause none of them graduated.
That settles it with these four.
I guess so.

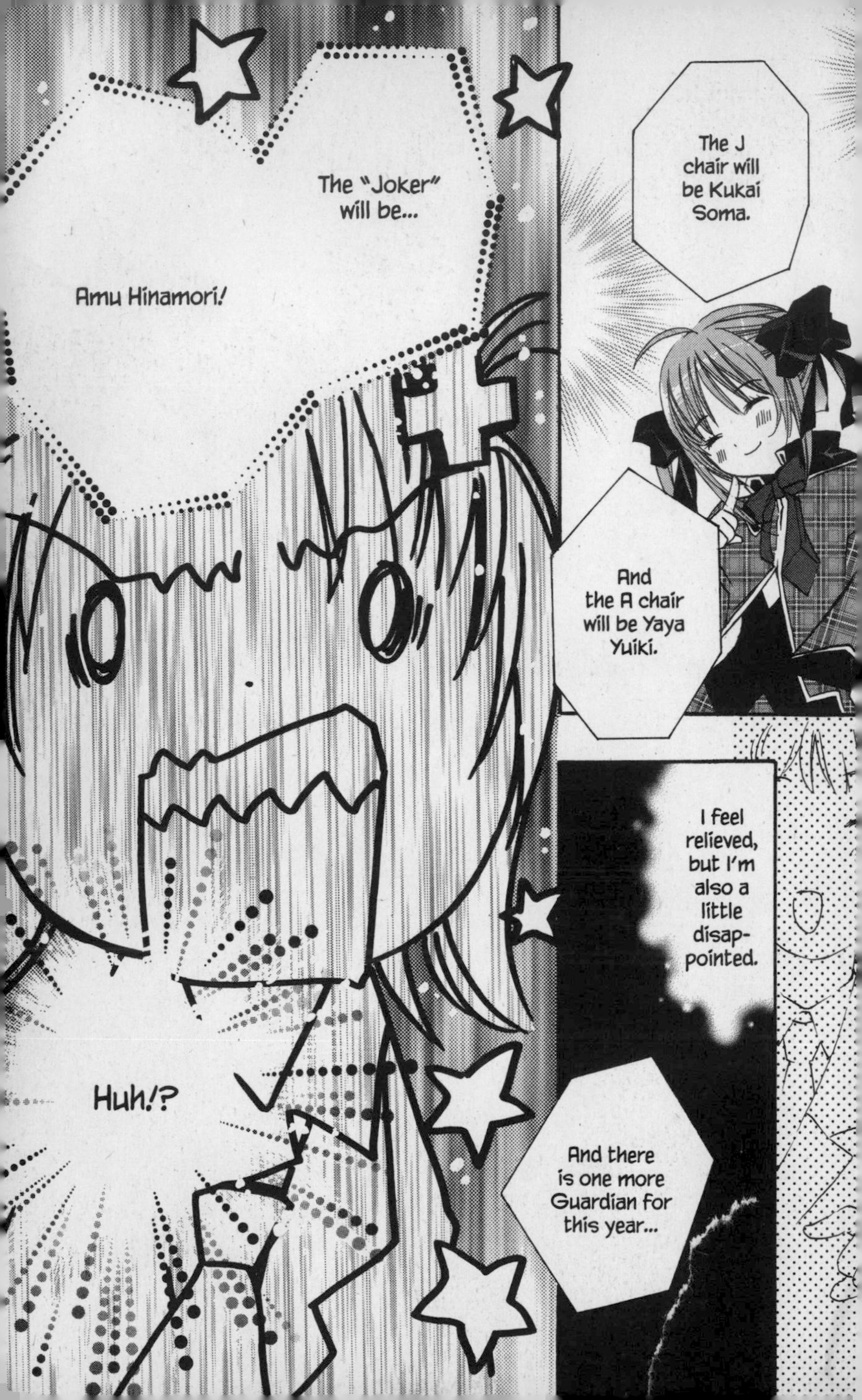
The J chair will be Kukai Soma.
And the A chair will be Yaya Yuiki.
I feel relieved, but I'm also a little disap-pointed.
And there is one more Guardian for this year...
The "Joker" will be...
Amu Hinamori!
Huh!?

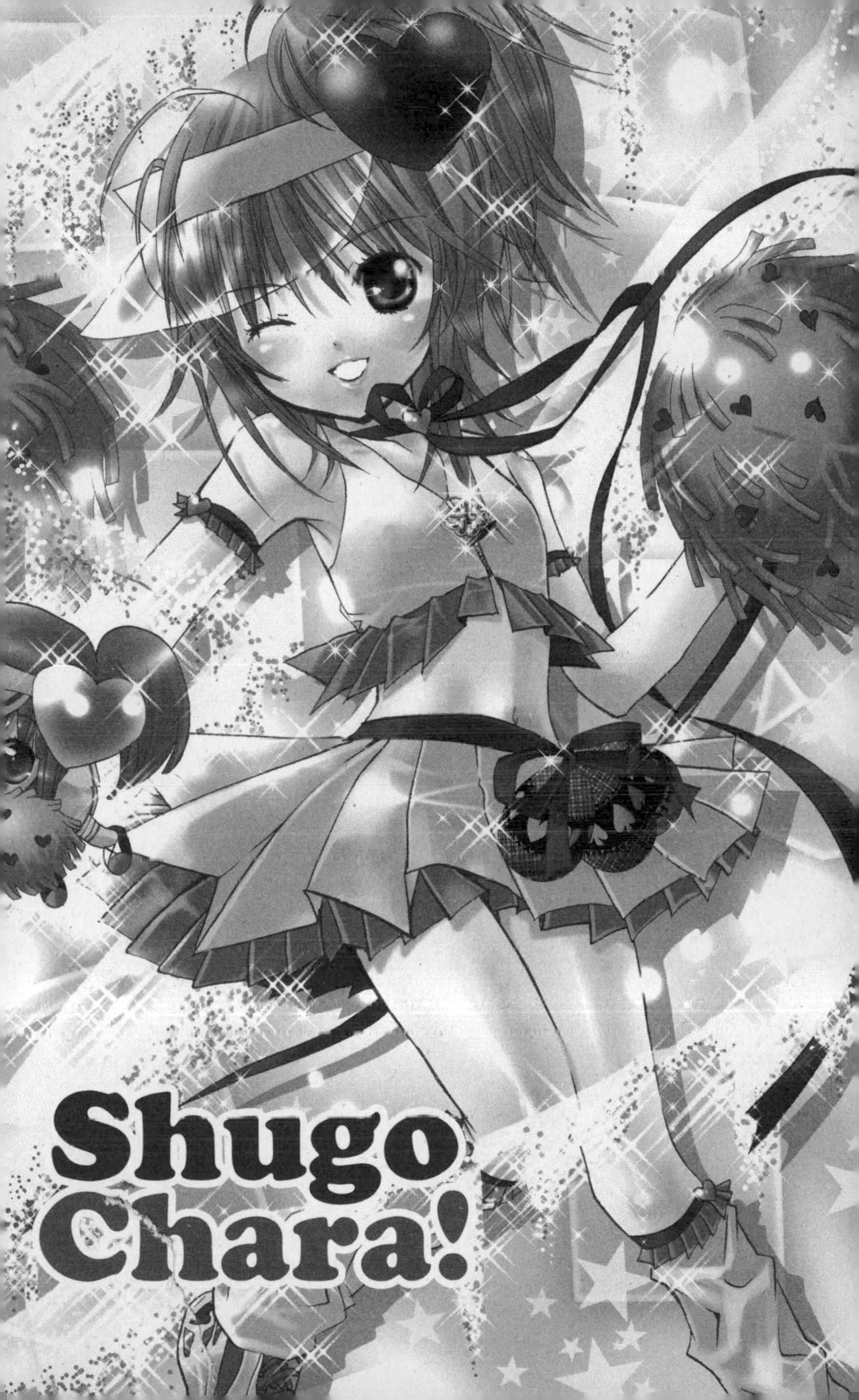
Shugo Chara!

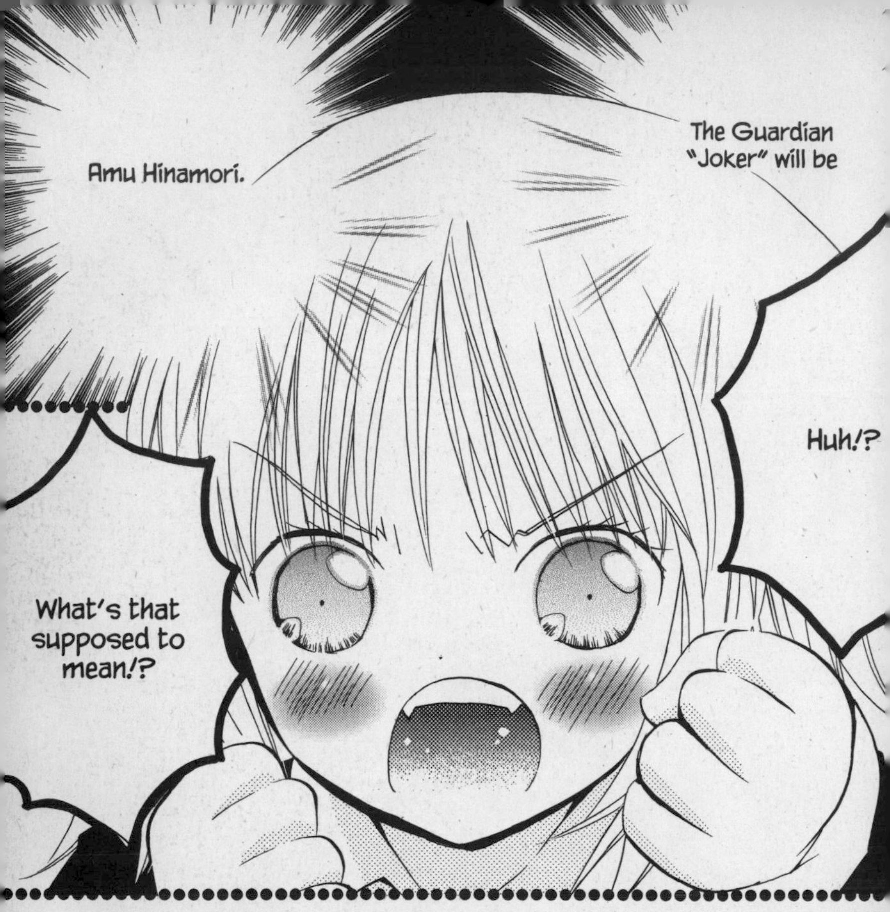
The Guardian "Joker" will be
Amu Hinamori.
Huh!?
What's that supposed to mean!?

Shugo Chara!

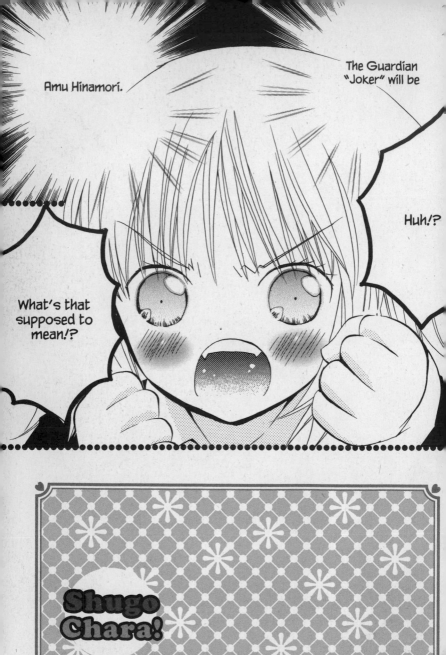

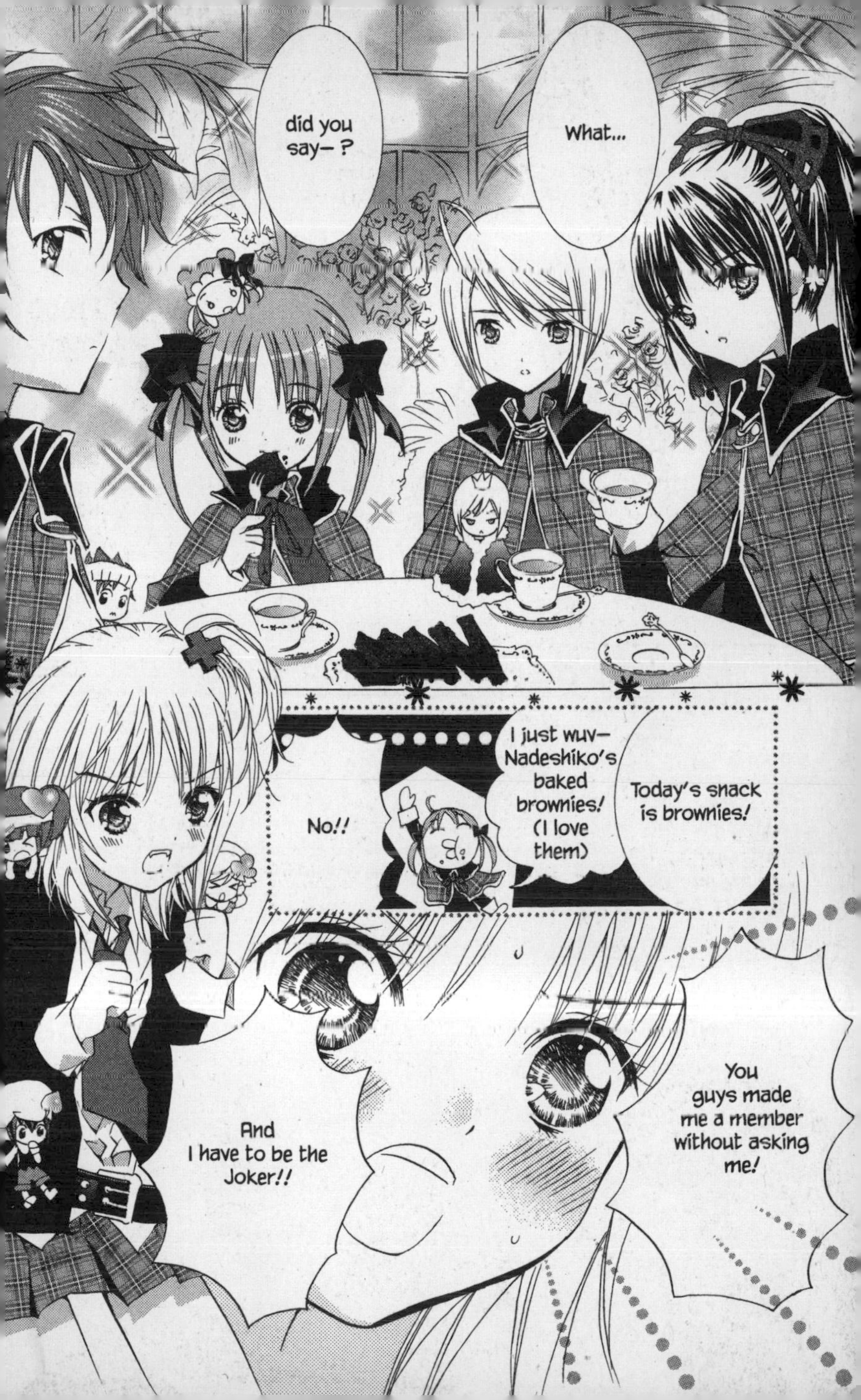
What...
did you say—?
Today's snack is brownies!
I just wuv— Nadeshiko's baked brownies! (I love them)
No!!
You guys made me a member without asking me!
And I have to be the Joker!!

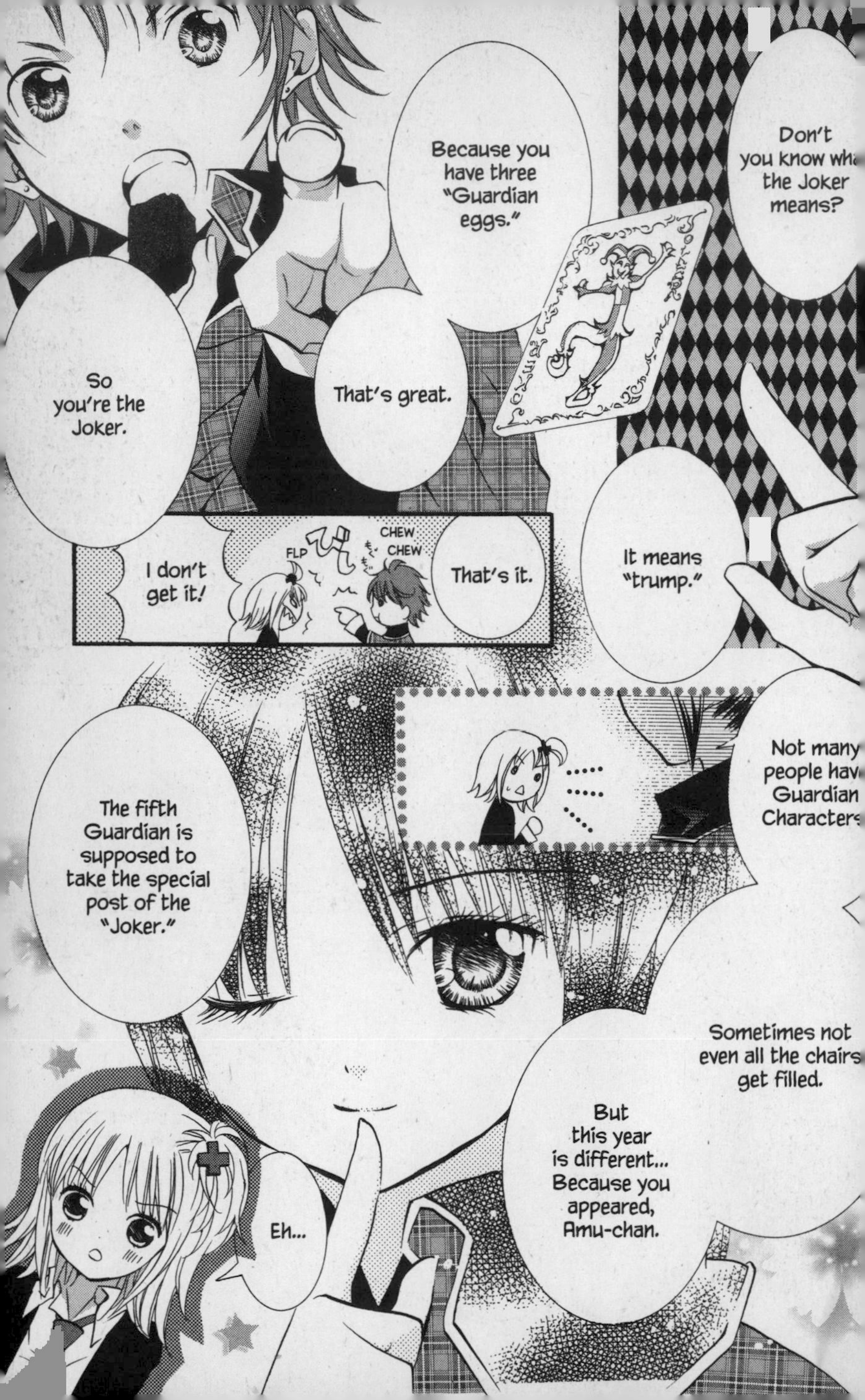
Don't you know wha the Joker means?
It means "trump."
Because you have three "Guardian eggs."
That's great.
So you're the Joker.
That's it.
CHEW CHEW
FLP
I don't get it!
Not many people hav Guardian Characters
.....
The fifth Guardian is supposed to take the special post of the "Joker."
Sometimes not even all the chairs get filled.
But this year is different... Because you appeared, Amu-chan.
Eh...

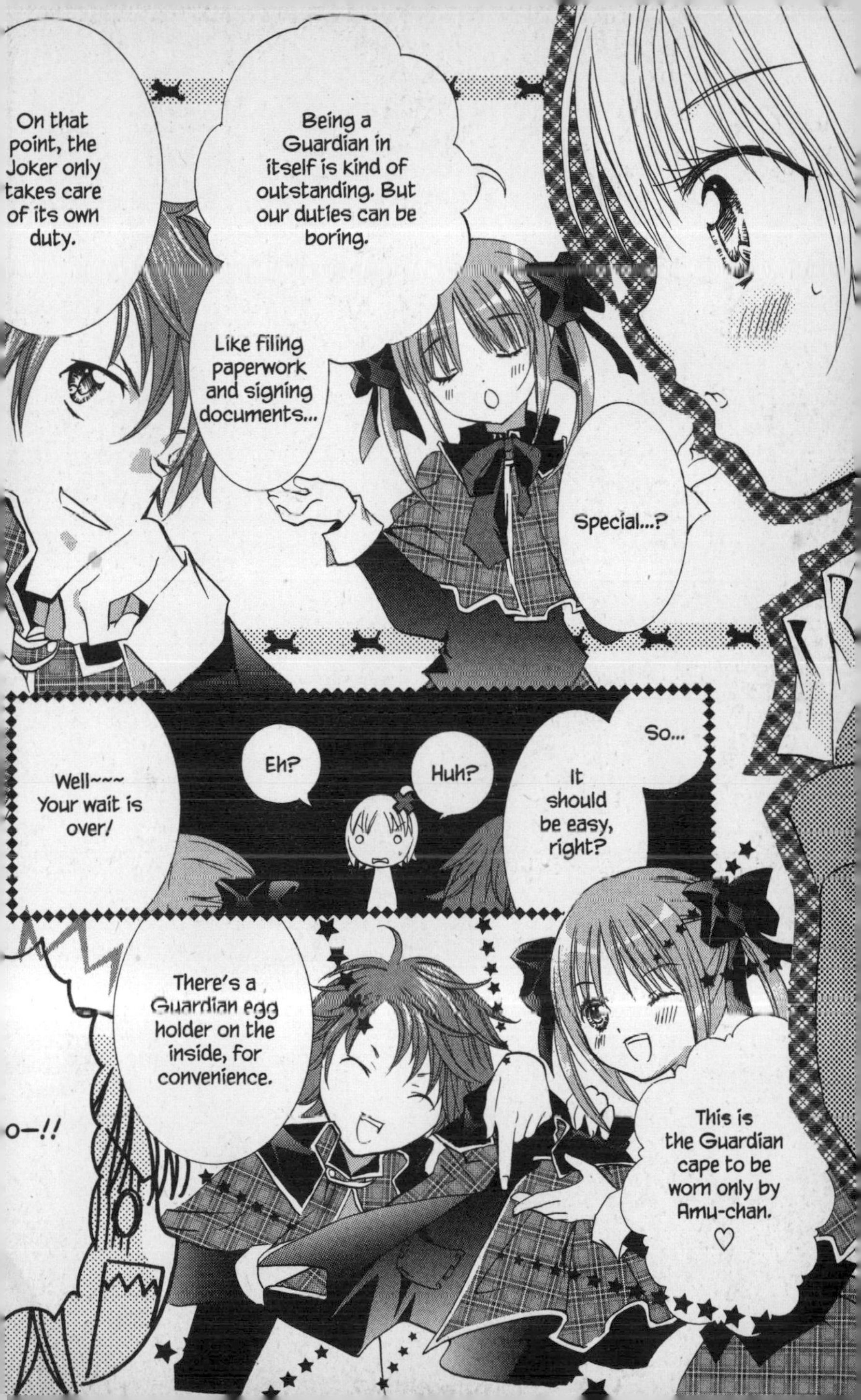
Special...?
Being a Guardian in itself is kind of outstanding. But our duties can be boring.
Like filing paperwork and signing documents...
On that point, the Joker only takes care of its own duty.
So...
It should be easy, right?
Huh?
Eh?
Well~~~ Your wait is over!
This is the Guardian cape to be worn only by Amu-chan. ♡
There's a Guardian egg holder on the inside, for convenience.
o–!!

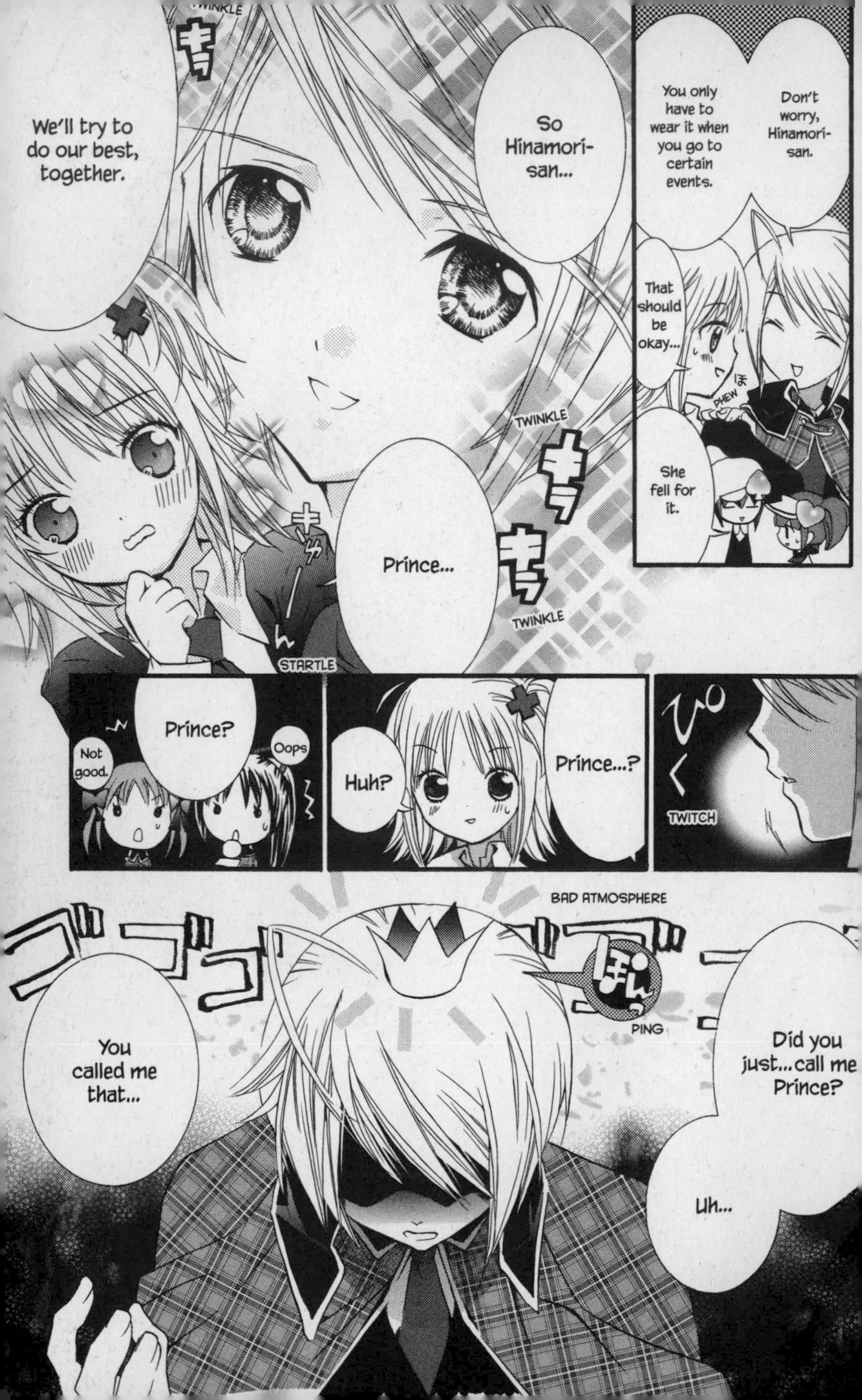
Don't worry, Hinamori-san.
You only have to wear it when you go to certain events.
That should be okay...
PHEW
She fell for it.
So Hinamori-san...
We'll try to do our best, together.
TWINKLE
Prince...
TWINKLE
STARTLE
TWITCH
Prince...?
Huh?
Oops
Prince?
Not good.
BAD ATMOSPHERE
PING
Did you just...call me Prince?
Uh...
You called me that...

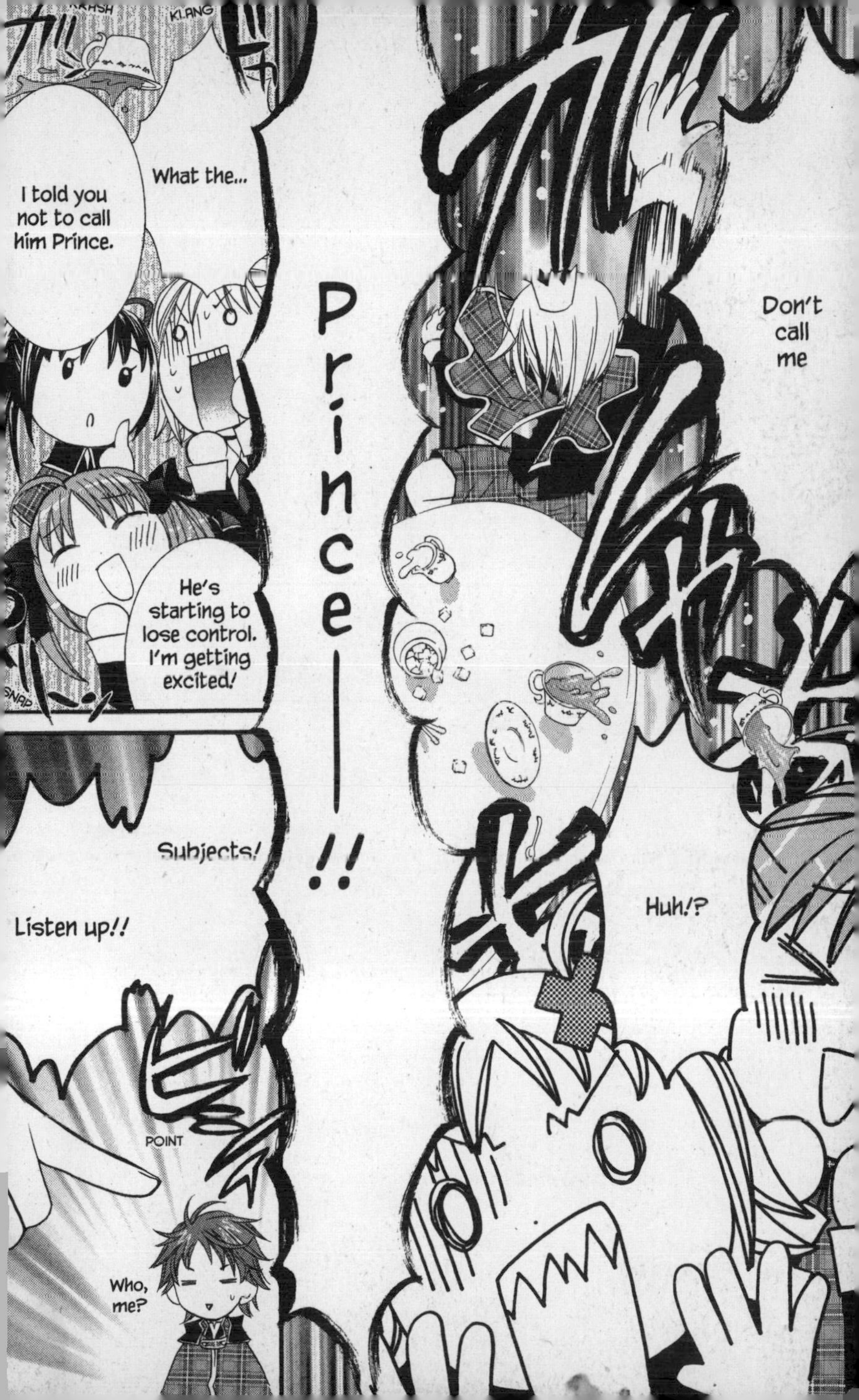

Don't call me
Prince——!!
Huh!?
KRASH
KLANG
What the...
I told you not to call him Prince.
He's starting to lose control. I'm getting excited!
SNAP
Subjects!
Listen up!!
POINT
Who, me?

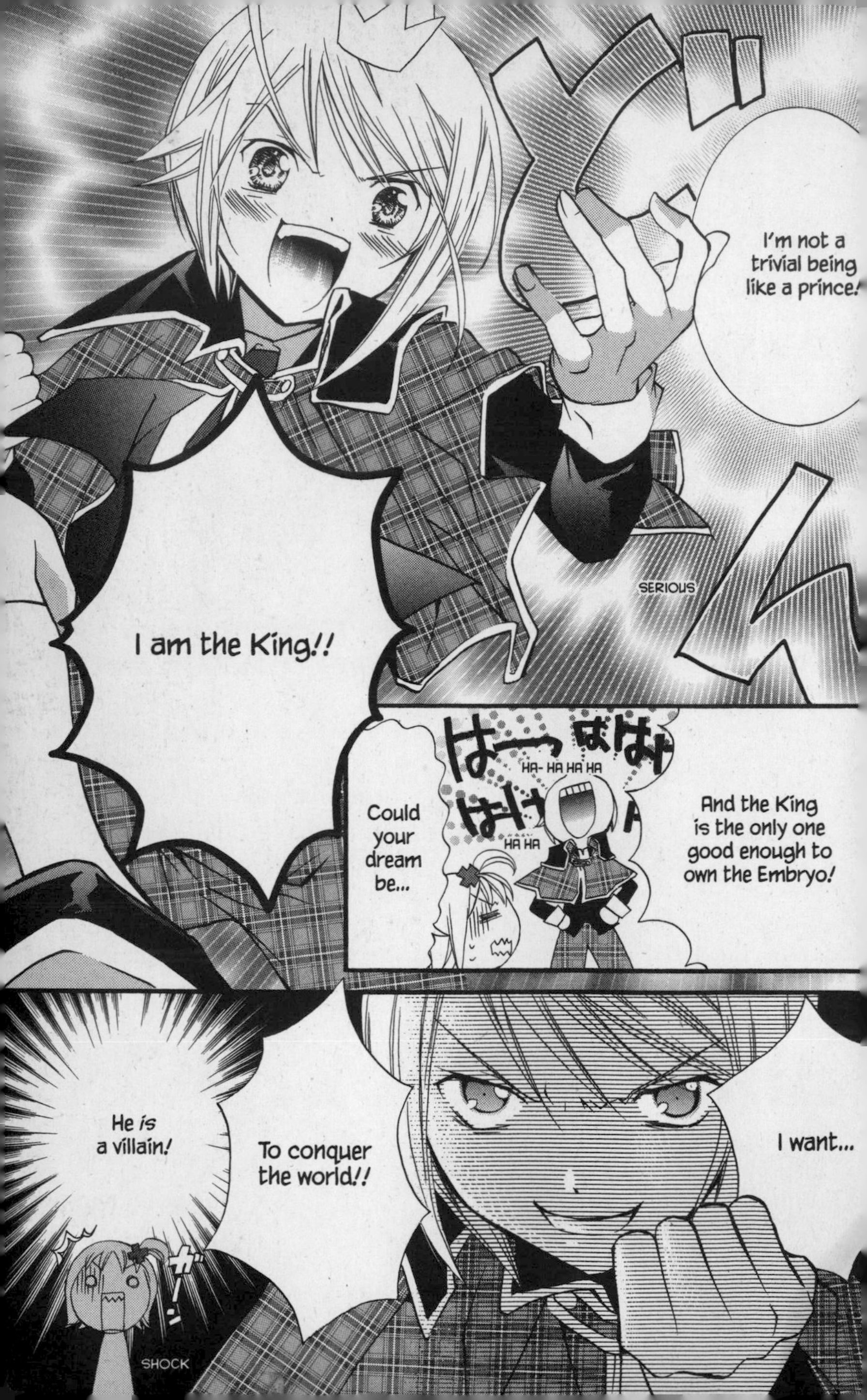
I'm not a trivial being like a prince!
SERIOUS
I am the King!!
And the King is the only one good enough to own the Embryo!
HA- HA HA HA
HA HA
Could your dream be...
I want...
To conquer the world!!
He *is* a villain!
SHOCK

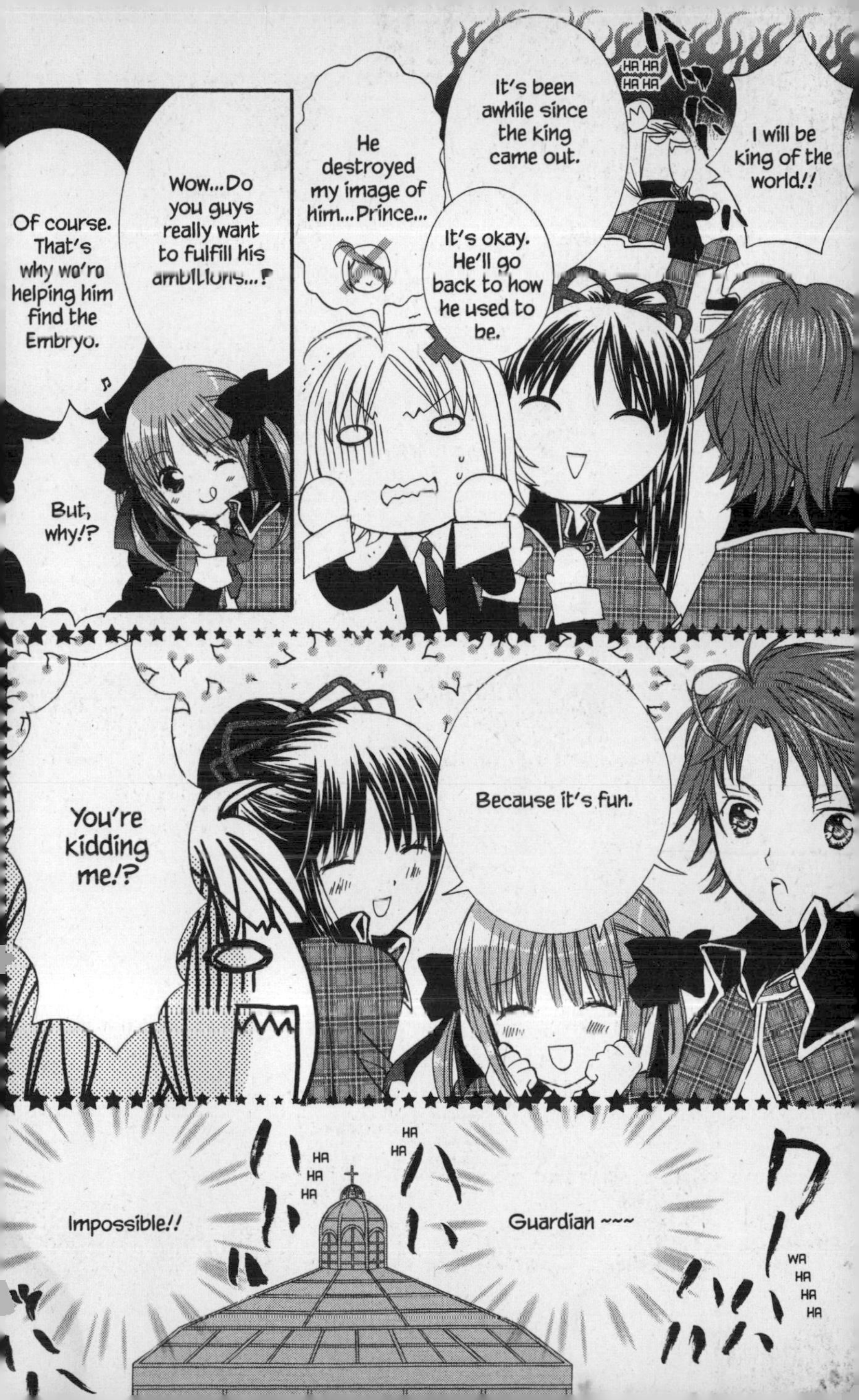
I will be king of the world!!
HA HA
HA HA
It's been awhile since the king came out.
He destroyed my image of him...Prince...
It's okay. He'll go back to how he used to be.
Wow...Do you guys really want to fulfill his ambitions...!?
Of course. That's why we're helping him find the Embryo.
But, why!?
Because it's fun.
You're kidding me!?
WA
HA
HA
HA
Guardian ~~~
HA
HA
HA
HA
HA
Impossible!!

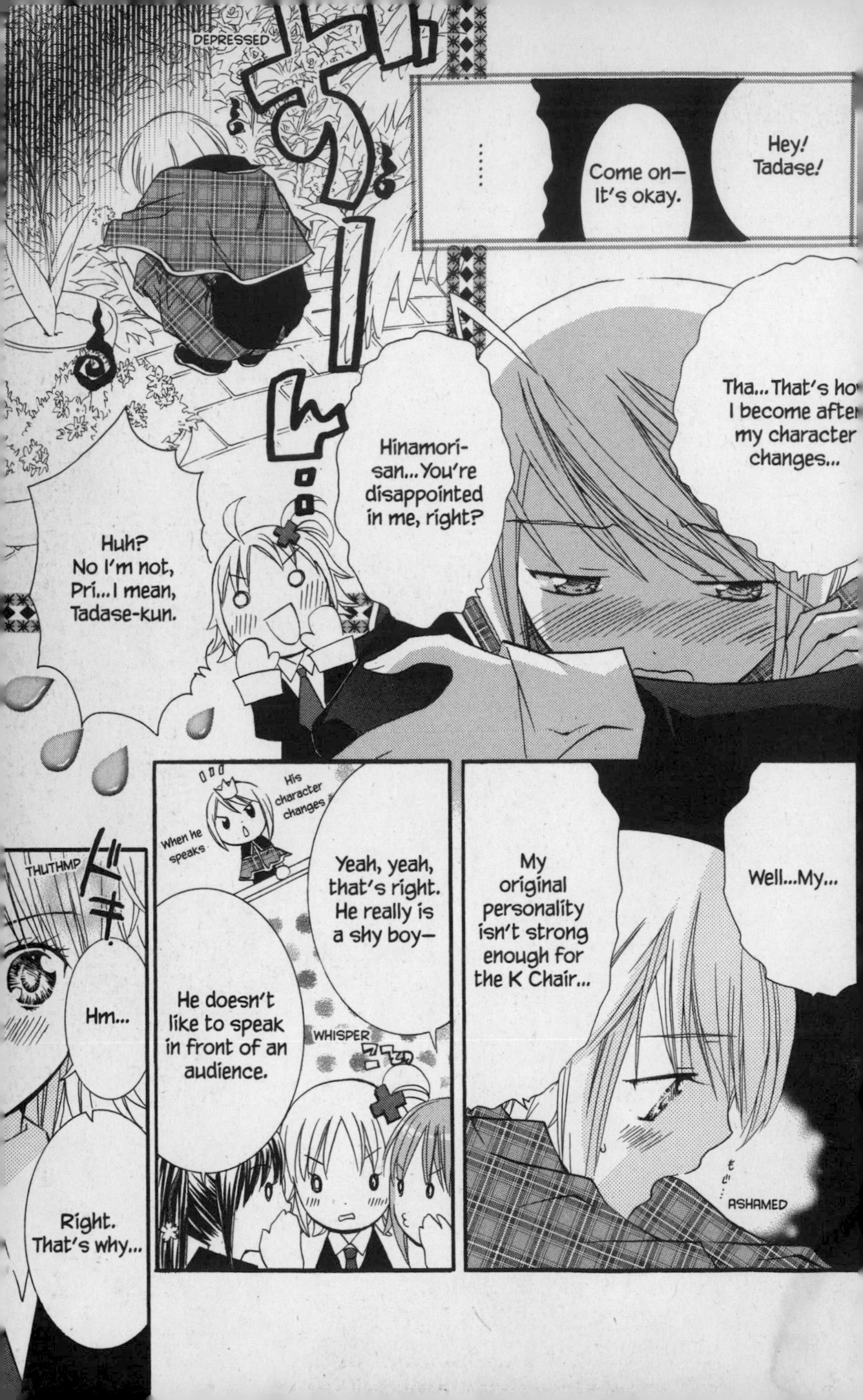
Hey! Tadase!
Come on— It's okay.
......
DEPRESSED
Tha... That's ho
I become afte
my character changes...
Hinamori-san... You're disappointed in me, right?
Huh? No I'm not, Pri...I mean, Tadase-kun.
Well...My...
My original personality isn't strong enough for the K Chair...
ASHAMED
Yeah, yeah, that's right. He really is a shy boy—
His character changes
When he speaks
He doesn't like to speak in front of an audience.
WHISPER
THUTHMP
Hm...
Right. That's why...

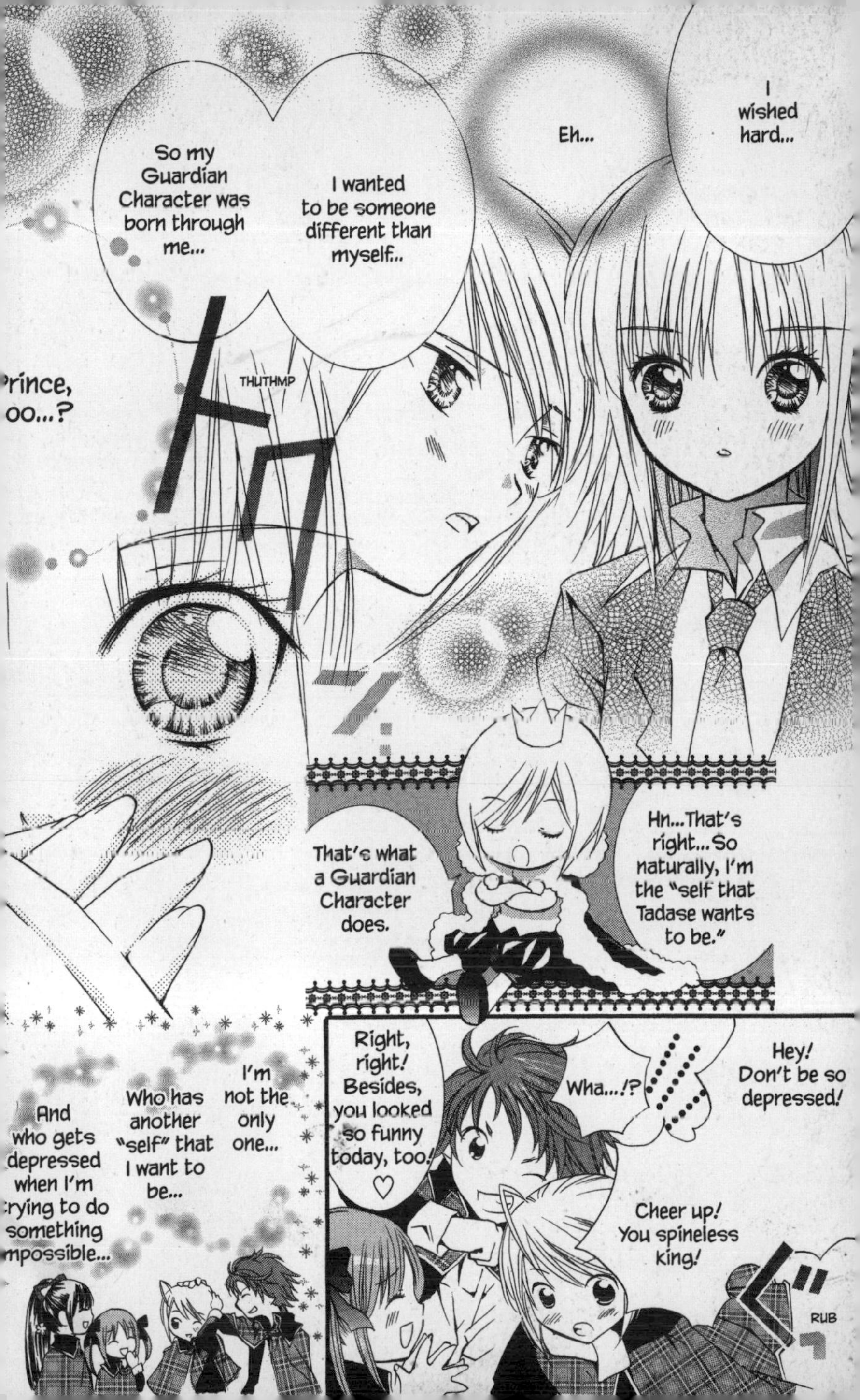
I wished hard...
Eh...
I wanted to be someone different than myself...
So my Guardian Character was born through me...
THUTHMP
Prince, oo...?
Hn...That's right... So naturally, I'm the "self that Tadase wants to be."
That's what a Guardian Character does.
Hey! Don't be so depressed!
Wha...!?
Right, right! Besides, you looked so funny today, too! ♡
Cheer up! You spineless king!
RUB
I'm not the only one...
Who has another "self" that I want to be...
And who gets depressed when I'm rying to do something mpossible...

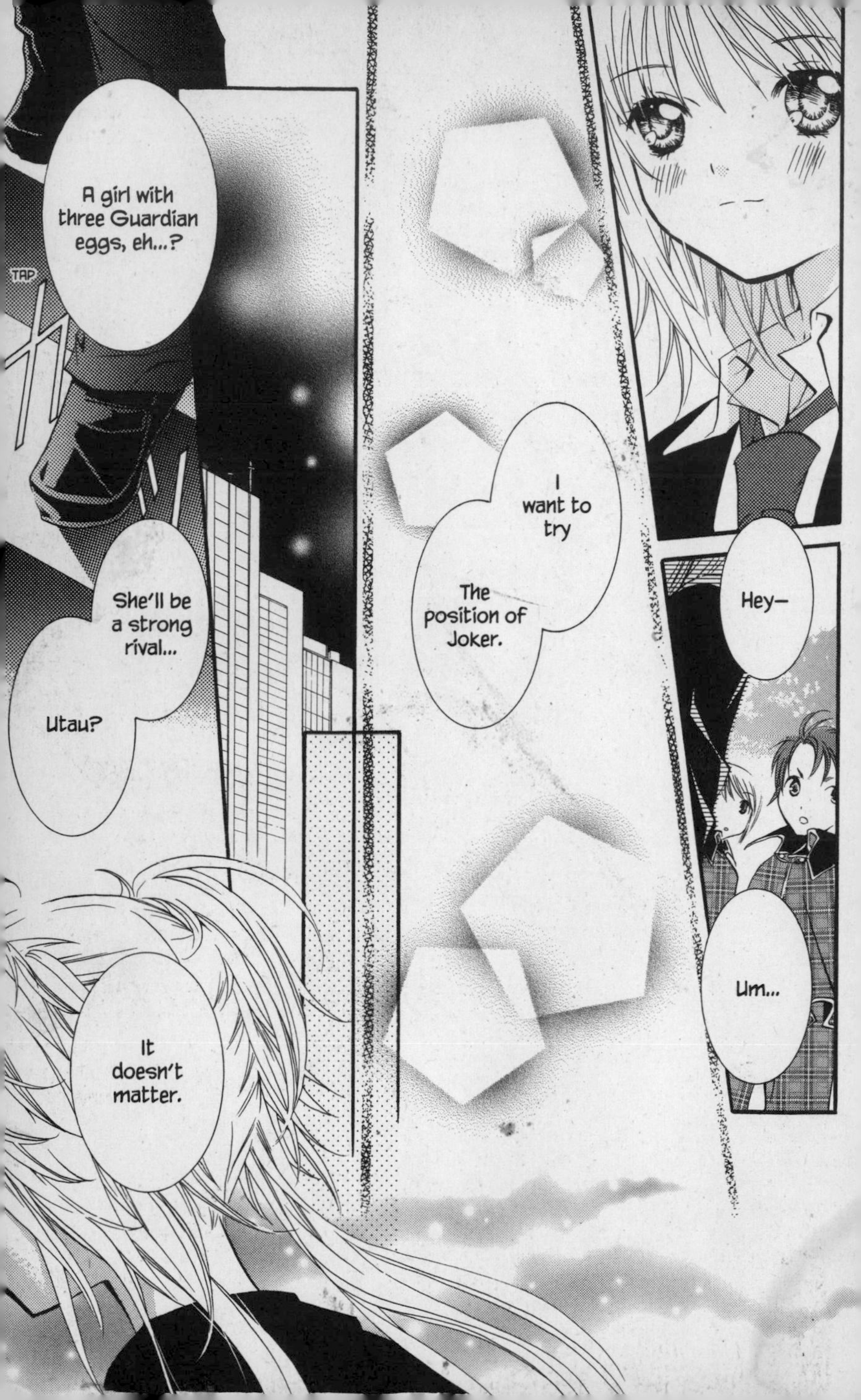
Hey—
Um...
I want to try
The position of Joker.
A girl with three Guardian eggs, eh...?
TAP
She'll be a strong rival...
Utau?
It doesn't matter.

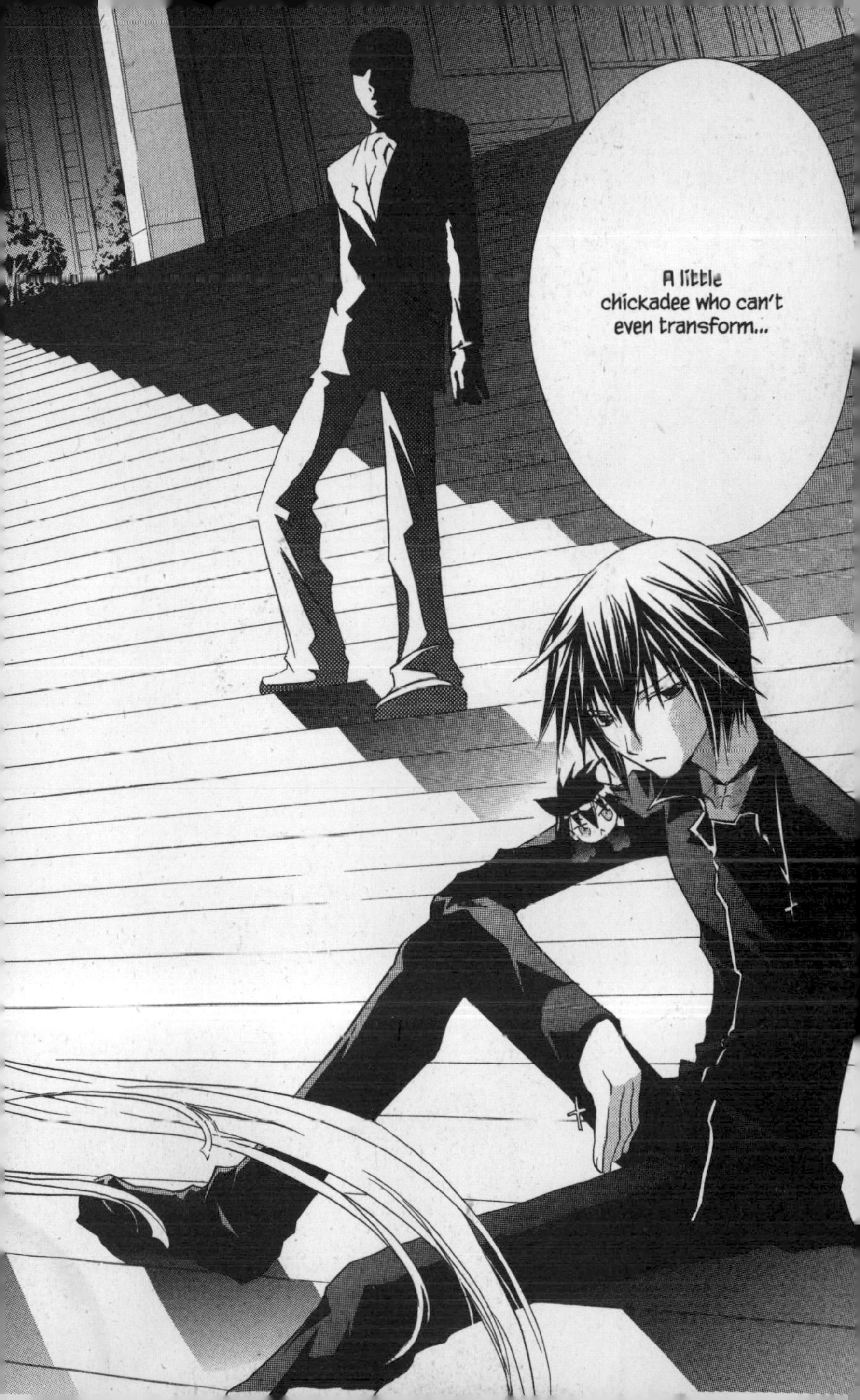
A little chickadee who can't even transform...

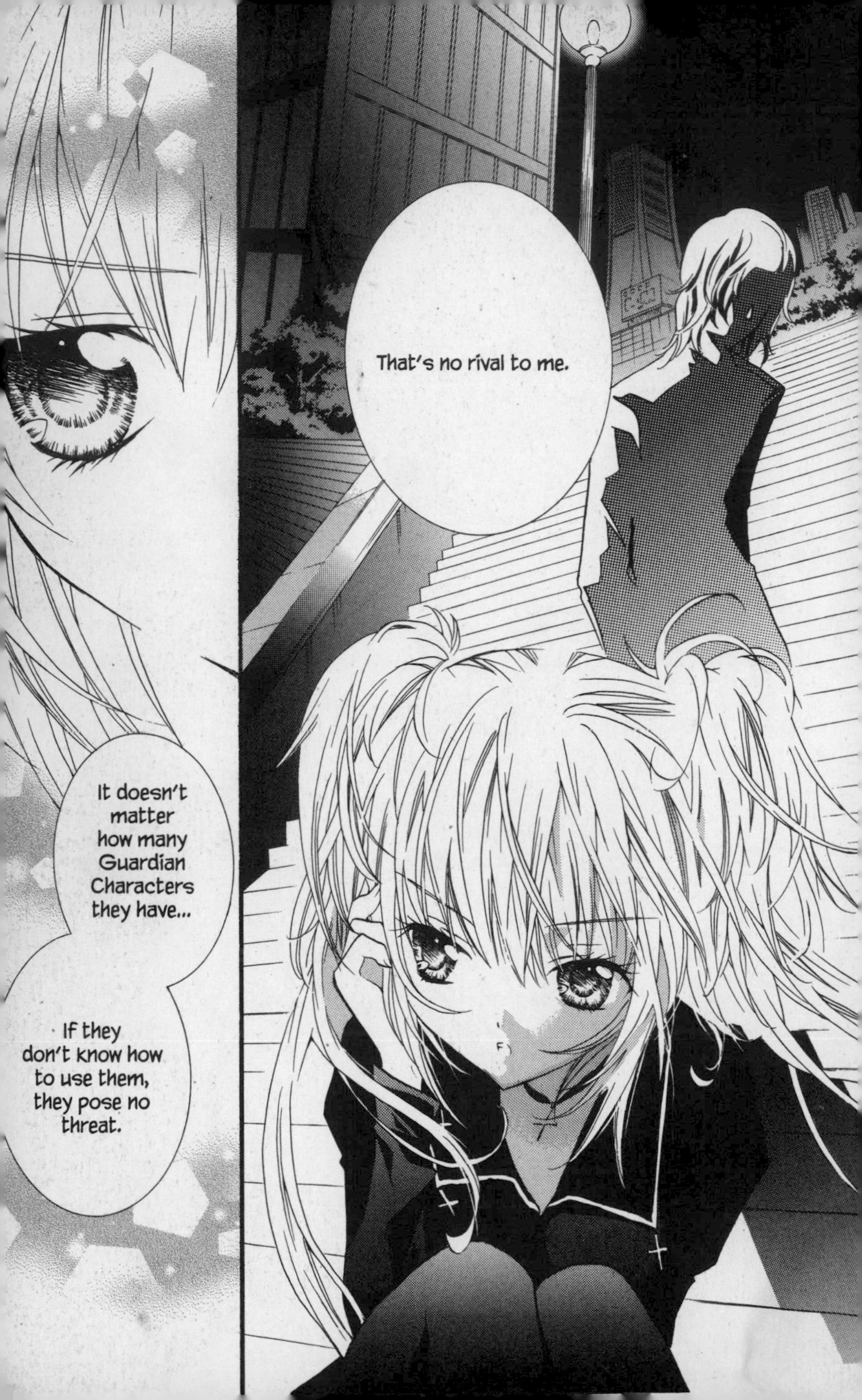
That's no rival to me.
It doesn't matter how many Guardian Characters they have...
If they don't know how to use them, they pose no threat.

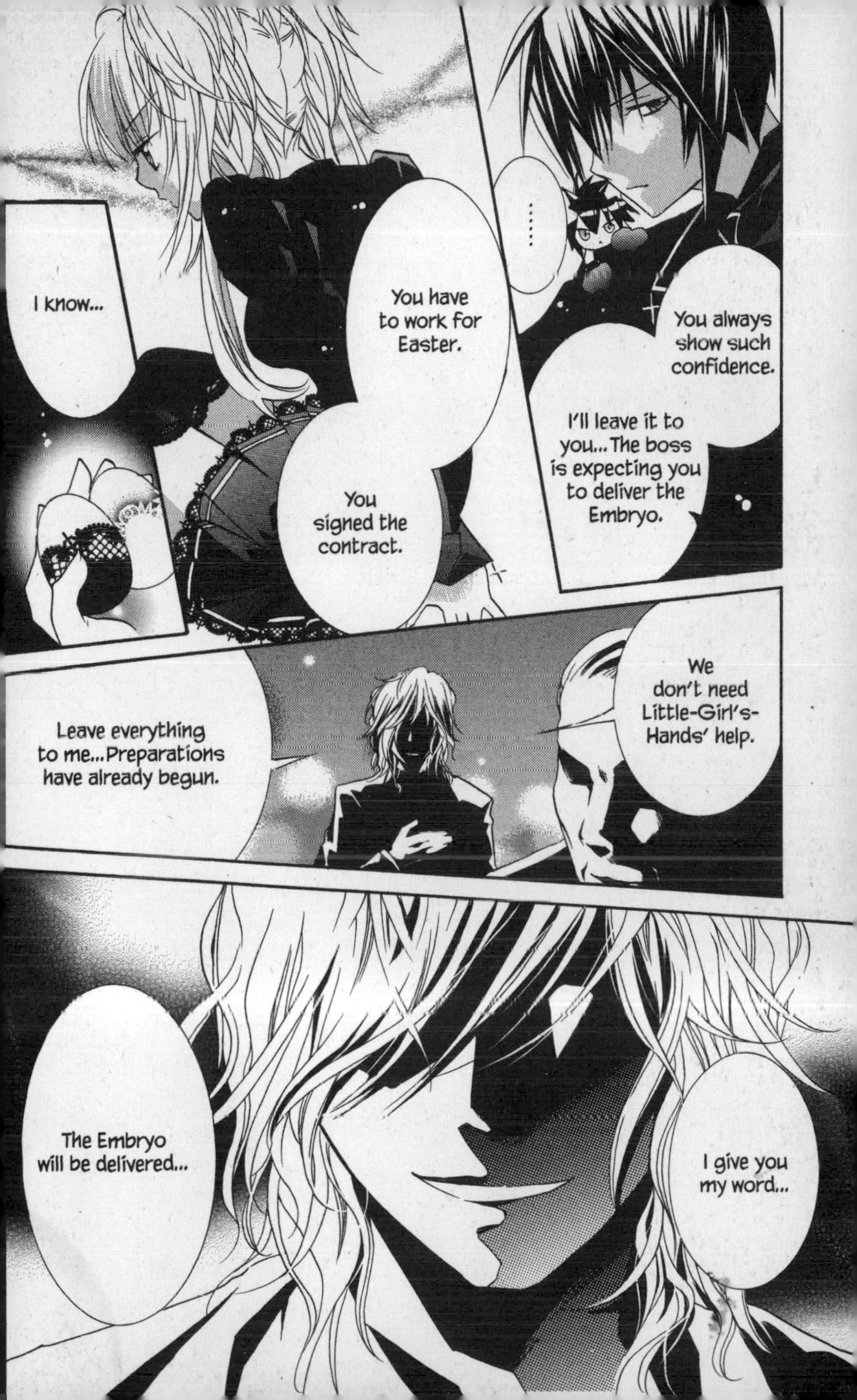
……
You always show such confidence.
I'll leave it to you... The boss is expecting you to deliver the Embryo.
You have to work for Easter.
You signed the contract.
I know...
We don't need Little-Girl's-Hands' help.
Leave everything to me...Preparations have already begun.
I give you my word...
The Embryo will be delivered...

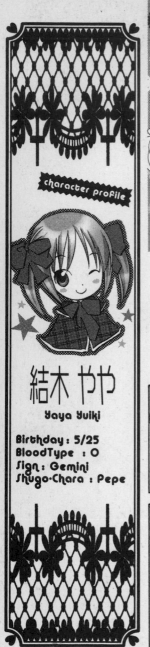

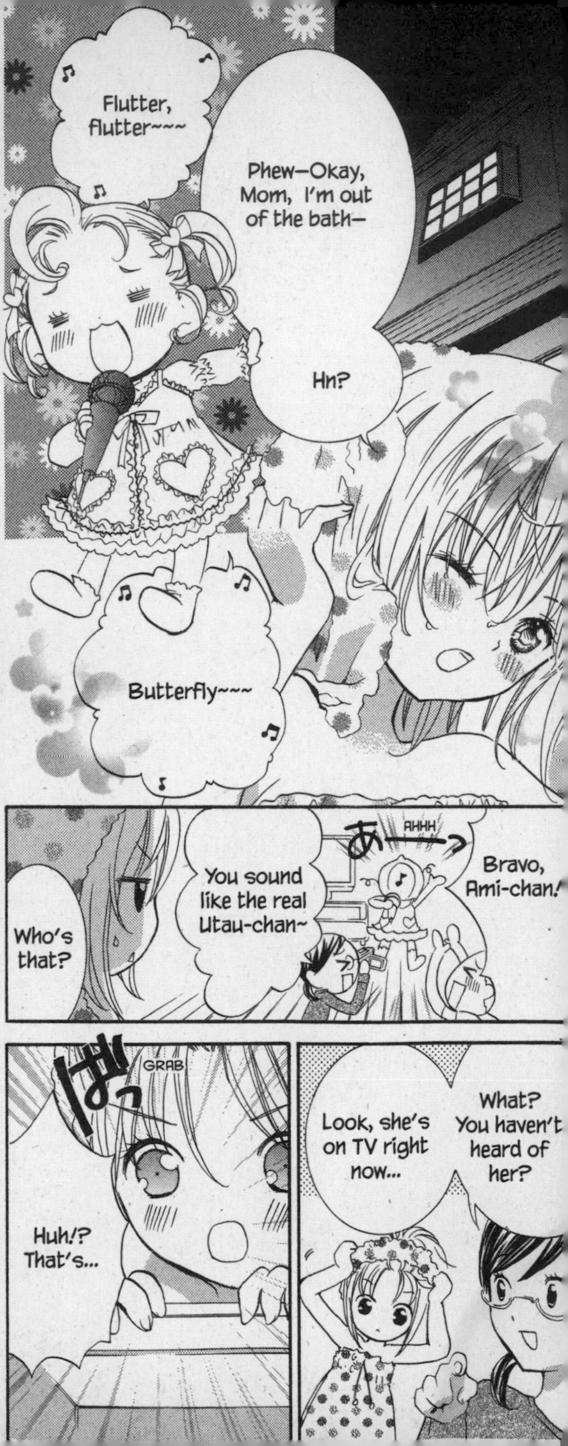
Phew—Okay, Mom, I'm out of the bath—
Flutter, flutter~~~
Hn?
Butterfly~~~
Bravo, Ami-chan!
あーーっ
AHHH
You sound like the real Utau-chan~
Who's that?
What? You haven't heard of her?
Look, she's on TV right now...
ぱっ
GRAB
Huh!? That's...

character profile

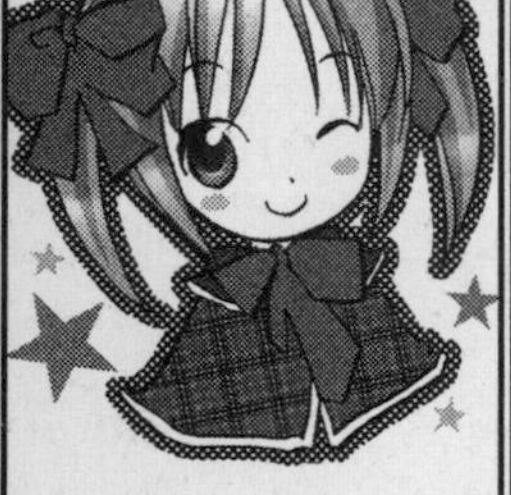

結木 やや

Yaya Yuiki

Birthday : 5/25
BloodType : O
Sign : Gemini
Shugo-Chara : Pepe

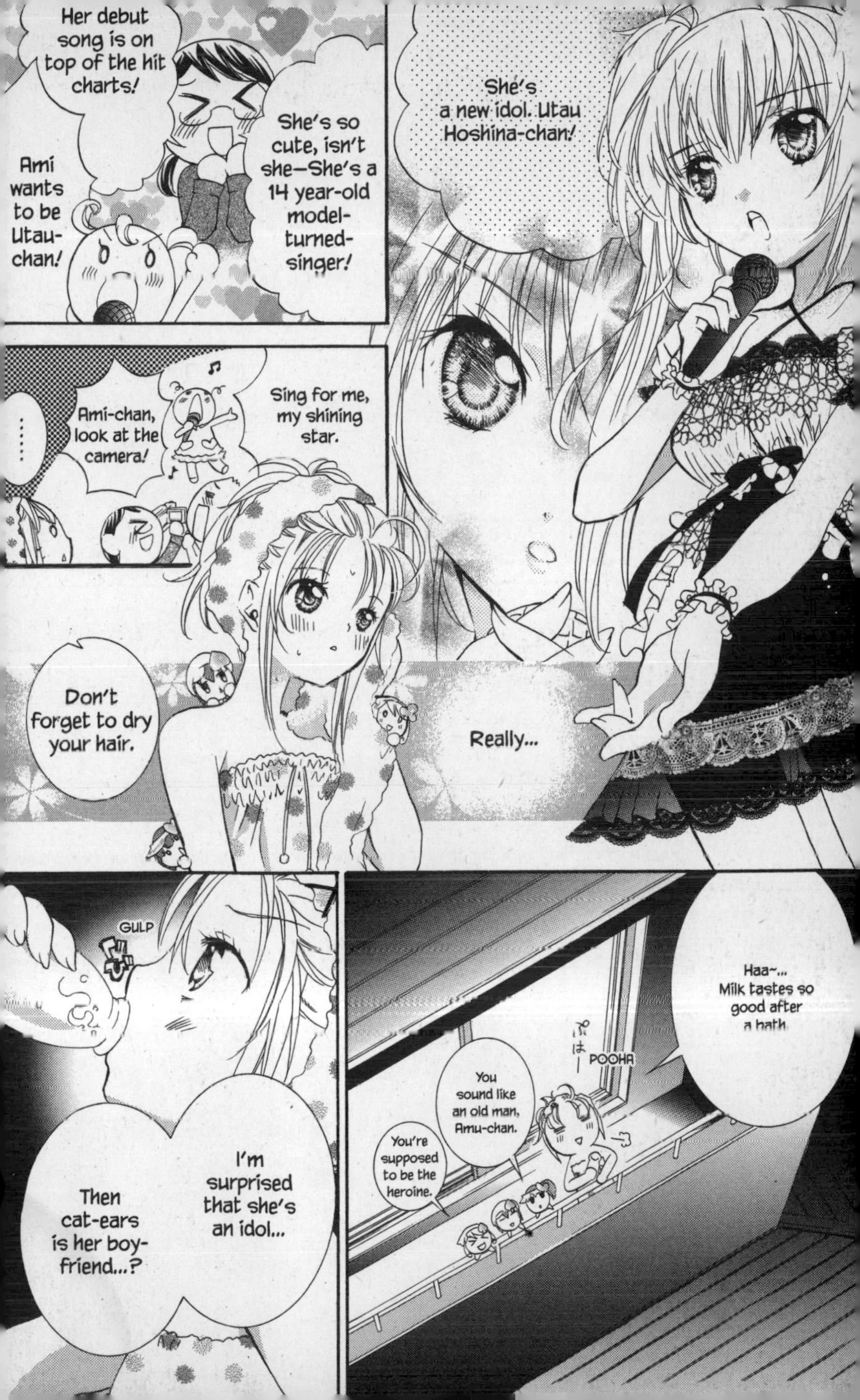

She's a new idol. Utau Hoshina-chan!
Her debut song is on top of the hit charts!
She's so cute, isn't she—She's a 14 year-old model-turned-singer!
Ami wants to be Utau-chan!
Sing for me, my shining star.
Ami-chan, look at the camera!
......
Really...
Don't forget to dry your hair.
Haa~... Milk tastes so good after a bath.
ぷはー
POOHA
You sound like an old man, Amu-chan.
You're supposed to be the heroine.
GULP
I'm surprised that she's an idol...
Then cat-ears is her boy-friend...?

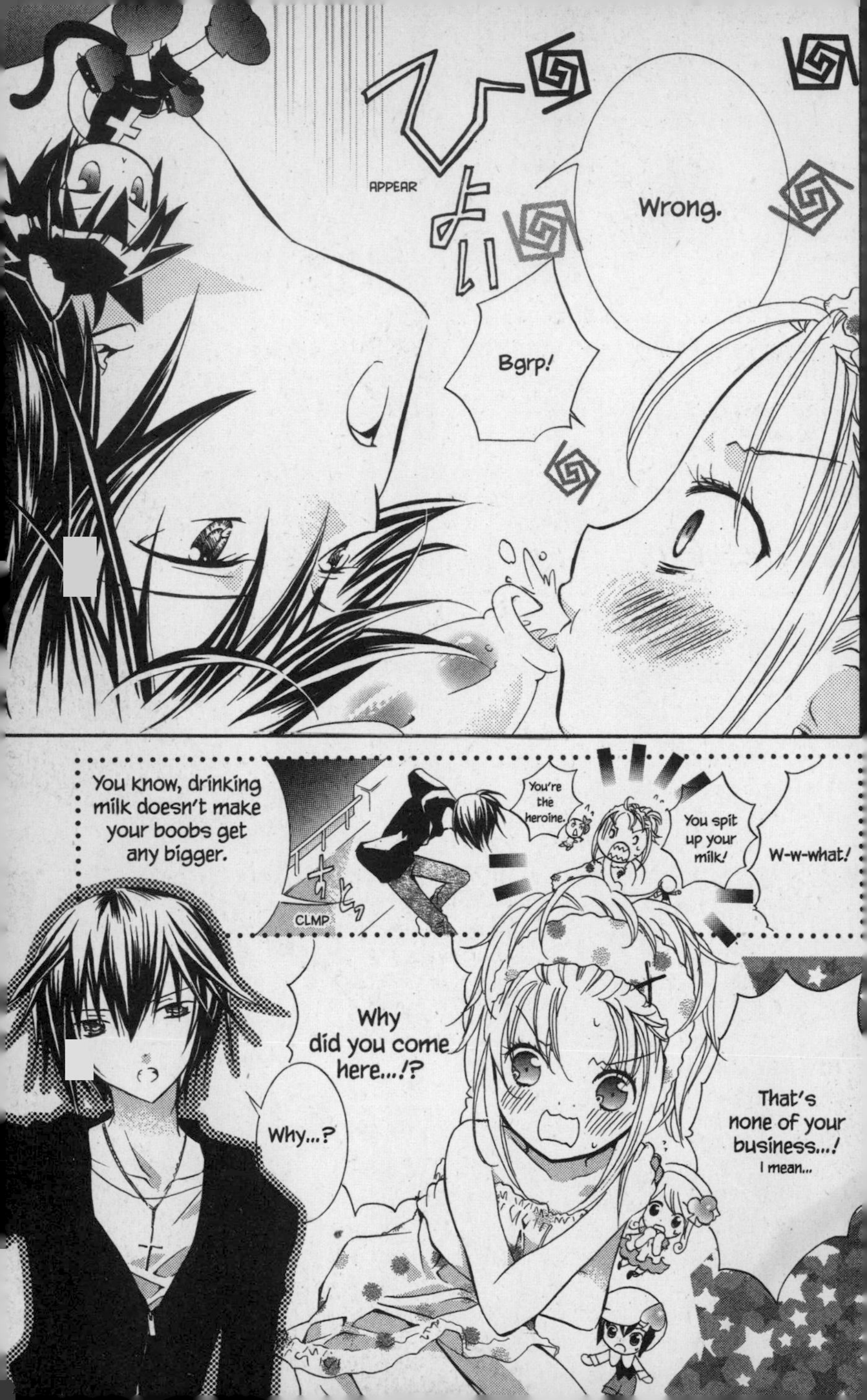
Wrong.
APPEAR
Bgrp!
W-w-what!
You spit up your milk!
You're the heroine.
CLMP
You know, drinking milk doesn't make your boobs get any bigger.
That's none of your business...!
I mean...
Why did you come here...!?
Why...?

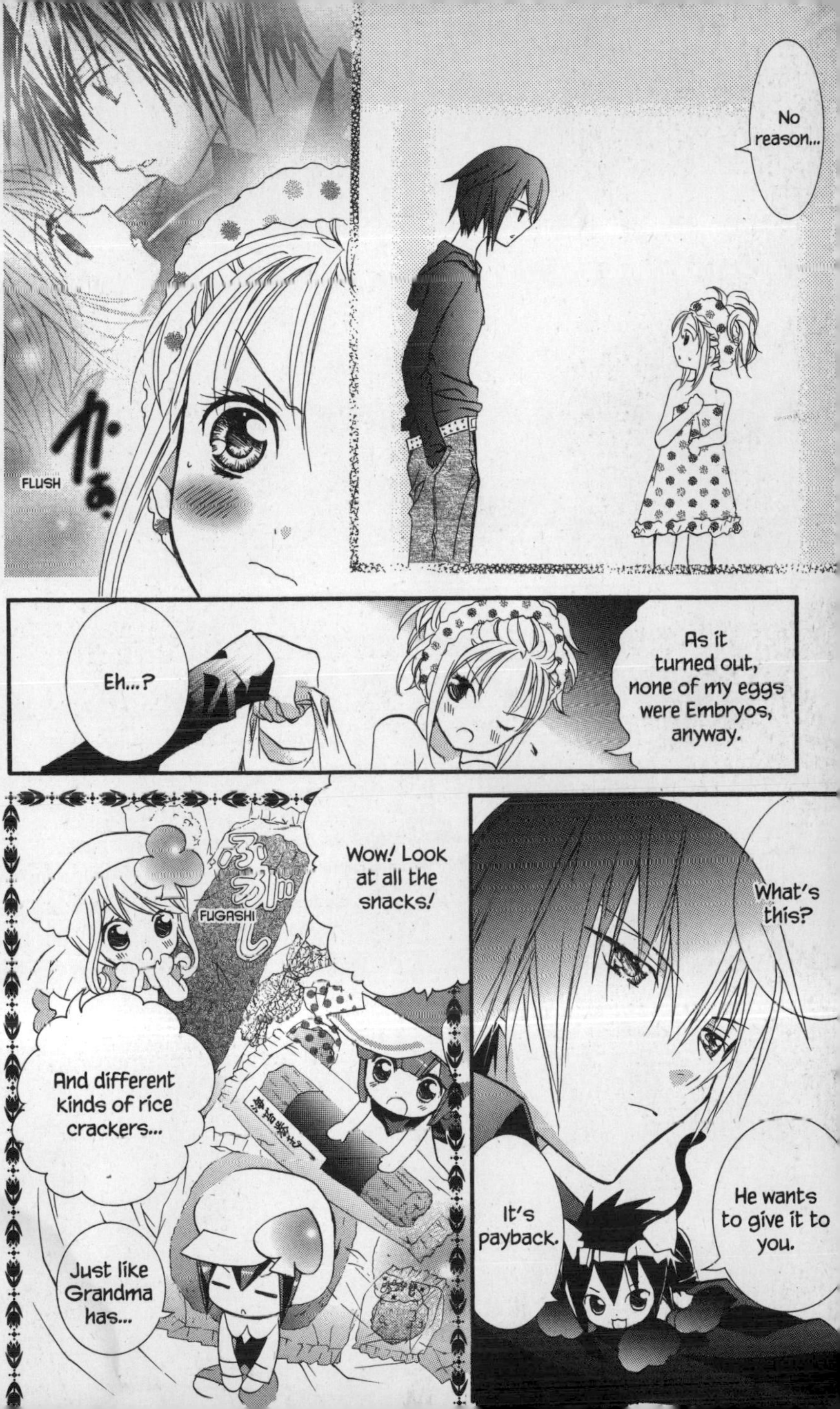
No reason...
FLUSH
As it turned out, none of my eggs were Embryos, anyway.
Eh...?
What's this?
He wants to give it to you.
It's payback.
Wow! Look at all the snacks!
FUGASHI
And different kinds of rice crackers...
Just like Grandma has...

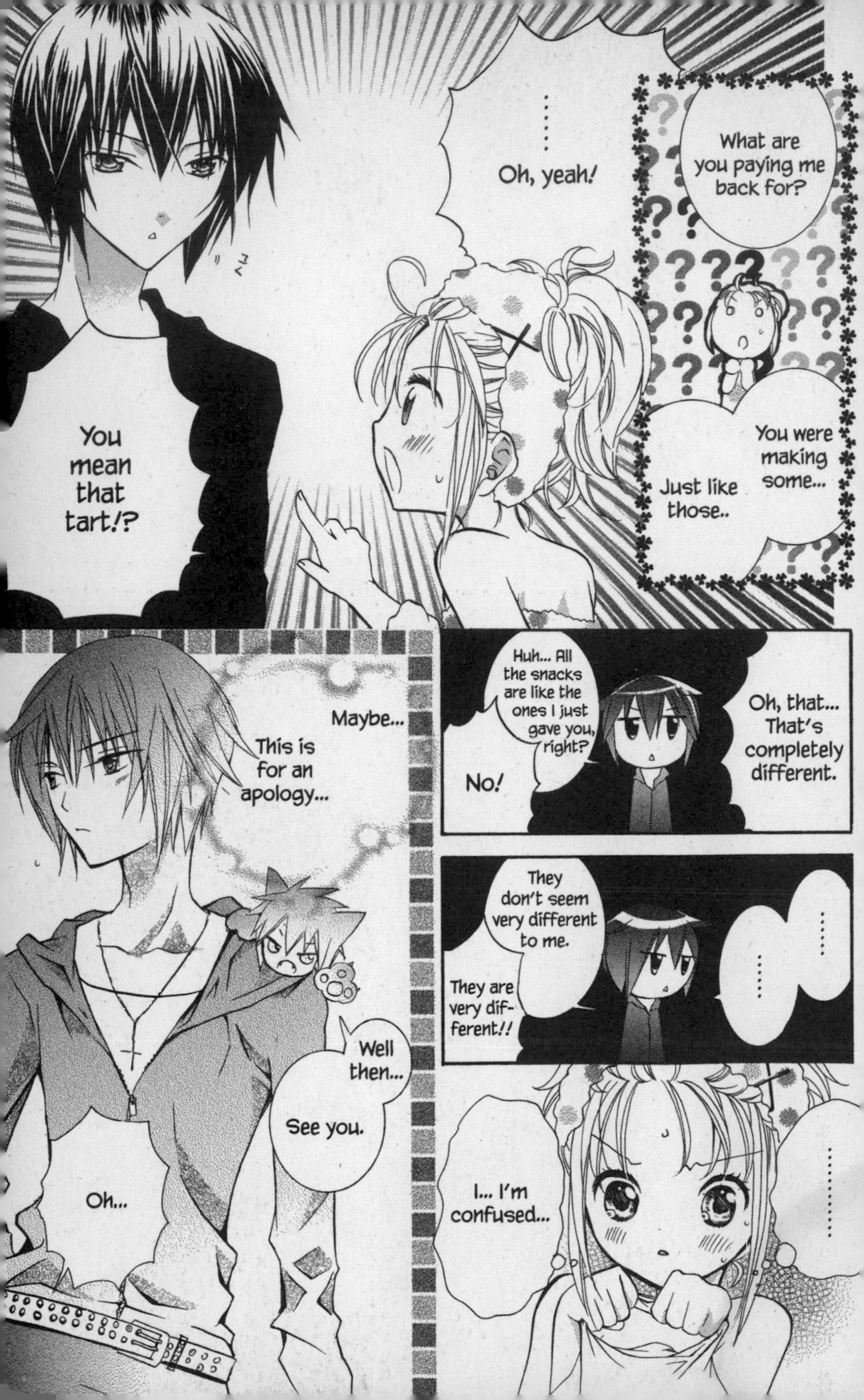
What are you paying me back for?
You were making some...
Just like those..
......
Oh, yeah!
You mean that tart!?
Oh, that... That's completely different.
Huh... All the snacks are like the ones I just gave you, right?
No!
......
......
They don't seem very different to me.
They are very dif-ferent!!
......
I... I'm confused...
Maybe...
This is for an apology...
Well then...
See you.
Oh...

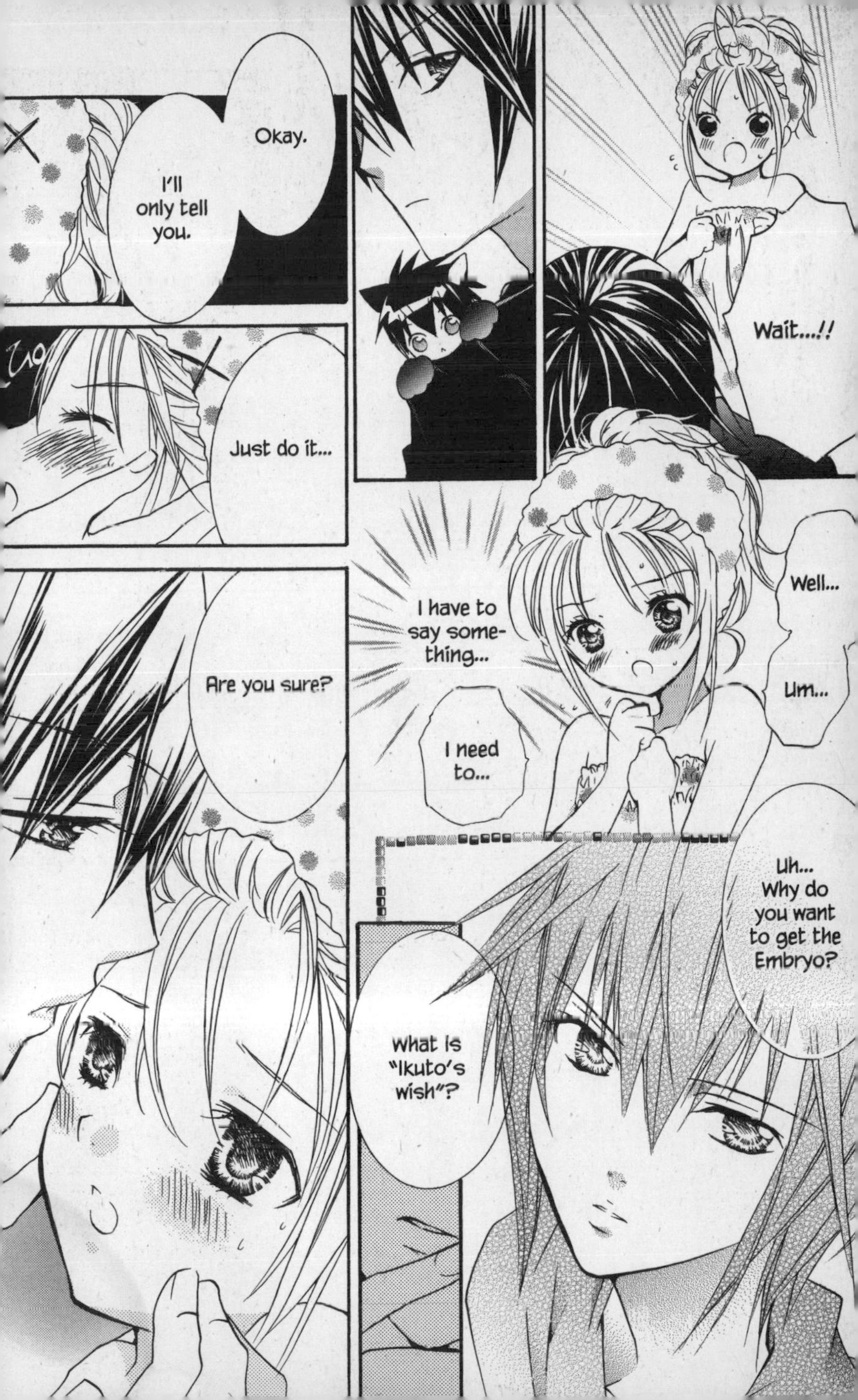
Wait...!!
Well...
Um...
I have to say something...
I need to...
Uh... Why do you want to get the Embryo?
What is "Ikuto's wish"?
Okay.
I'll only tell you.
Just do it...
Are you sure?

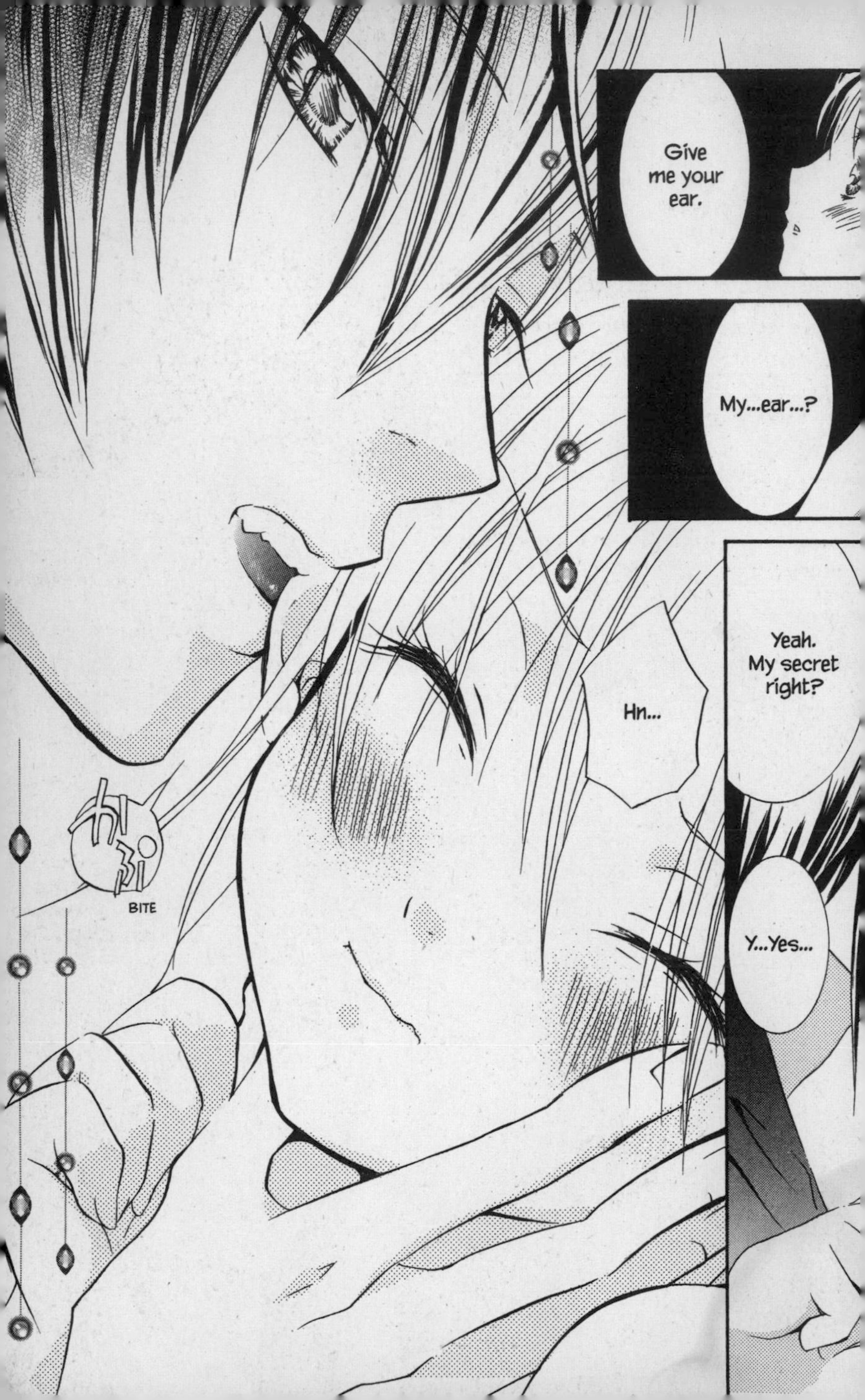
Give me your ear.
My...ear...?
Yeah. My secret right?
Y...Yes...
Hn...
BITE

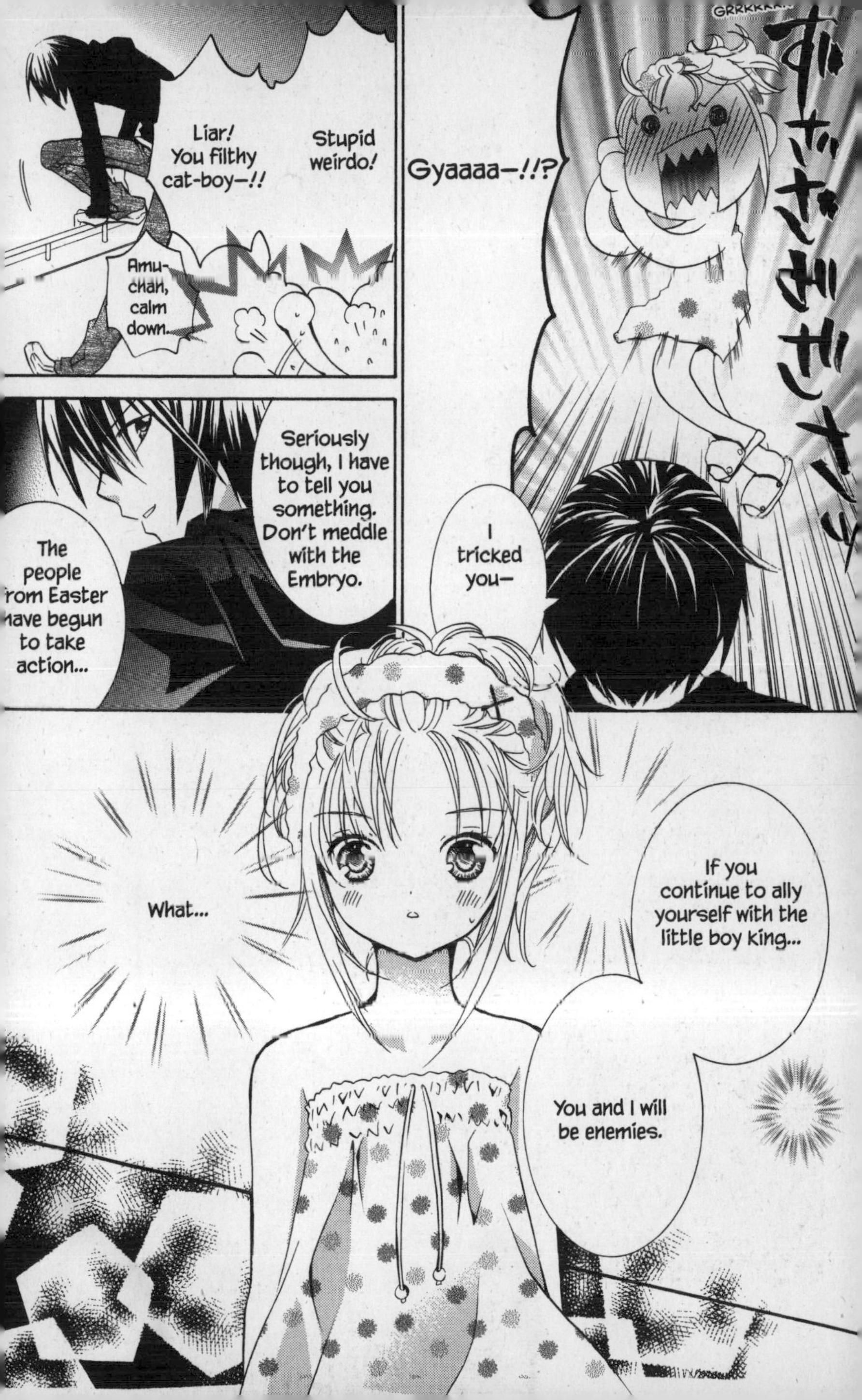
GRRKKKK
Gyaaaa—!!?
I tricked you—
Stupid weirdo!
Liar! You filthy cat-boy—!!
Amu-chan, calm down...
Seriously though, I have to tell you something. Don't meddle with the Embryo.
The people from Easter have begun to take action...
If you continue to ally yourself with the little boy king...
You and I will be enemies.
What...

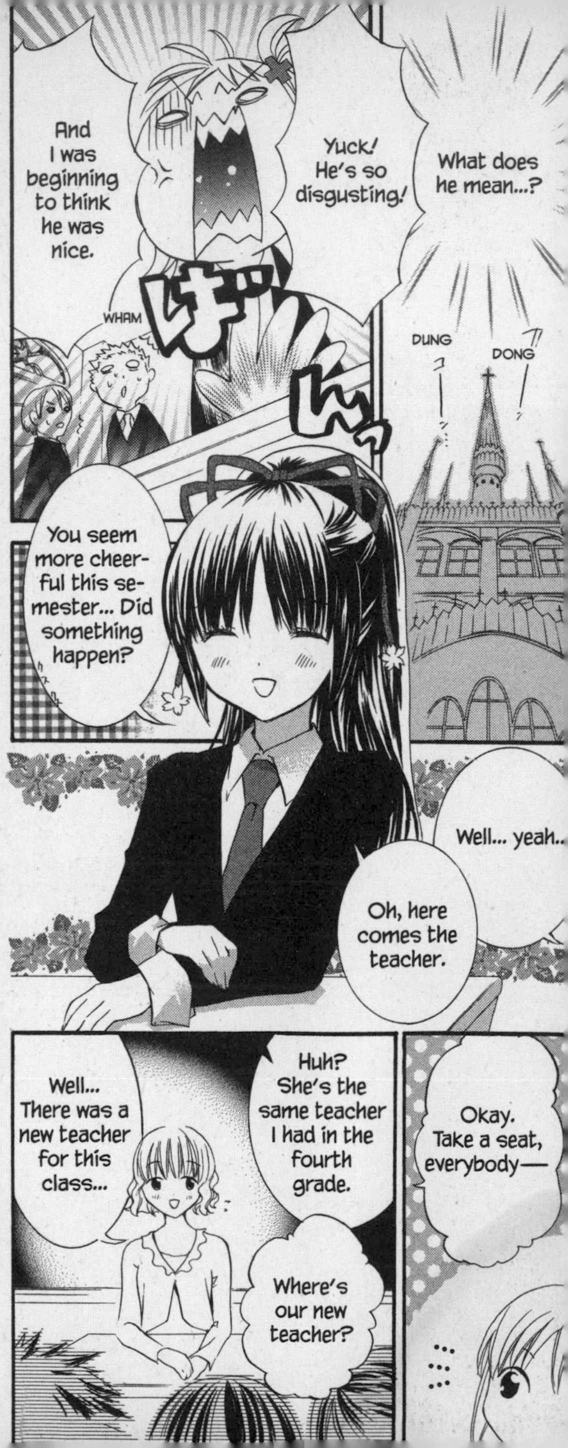
What does he mean...?
DUNG
DONG
Yuck! He's so disgusting!
And I was beginning to think he was nice.
ぼんっ
WHAM
You seem more cheerful this semester... Did something happen?
Well... yeah..
Oh, here comes the teacher.
Okay. Take a seat, everybody—
...
...
Huh? She's the same teacher I had in the fourth grade.
Well... There was a new teacher for this class...
Where's our new teacher?

character profile

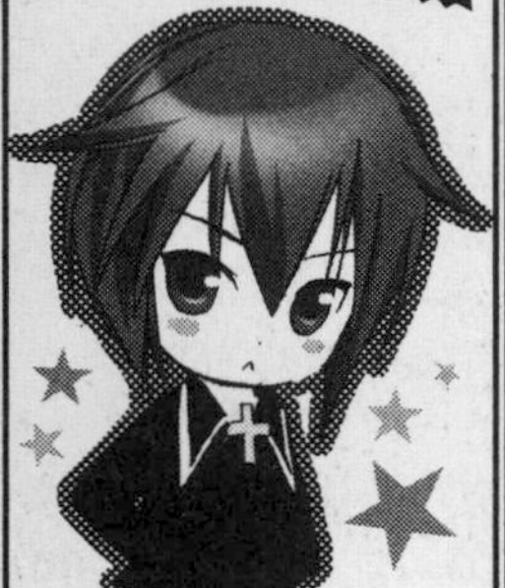

月詠 幾斗

Ikuto Tsukiyomi

Birthday : 12/1
BloodType : AB
Sign : Sagittarius
Shugo-Chara : Yoru

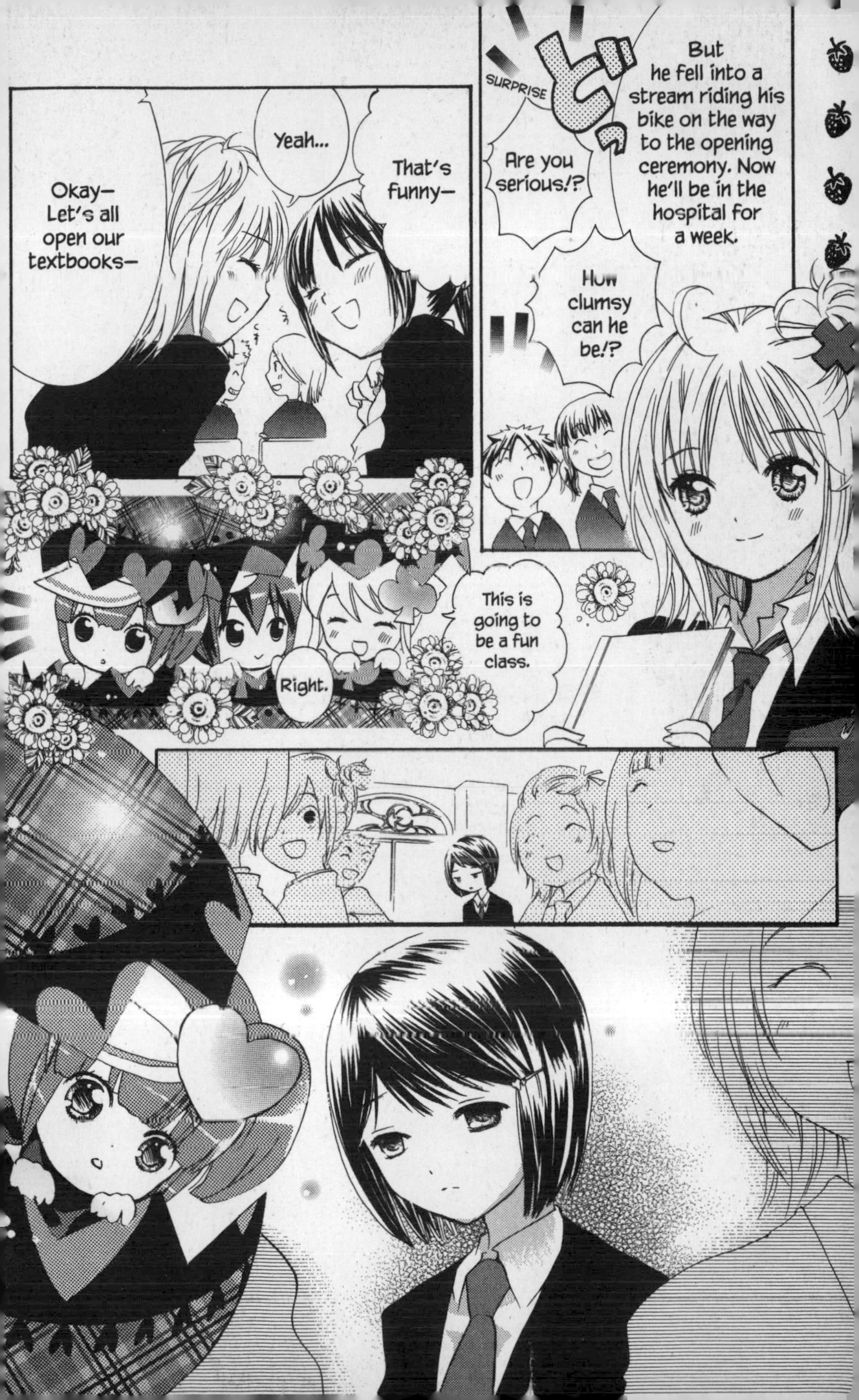
But he fell into a stream riding his bike on the way to the opening ceremony. Now he'll be in the hospital for a week.
SURPRISE
Are you serious!?
How clumsy can he be!?
That's funny—
Yeah...
Okay— Let's all open our textbooks—
This is going to be a fun class.
Right.

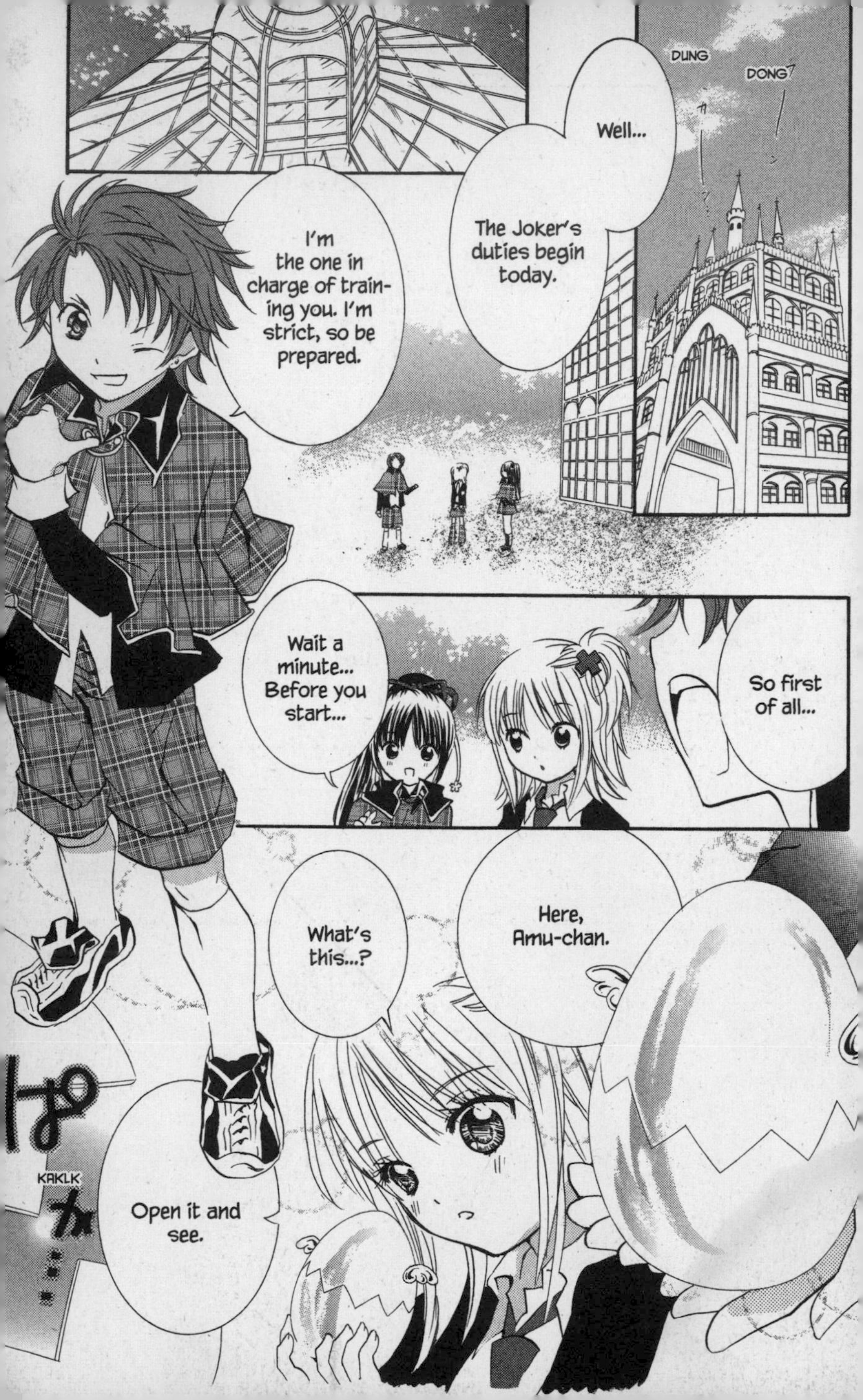

DUNG
DONG
Well...
The Joker's duties begin today.
I'm the one in charge of training you. I'm strict, so be prepared.
So first of all...
Wait a minute... Before you start...
Here, Amu-chan.
What's this...?
ぱか…
KAKLK
Open it and see.

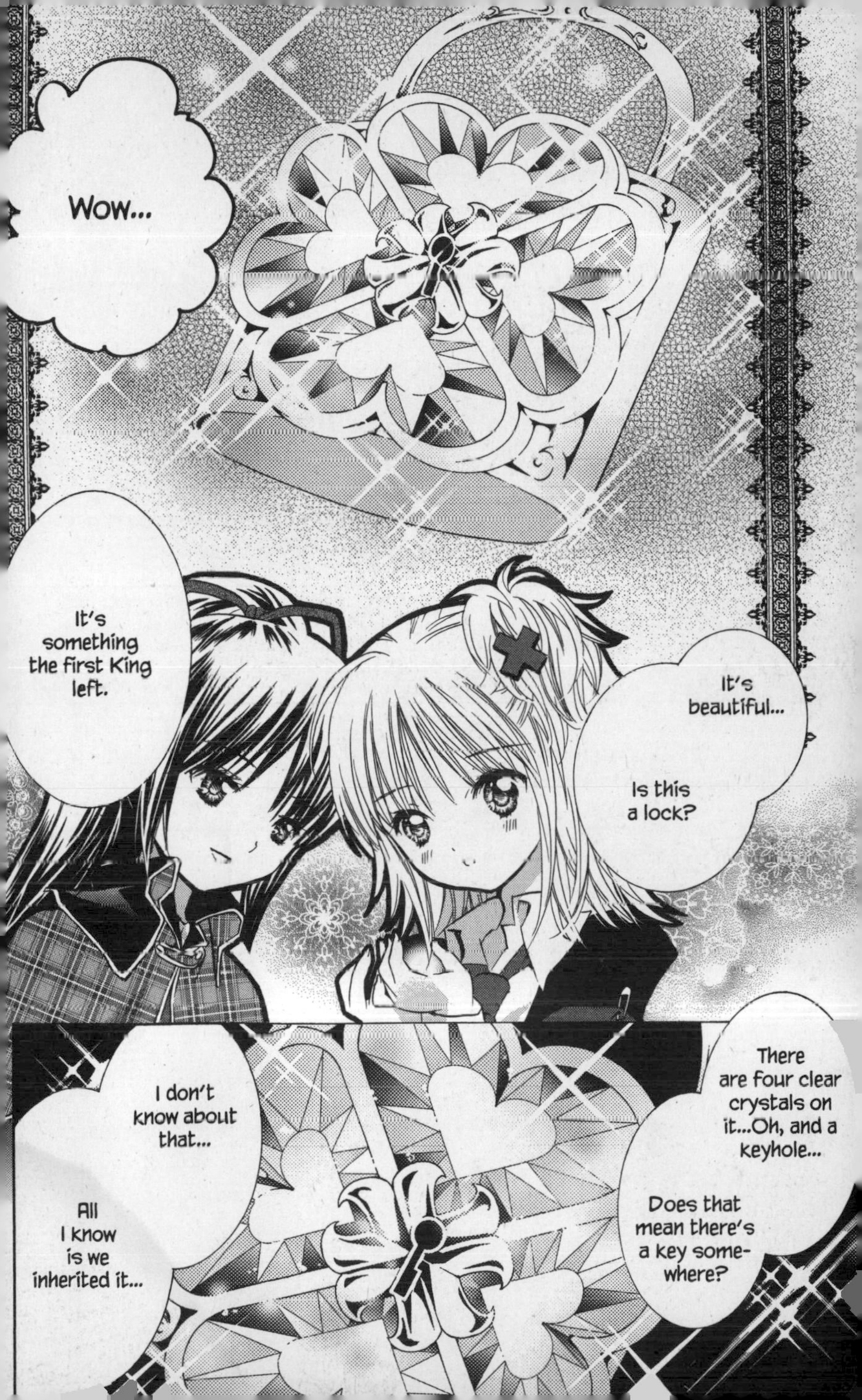
Wow...
It's beautiful...
Is this a lock?
It's something the first King left.
There are four clear crystals on it...Oh, and a keyhole...
Does that mean there's a key some-where?
I don't know about that...
All I know is we inherited it...

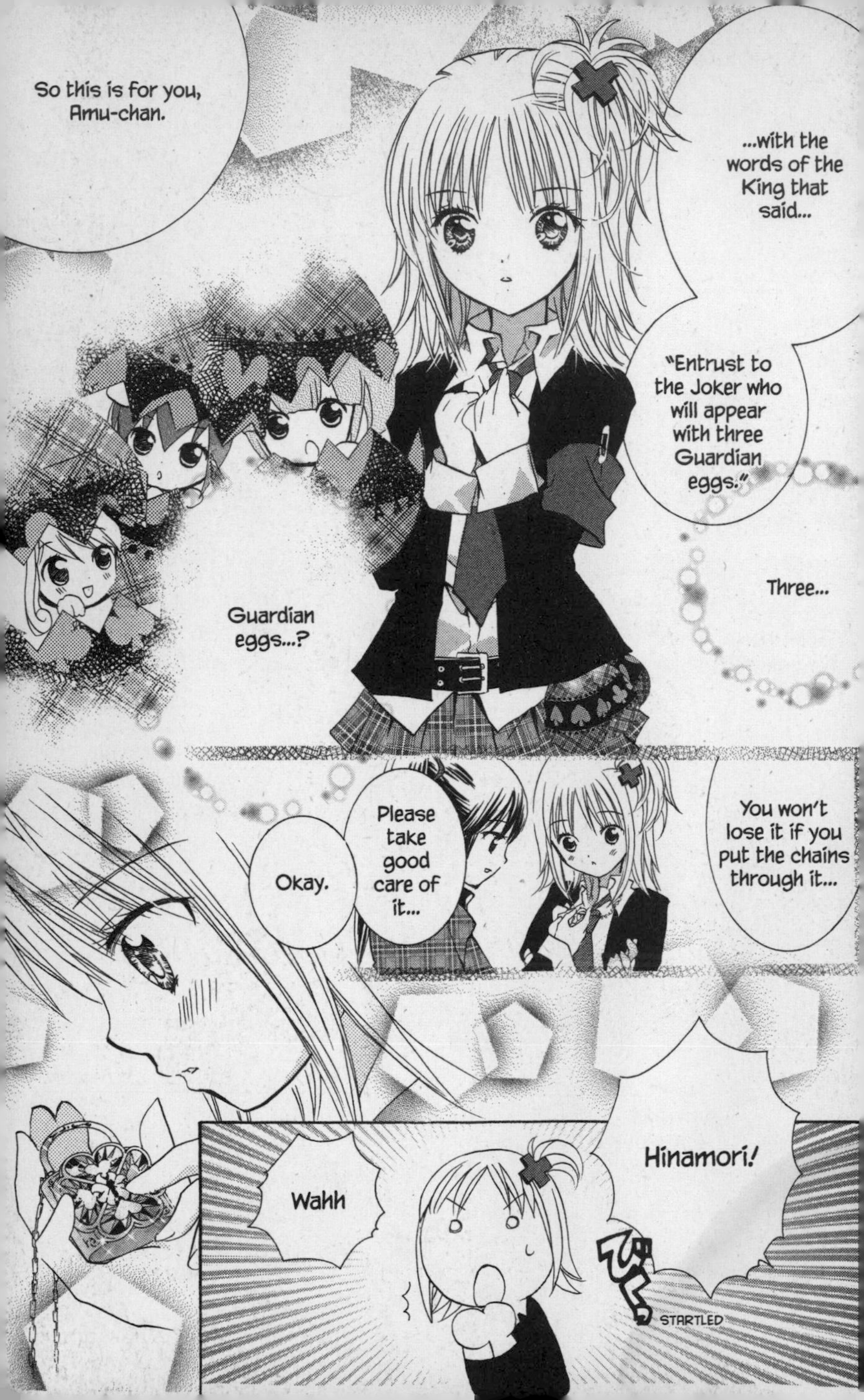

...with the words of the King that said...
"Entrust to the Joker who will appear with three Guardian eggs."
Three...
So this is for you, Amu-chan.
Guardian eggs...?
You won't lose it if you put the chains through it...
Please take good care of it...
Okay.
Hinamori!
Wahh
STARTLED

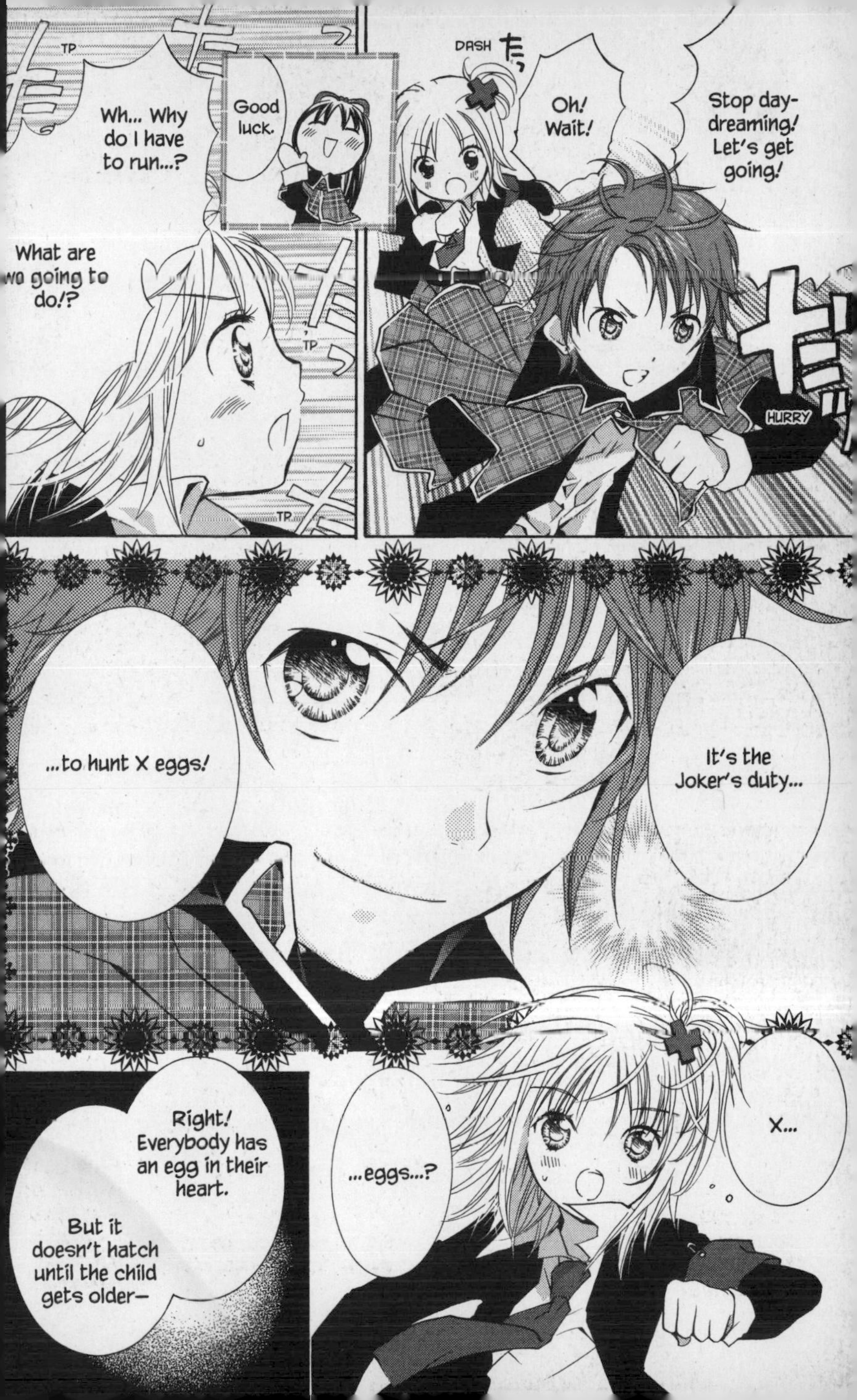
Stop day-dreaming! Let's get going!
Oh! Wait!
DASH
HURRY
Good luck.
TP
Wh... Why do I have to run...?
What are we going to do!?
TP
TP
It's the Joker's duty...
...to hunt X eggs!
X...
...eggs...?
Right! Everybody has an egg in their heart.
But it doesn't hatch until the child gets older—

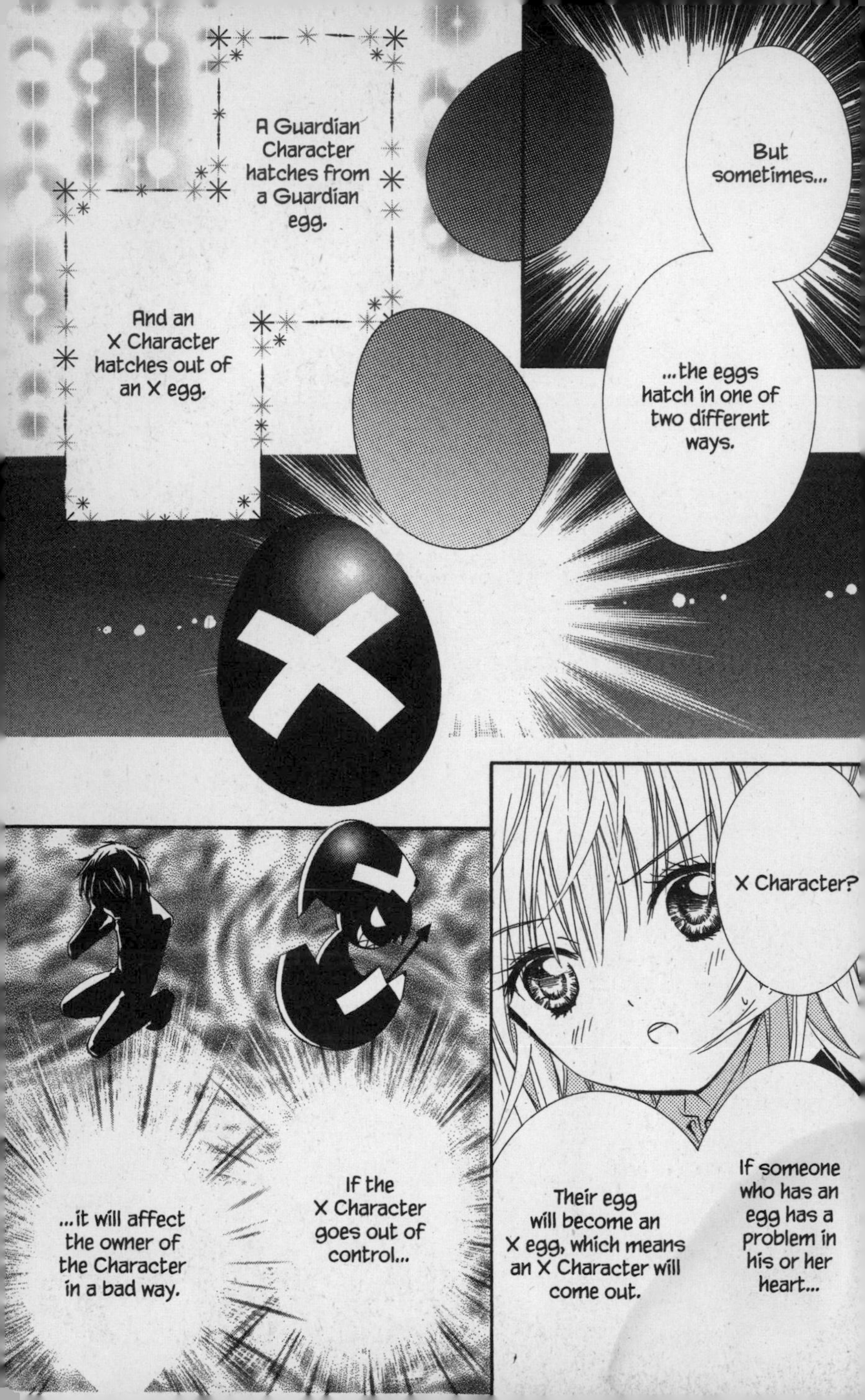
But sometimes...
...the eggs hatch in one of two different ways.
A Guardian Character hatches from a Guardian egg.
And an X Character hatches out of an X egg.
X Character?
If someone who has an egg has a problem in his or her heart...
Their egg will become an X egg, which means an X Character will come out.
If the X Character goes out of control...
...it will affect the owner of the Character in a bad way.

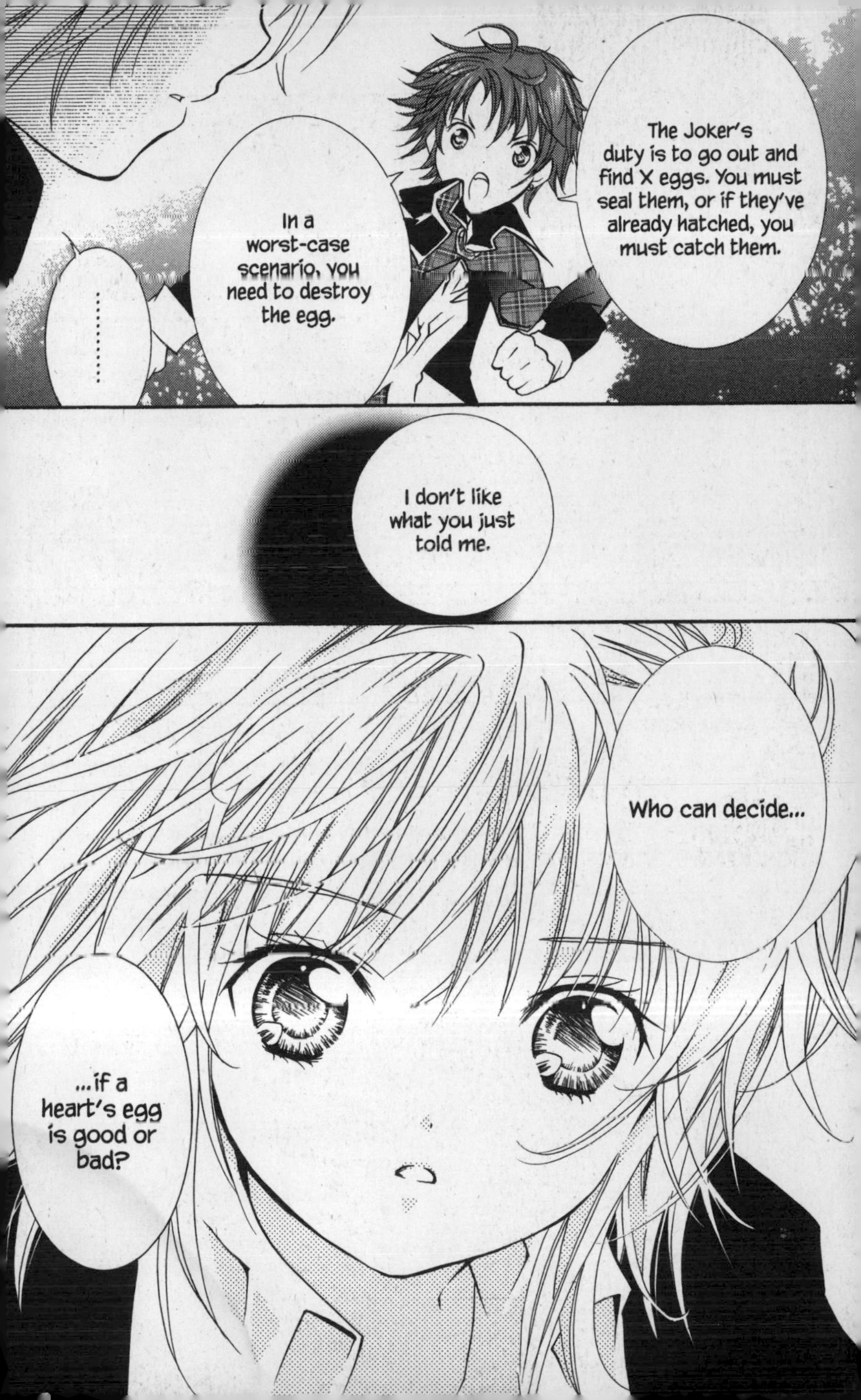
The Joker's duty is to go out and find X eggs. You must seal them, or if they've already hatched, you must catch them.
In a worst-case scenario, you need to destroy the egg.
....
I don't like what you just told me.
Who can decide...
...if a heart's egg is good or bad?

Published = 2006 "Nakayoshi" issues Feb ~ Jun

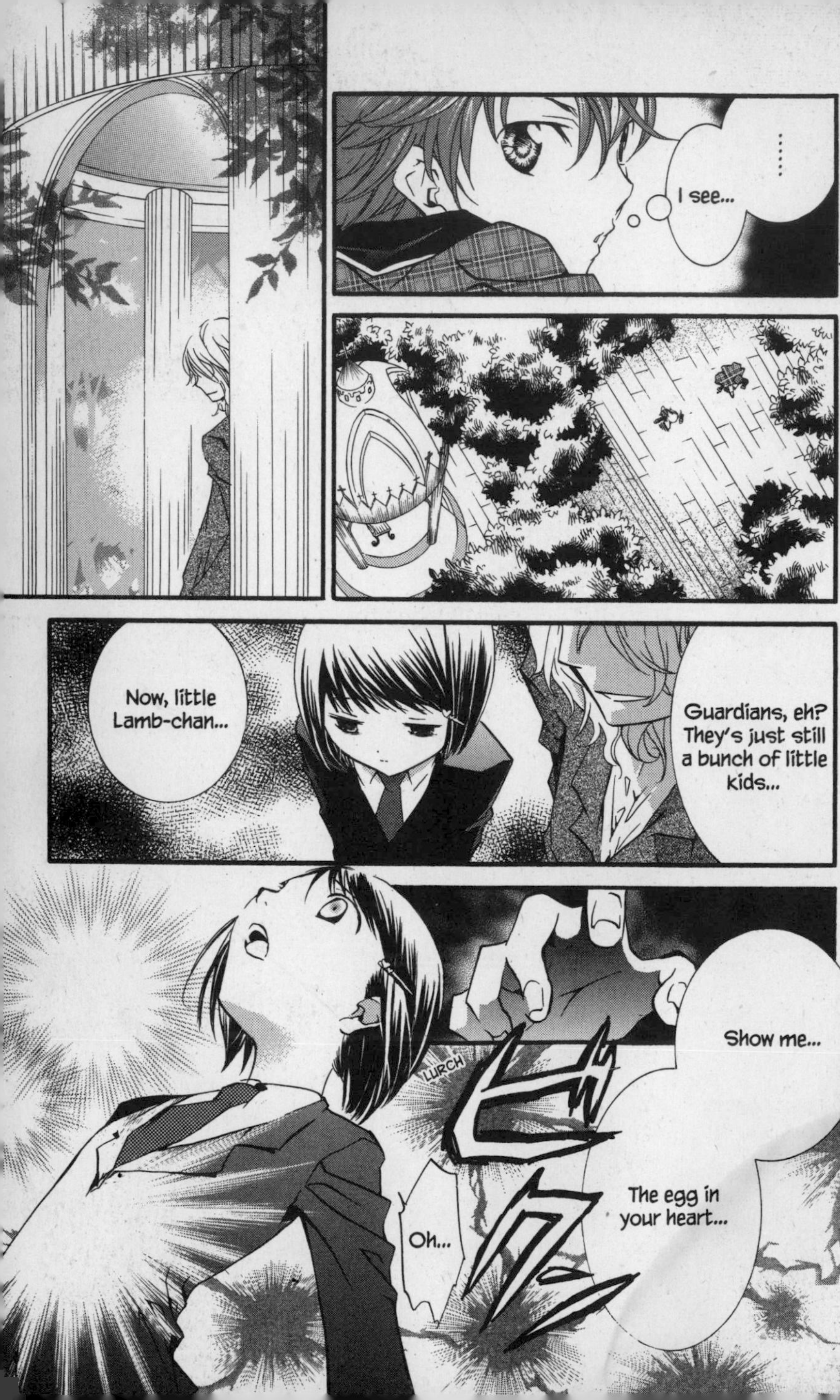
......
I see...
Guardians, eh? They's just still a bunch of little kids...
Now, little Lamb-chan...
Show me...
The egg in your heart...
LURCH
Oh...

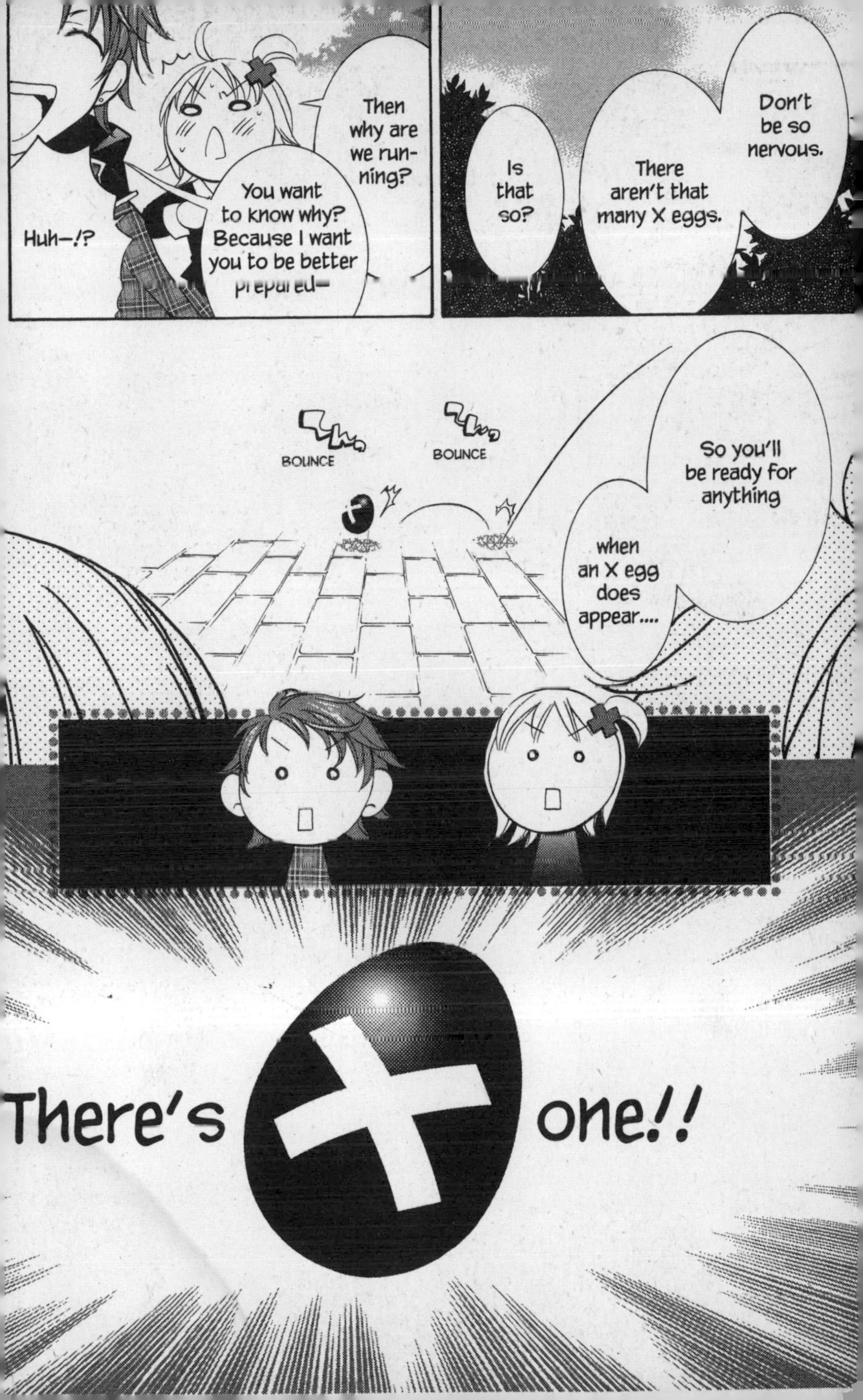
Don't be so nervous.
There aren't that many X eggs.
Is that so?
Then why are we running?
You want to know why? Because I want you to be better prepared—
Huh—!?
So you'll be ready for anything
when an X egg does appear....
BOUNCE
BOUNCE
There's one!!

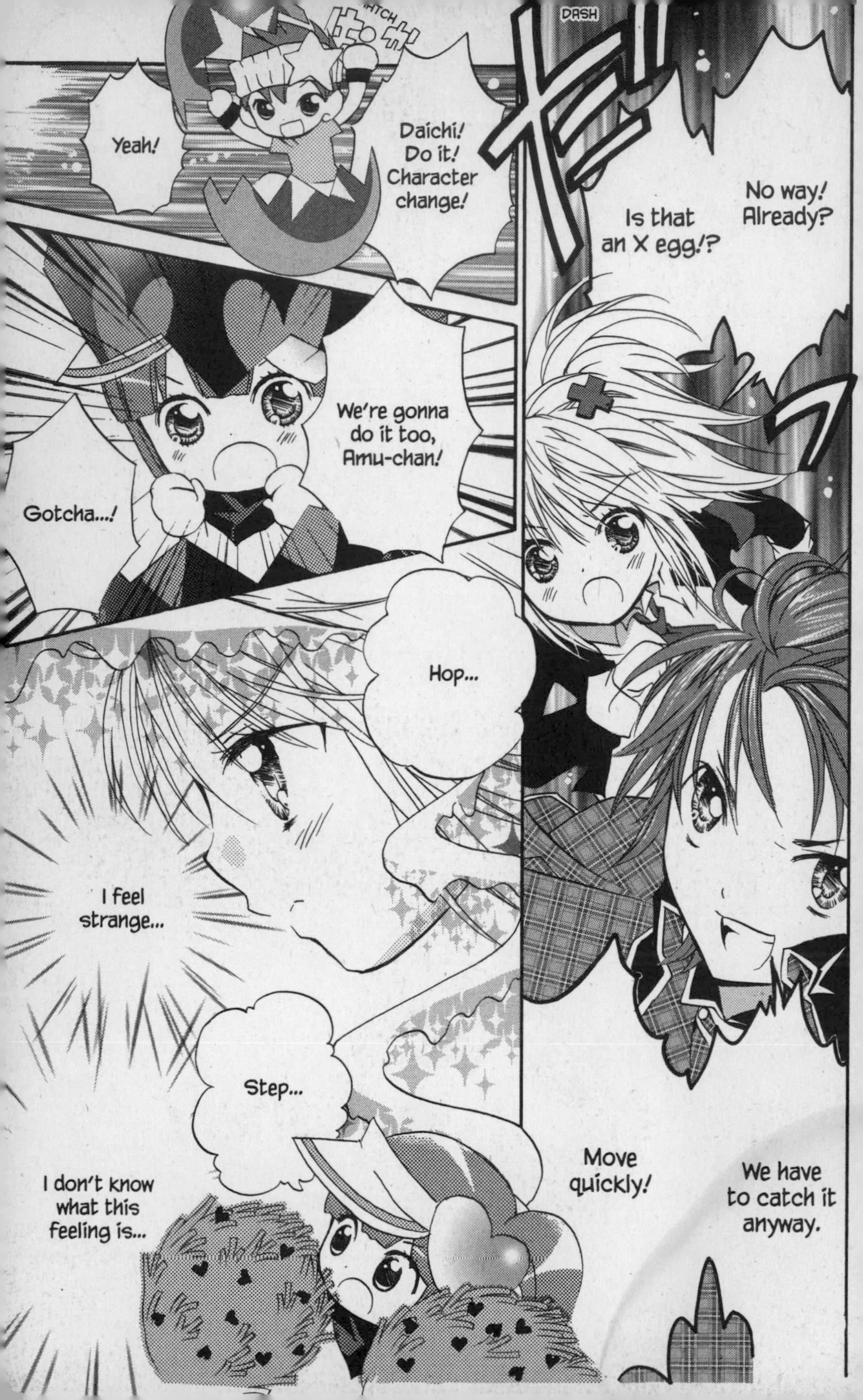
DASH
No way! Already?
Is that an X egg!?
We have to catch it anyway.
Move quickly!
Daichi! Do it! Character change!
Yeah!
We're gonna do it too, Amu-chan!
Gotcha...!
Hop...
I feel strange...
Step...
I don't know what this feeling is...

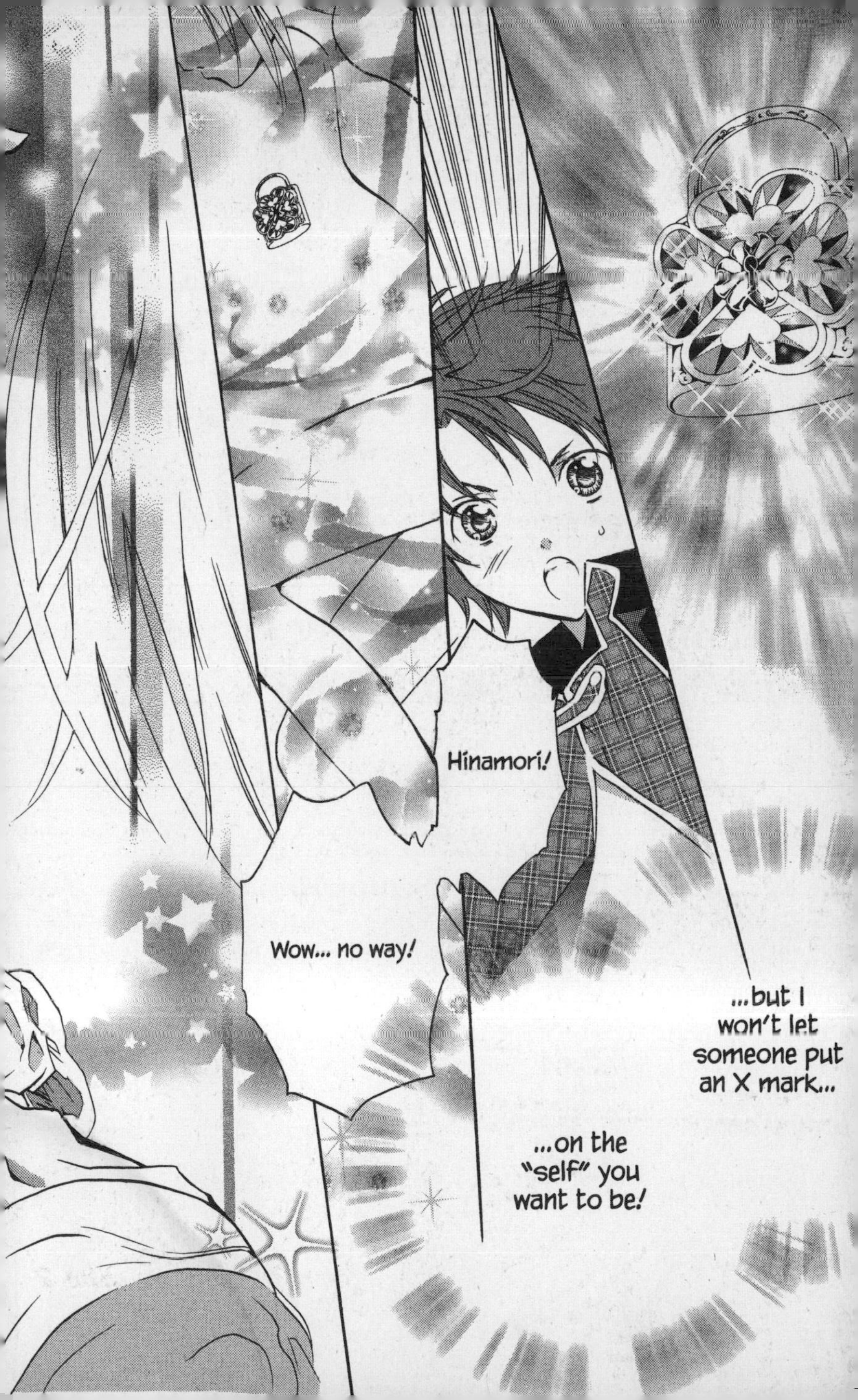
Hinamori!
Wow... no way!
...but I won't let someone put an X mark...
...on the "self" you want to be!

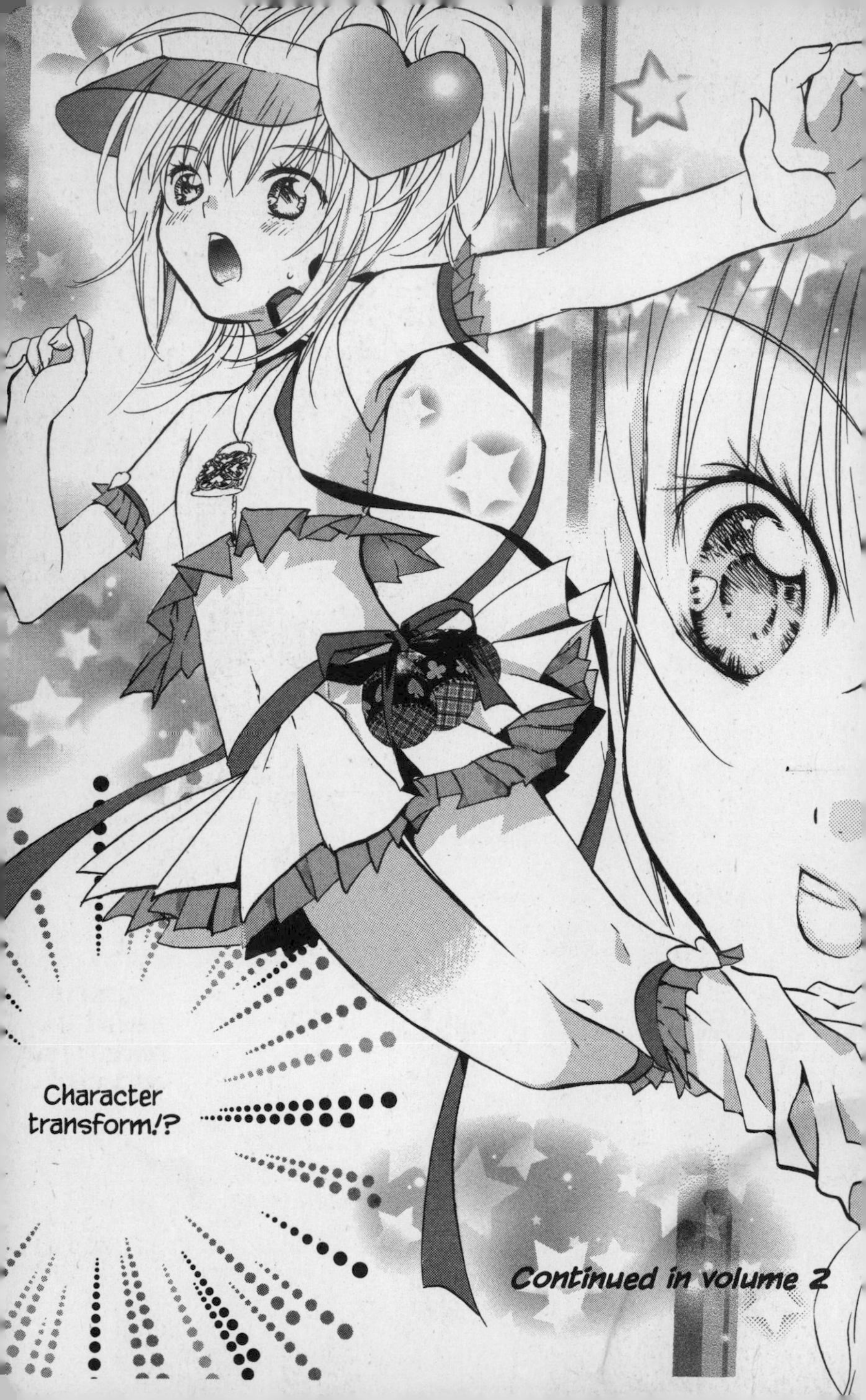
Character transform!?
Continued in volume 2

About the Creators

PEACH-PIT is:

Banri Sendo, born on June 7th

Shibuko Ebara, born on June 21st

We both are Gemini. We're a pair of manga artists.
Sendo enjoys sweets, but Ebara prefers spicy food. Our favorite
animals are cats and rabbits, and our recent hobbies are making
the ultimate *ajitama* and doing fingernail art.

Translation Notes

Japanese is a tricky language for most Westerners, and translation is often more art than science. For your edification and reading pleasure, here are notes on some of the places where we could have gone in a different direction with our translation of the work, or where a Japanese cultural reference is used.

Mushi Champ, page 3

This name is a play on *Mushi King*, a game by Sega that combines trading card and video gameplay. It's very popular among young boys in Japan, because the game features *mushi*, or bugs such as beetles and stag beetles.

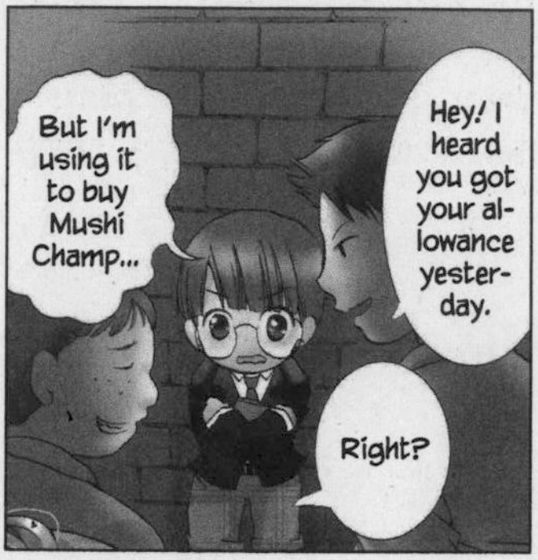
Hey! I heard you got your allowance yesterday.
Right?
But I'm using it to buy Mushi Champ...

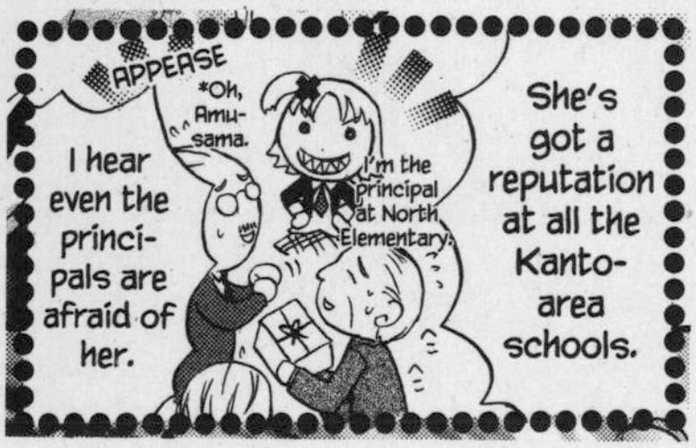
She's got a reputation at all the Kanto-area schools.
APPEASE
*Oh, Amu-sama.
I'm the principal at North Elementary.
I hear even the principals are afraid of her.

Kanto-area schools, page 7

The boy is referring to schools in the area surrounding and including Tokyo, which is known as the "Kanto area."

Bonjour and *Je t'aime*, page 10

Amu's classmates are imagining that Amu probably has a super-cool French boyfriend. It is typical of Japanese girls (and women) to think another girl is awesome if she's dating a foreigner. *Bonjour* means "hello," and *je t'aime* means "I love you" in French.

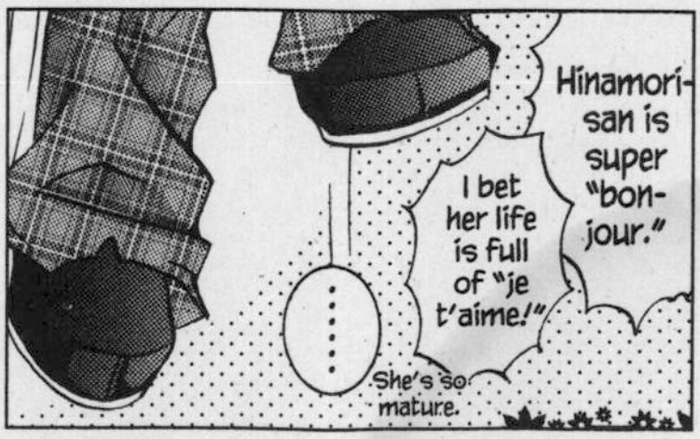
Hinamori-san is super "bonjour."
I bet her life is full of "je t'aime!"
She's so mature.

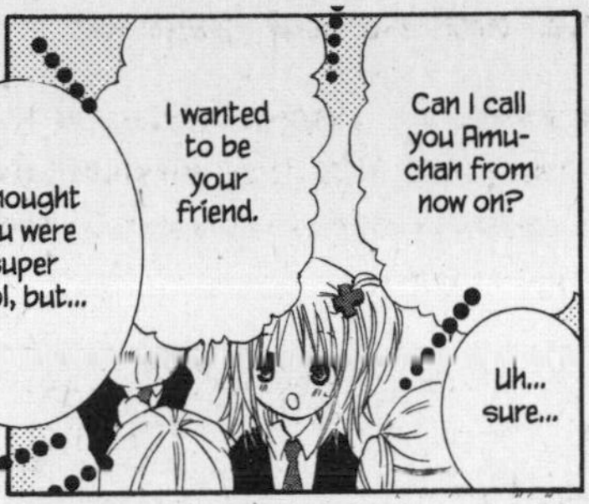
Can I call you Amu-chan from now on?
I wanted to be your friend.
I thought you were super cool, but...
Uh... sure...

"Can I call you Amu-chan?" page 63

In Japan, before you get to know someone a little better, it is most acceptable to call a person by their family name, such as Hinamori-san. This girl wants to feel closer to Amu so she is asking permission to call her by her first name.

Burglar Alarm, page 113

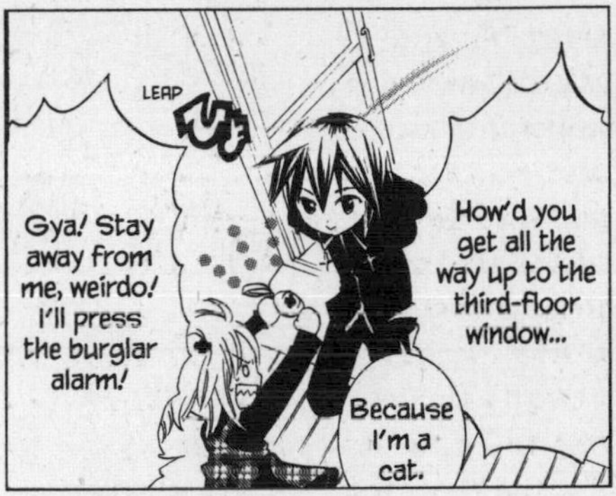
LEAP
How'd you get all the way up to the third-floor window...
Gya! Stay away from me, weirdo! I'll press the burglar alarm!
Because I'm a cat.

Amu is holding a little plastic burglar alarm that young children and women commonly carry when going out. These alarms are usually round devices on a strap, with a string hanging out from the other side. When you pull out the string, a loud alarm sounds. There are also some kinds of burglar alarms that are shaped like cartoon characters.

Chin, ton, chan, page 116

Chin, ton, and *chan* are three sounds the Japanese use to augment moves in a dance. It's nothing specific to any dance; it's just a way of singing a rhythm.

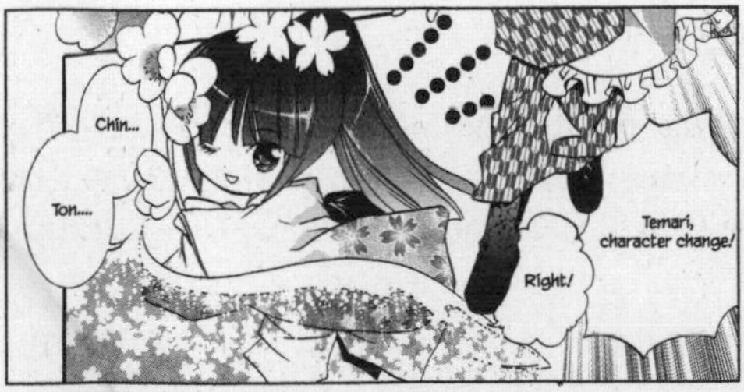
Temari, character change!
Right!
Chin...
Ton....

Kamenashi-kun, Akanishi-kun, and Yamapi, page 121

These are all names of popular idol singers in Japan. Kamenashi-kun and Akanishi-kun are from the same group of six known as KAT-TUN. They are known for looking alike, so that it would be tough for a non-fan to tell them apart. Tomohisa Yamashita, also known as Yamapi, is another pop idol.

Dollies, page 132

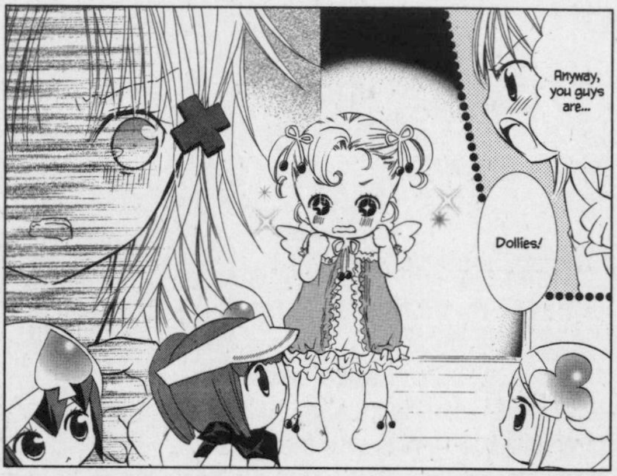
Anyway, you guys are...
Dollies!

In the Japanese version, when Ami first sees the Guardian Characters she yells "Sugoi!" which in this case is similar to yelling "Wow!" In the original Japanese, it's written in a "baby talk" style, making it "Shugoi!" Since the Japanese name of the series is *Shugo Chara!*, which means "Guardian Characters," the characters think Ami is mispronouncing their name. It was difficult to find an equivalent for this pun in English, so we went with "dollies," which is something a 3-year old would say, but also something the Guardian Characters most certainly are not.

Fugashi, page 174

Fugashi is an old-fashioned Japanese snack made with gluten and flour and then baked and covered with black sugar. It was popular before the 1980s in Japan.

Ajitama, page 192

Ajitama can be translated to "flavored eggs," which are boiled eggs made when boiled in flavored soup. They sell them at certain markets, but since they are easy to make, it seems PEACH-PIT is trying to make the "ultimate flavored one."

KITCHEN PRINCESS

STORY BY MIYUKI KOBAYASHI
MANGA BY NATSUMI ANDO
CREATOR OF ZODIAC P.I.

HUNGRY HEART

Najika is a great cook and likes to make meals for the people she loves. But something is missing from her life. When she was a child, she met a boy who touched her heart—and now Najika is determined to find him. The only clue she has is a silver spoon that leads her to the prestigious Seika Academy.

Attending Seika will be a challenge. Every kid at the school has a special talent, and the girls in Najika's class think she doesn't deserve to be there. But Sora and Daichi, two popular brothers who barely speak to each other, recognize Najika's cooking for what it is—magical. Could one of the boys be Najika's mysterious prince?

Special extras in each volume! Read them all!

MICHIYO KIKUTA

BOY CRAZY

Junior high schooler Nina is ready to fall in love. She's looking for a boy who's cute and sweet—and strong enough to support her when the chips are down. But what happens when Nina's dream comes true . . . twice? One day, two cute boys literally fall from the sky. They're both wizards who've come to the Human World to take the Magic Exam. The boys' success on this test depends on protecting Nina from evil, so now Nina has a pair of cute magical boys chasing her everywhere! One of these wizards just might be the boy of her dreams . . . but which one?

Special extras in each volume! Read them all!

VISIT WWW.DELREYMANGA.COM TO:
- Read sample pages
- View release date calendars for upcoming volumes
- Sign up for Del Rey's free manga e-newsletter
- Find out the latest about new Del Rey Manga series

DEL REY MANGA

The Otaku's Choice

Sugar Sugar Rune

BY MOYOCO ANNO

QUEEN OF HEARTS

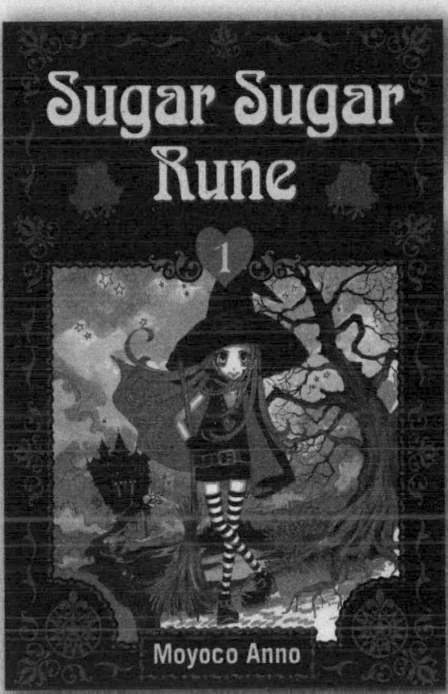
Sugar Sugar Rune
1
Moyoco Anno

Chocolat and Vanilla are young witch princesses from a magical land. They've come to Earth to compete in a contest—whichever girl captures the most hearts will become queen! While living in a boarding school, they must make as many boys fall in love with them as possible if they want to achieve their goal. Standing against them are a pair of rival princes looking to capture their hearts because they want to be king!

There's danger for the witch-girls, though: If they give their hearts to a human, they may never return to the Magical World....

Ages: 10 +

Special extras in each volume! Read them all!

DEL REY

VISIT WWW.DELREYMANGA.COM TO:

- View release date calendars for upcoming volumes
- Sign up for Del Rey's free manga e-newsletter
- Find out the latest about new Del Rey Manga series

Guru Guru Pon-Chan

BY SATOMI IKEZAWA

WINNER OF THE KODANSHA MANGA OF THE YEAR AWARD!

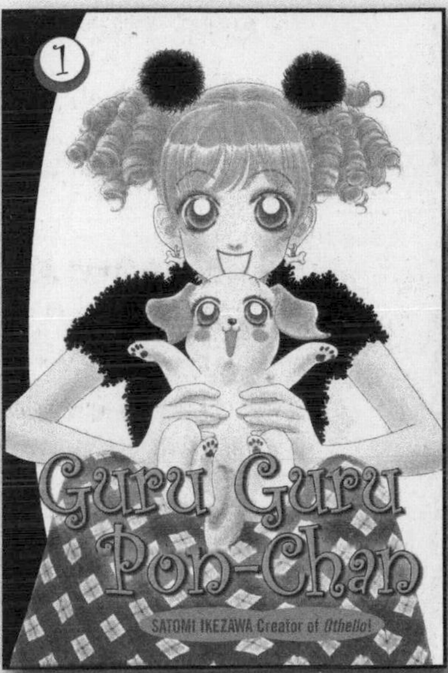
1
Guru Guru Pon-Chan
SATOMI IKEZAWA Creator of Othello!

Ages: 13 +

Ponta is a normal Labrador retriever puppy, the Koizumi family's pet. Full of energy, she is always up to some kind of trouble. However, when Grandpa Koizumi, a passionate amateur inventor, creates the "Guru Guru Bone," which empowers animals with human speech, Ponta turns into a human girl!

Ponta dashes out into the street and is saved by Mirai Iwaki, the most popular boy at school! Her heart pounds and her face flushes. Why does she feel this way? Can there be love between a human and a dog?

The effects of the "Guru Guru Bone" are not permanent, and Ponta turns back and forth between dog and girl.

Special extras in each volume! Read them all!

VISIT WWW.DELREYMANGA.COM TO:
- **View release date calendars for upcoming volumes**
- **Sign up for Del Rey's free manga e-newsletter**
- **Find out the latest about new Del Rey Manga series**

TOMARE!

[STOP!]

You're going the wrong way!

Manga is a completely different type of reading experience.

To start at the *beginning,* go to the *end!*

That's right! Authentic manga is read the traditional Japanese way—from right to left. Exactly the opposite of how American books are read. It's easy to follow: Just go to the other end of the book, and read each page—and each panel—from right side to left side, starting at the top right. Now you're experiencing manga as it was meant to be!